Linux® Programming For Dummies®

Cheat Sheet

Check out the manual

If you want to know more about a Linux utility, use the on-screen manual for that utility. For example, if you want to know more about the sort utility, type **man sort** at the Linux prompt and press Enter.

If the manual pages scroll off the screen, use the more command so that you can see one screen at a time:

```
man sort | more
```

Shortcuts for Writing Linux Code

To Do This	Follow This Example
Display text on the screen	echo "**type_text_here**"
Declare a variable	declare *variable_name*
Assign a value to a string variable	declare *variable_name* ="Bob"
Assign a value to a numeric variable	let *variable_name*=500
Display a variable	echo "$*variable_name* "
Save data to a file (instead of to the screen)	echo " *variable_name* " > file
Append data to a file (instead of to the screen)	echo " *variable_name* " > file
Comment on a program	#Written by John Grace
Disable an instruction	#declare *variable_name* ="Bob"

case

```
case variable_name in
    value_1)
        instruction
        ;;

    value_2)
        instruction
        ;;
esac
```

Beginning with the case reserved word and ending with the ;; reserved word , your program first looks at the value of *variable_name*. If this value is equal to *value_1*, the program follows the first set of instructions. If this is equal to *value_2,* the program follows the second set of instructions. The program follows all the instructions that appear between the) reserved word and the ; ; reserved word if there is a match.

for in

```
for variable_na
    do
        instruct
done
```

wordlist is a list of string values that are
...gned to the *variable_name*. The *variable_name*
...be used by the instruction inside the for in

DI091856

Linux® Programming For Dummies®

Cheat Sheet

if

```
if [ condition ]
then
        instruction
fi
```

Your program follows the instruction if a certain *condition* exists — meaning the *condition* is true.

if elif

```
if [ condition_1]
then
        instruction_1
elif [ condition_2 ]
then
        instruction_2
fi
```

Your program obeys the first group of instructions if *condition_1* is true. However, if *condition_1* is false, your program determines if *condition_2* is true. If *condition_2* is true, your program obeys the second group of instructions. If *condition_2* is false, your program skips the second group of instructions.

if else

```
if [ condition ]
    then
        instruction_1
else
        instruction_2
fi
```

Your program obeys the first group of instructions if the *condition* is true . . . but obeys the second group of instructions if the *condition* is false.

while

```
while [ condition ]
    do
        instruction
done
```

The *condition* must be a variable or expression that results in a true or false value.

IDG BOOKS WORLDWIDE

Copyright © 2001 IDG Books Worldwide, Inc.
All rights reserved.

Cheat Sheet $2.95 value. Item 0691-9.

For more information about IDG Books,
call 1-800-762-2974.

For Dummies®: Bestselling Book Series for Beginners

...FOR DUMMIES™

References for the Rest of Us!®

BESTSELLING BOOK SERIES

Are you intimidated and confused by computers? Do you find that traditional manuals are overloaded with technical details you'll never use? Do your friends and family always call you to fix simple problems on their PCs? Then the *...For Dummies*® computer book series from IDG Books Worldwide is for you.

...For Dummies books are written for those frustrated computer users who know they aren't really dumb but find that PC hardware, software, and indeed the unique vocabulary of computing make them feel helpless. *...For Dummies* books use a lighthearted approach, a down-to-earth style, and even cartoons and humorous icons to dispel computer novices' fears and build their confidence. Lighthearted but not lightweight, these books are a perfect survival guide for anyone forced to use a computer.

> *"I like my copy so much I told friends; now they bought copies."*
>
> — Irene C., Orwell, Ohio

> *"Quick, concise, nontechnical, and humorous."*
>
> — Jay A., Elburn, Illinois

> *"Thanks, I needed this book. Now I can sleep at night."*
>
> — Robin F., British Columbia, Canada

Already, millions of satisfied readers agree. They have made *...For Dummies* books the #1 introductory level computer book series and have written asking for more. So, if you're looking for the most fun and easy way to learn about computers, look to *...For Dummies* books to give you a helping hand.

IDG BOOKS WORLDWIDE®

by Jim Keogh

IDG Books Worldwide, Inc.
An International Data Group Company

Foster City, CA ◆ Chicago, IL ◆ Indianapolis, IN ◆ New York, NY

Linux® Programming For Dummies®

Published by
IDG Books Worldwide, Inc.
An International Data Group Company
919 E. Hillsdale Blvd.
Suite 300
Foster City, CA 94404
www.idgbooks.com (IDG Books Worldwide Web Site)
www.dummies.com (Dummies Press Web Site)

Library of Congress Control Number: 99-69377

ISBN: 0-7645-0691-9

Printed in the United States of America

10 9 8 7 6 5 4 3 2 1

1B/IQ/RQ/QQ/IN

Distributed in the United States by IDG Books Worldwide, Inc.

Distributed by CDG Books Canada Inc. for Canada; by Transworld Publishers Limited in the United Kingdom; by IDG Norge Books for Norway; by IDG Sweden Books for Sweden; by IDG Books Australia Publishing Corporation Pty. Ltd. for Australia and New Zealand; by TransQuest Publishers Pte Ltd. for Singapore, Malaysia, Thailand, Indonesia, and Hong Kong; by Gotop Information Inc. for Taiwan; by ICG Muse, Inc. for Japan; by Intersoft for South Africa; by Eyrolles for France; by International Thomson Publishing for Germany, Austria and Switzerland; by Distribuidora Cuspide for Argentina; by LR International for Brazil; by Galileo Libros for Chile; by Ediciones ZETA S.C.R. Ltda. for Peru; by WS Computer Publishing Corporation, Inc., for the Philippines; by Contemporanea de Ediciones for Venezuela; by Express Computer Distributors for the Caribbean and West Indies; by Micronesia Media Distributor, Inc. for Micronesia; by Chips Computadoras S.A. de C.V. for Mexico; by Editorial Norma de Panama S.A. for Panama; by American Bookshops for Finland.

For general information on IDG Books Worldwide's books in the U.S., please call our Consumer Customer Service department at 800-762-2974. For reseller information, including discounts and premium sales, please call our Reseller Customer Service department at 800-434-3422.

For information on where to purchase IDG Books Worldwide's books outside the U.S., please contact our International Sales department at 317-572-3993 or fax 317-572-4002.

For consumer information on foreign language translations, please contact our Customer Service department at 1-800-434-3422, fax 317-572-4002, or e-mail rights@idgbooks.com.

For information on licensing foreign or domestic rights, please phone +1-650-653-7098.

For sales inquiries and special prices for bulk quantities, please contact our Order Services department at 800-434-3422 or write to the address above.

For information on using IDG Books Worldwide's books in the classroom or for ordering examination copies, please contact our Educational Sales department at 800-434-2086 or fax 317-572-4005.

For press review copies, author interviews, or other publicity information, please contact our Public Relations department at 650-653-7000 or fax 650-653-7500.

For authorization to photocopy items for corporate, personal, or educational use, please contact Copyright Clearance Center, 222 Rosewood Drive, Danvers, MA 01923, or fax 978-750-4470.

About the Author

Jim Keogh is chair of the Electronic Commerce Track at Columbia University. He has developed Unix and Linux systems for major Wall Street firms and is the author of more than 45 books on computers and computer programming, including the popular *UNIX Programming for Dummies*. He was one of the first to introduce PC programming internationally in his "Programmer's Notebook" column in *Popular Electronics Magazine*, four years after Apple Computer was born in a garage. Keogh is also a former contributing editor to *Popular Electronics Magazine* and associate editor for *Personal Computing Magazine*.

ABOUT IDG BOOKS WORLDWIDE

Welcome to the world of IDG Books Worldwide.

IDG Books Worldwide, Inc., is a subsidiary of International Data Group, the world's largest publisher of computer-related information and the leading global provider of information services on information technology. IDG was founded more than 30 years ago by Patrick J. McGovern and now employs more than 9,000 people worldwide. IDG publishes more than 290 computer publications in over 75 countries. More than 90 million people read one or more IDG publications each month.

Launched in 1990, IDG Books Worldwide is today the #1 publisher of best-selling computer books in the United States. We are proud to have received eight awards from the Computer Press Association in recognition of editorial excellence and three from Computer Currents' First Annual Readers' Choice Awards. Our best-selling *...For Dummies*® series has more than 50 million copies in print with translations in 31 languages. IDG Books Worldwide, through a joint venture with IDG's Hi-Tech Beijing, became the first U.S. publisher to publish a computer book in the People's Republic of China. In record time, IDG Books Worldwide has become the first choice for millions of readers around the world who want to learn how to better manage their businesses.

Our mission is simple: Every one of our books is designed to bring extra value and skill-building instructions to the reader. Our books are written by experts who understand and care about our readers. The knowledge base of our editorial staff comes from years of experience in publishing, education, and journalism — experience we use to produce books to carry us into the new millennium. In short, we care about books, so we attract the best people. We devote special attention to details such as audience, interior design, use of icons, and illustrations. And because we use an efficient process of authoring, editing, and desktop publishing our books electronically, we can spend more time ensuring superior content and less time on the technicalities of making books.

You can count on our commitment to deliver high-quality books at competitive prices on topics you want to read about. At IDG Books Worldwide, we continue in the IDG tradition of delivering quality for more than 30 years. You'll find no better book on a subject than one from IDG Books Worldwide.

John Kilcullen
Chairman and CEO
IDG Books Worldwide, Inc.

Eighth Annual
Computer Press
Awards ≥1992

WINNER
IX
Ninth Annual
Computer Press
Awards ≥1993

WINNER
X
Tenth Annual
Computer Press
Awards ≥1994

XI WINNER
Eleventh Annual
Computer Press
Awards ≥1995

IDG is the world's leading IT media, research and exposition company. Founded in 1964, IDG had 1997 revenues of $2.05 billion and has more than 9,000 employees worldwide. IDG offers the widest range of media options that reach IT buyers in 75 countries representing 95% of worldwide IT spending. IDG's diverse product and services portfolio spans six key areas including print publishing, online publishing, expositions and conferences, market research, education and training, and global marketing services. More than 90 million people read one or more of IDG's 290 magazines and newspapers, including IDG's leading global brands — Computerworld, PC World, Network World, Macworld and the Channel World family of publications. IDG Books Worldwide is one of the fastest-growing computer book publishers in the world, with more than 700 titles in 36 languages. The "...For Dummies®" series alone has more than 50 million copies in print. IDG offers online users the largest network of technology-specific Web sites around the world through IDG.net (http://www.idg.net), which comprises more than 225 targeted Web sites in 55 countries worldwide. International Data Corporation (IDC) is the world's largest provider of information technology data, analysis and consulting, with research centers in over 41 countries and more than 400 research analysts worldwide. IDG World Expo is a leading producer of more than 168 globally branded conferences and expositions in 35 countries including E3 (Electronic Entertainment Expo), Macworld Expo, ComNet, Windows World Expo, ICE (Internet Commerce Expo), Agenda, DEMO, and Spotlight. IDG's training subsidiary, ExecuTrain, is the world's largest computer training company, with more than 230 locations worldwide and 785 training courses. IDG Marketing Services helps industry-leading IT companies build international brand recognition by developing global integrated marketing programs via IDG's print, online and exposition products worldwide. Further information about the company can be found at www.idg.com.   1/26/00

Dedication

This book is dedicated to Anne, Sandra, and Joanne, without whose help this book wouldn't have been possible.

Publisher's Acknowledgments

We're proud of this book; please register your comments through our IDG Books Worldwide Online Registration Form located at `http://my2cents.dummies.com`.

Some of the people who helped bring this book to market include the following:

Acquisitions and Editorial

Project Editors: James H. Russell, Mica Johnson

Acquisitions Editor: Gregory S. Croy

Copy Editors: William A. Barton, Nicole Laux

Proof Editor: Teresa Artman

Technical Editor: Drew Michaels

Editorial Manager: Kyle Looper

Editorial Assistant: Sarah Shupert

Production

Project Coordinator: Emily Wichlinski

Layout and Graphics: Heather Pope, Julie Trippetti, Jeremey Unger, Erin Zeltner

Proofreaders: Laura Albert, Corey Bowen, Susan Moritz, York Production Services, Inc.

Indexer: York Production Services, Inc.

General and Administrative

IDG Books Worldwide, Inc.: John Kilcullen, CEO; Bill Barry, President and COO; John Ball, Executive VP, Operations & Administration; John Harris, CFO

IDG Books Technology Publishing Group: Richard Swadley, Senior Vice President and Publisher; Mary Bednarek, Vice President and Publisher; Walter R. Bruce III, Vice President and Publisher; Joseph Wikert, Vice President and Publisher; Mary C. Corder, Editorial Director; Andy Cummings, Publishing Director, General User Group; Barry Pruett, Publishing Director

IDG Books Manufacturing: Ivor Parker, Vice President, Manufacturing

IDG Books Marketing: John Helmus, Assistant Vice President, Director of Marketing

IDG Books Online Management: Brenda McLaughlin, Executive Vice President, Chief Internet Officer; Gary Millrood, Executive Vice President of Business Development, Sales and Marketing

IDG Books Packaging: Marc J. Mikulich, Vice President, Brand Strategy and Research

IDG Books Production for Branded Press: Debbie Stailey, Production Director

IDG Books Sales: Roland Elgey, Senior Vice President, Sales and Marketing; Michael Violano, Vice President, International Sales and Sub Rights

◆

The publisher would like to give special thanks to Patrick J. McGovern, without whom this book would not have been possible.

◆

Contents at a Glance

Cartoons at a Glance

By Rich Tennant

page 53

page 7

page 87

page 109

page 133

Fax: 978-546-7747
E-mail: richtennant@the5thwave.com
World Wide Web: www.the5thwave.com

Cartoons at a Glance

By Rich Tennant

"YEAH, I USED TO WORK ON REFRIGERATORS, WASHING MACHINES, STUFF LIKE THAT— HOW'D YOU GUESS?"

page 169

page 189

Real Programmers never laugh at science fiction movies regardless of how dumb they are.

page 209

After spending hours trying to get the system up and running, Carl discovers that everything had been plugged into a "Clapper" light socket when he tries to kill a mosquito.

page 245

Real Programmers love to talk "computer-eze" while ordinary citizens are listening.

page 273

Fax: 978-546-7747
E-mail: richtennant@the5thwave.com
World Wide Web: www.the5thwave.com

Table of Contents

Introduction

● ●

*W*elcome to the world of Linux programming. Just the thought of programming a computer is enough to make most people give up immediately because it usually seems too complicated. Clear your mind of that myth — it ain't that difficult.

Can you write a grocery list or directions to your house? Of course you can! You can also write a Linux program (seriously!).

This book is not like the other computer books that you may have attempted to read — I scrap all the confusing technical jargon. In its place, I use some honest-to-goodness, common-sense English words that tell you how to make a computer do what you want it to do.

Writing instructions to tell a computer to perform a certain task something doesn't need to be difficult. After you find out how to perform a few simple tricks, computer programming is a great deal of fun.

The pages of this book are full of simple explanations for things you may have believed you needed an engineering degree to understand. I provide plenty of examples for you to copy and try out on your computer.

About This Book

Pretend that this book is your private tutor who comes to your home to make sure that you understand how to write a program in Linux. Programming in Linux isn't difficult, but sometimes it requires that you provide many small details to tell your computer how to do something.

Following are a few samples of the subjects that I discuss in *Linux Programming For Dummies:*

- ✔ Planning a Linux program
- ✔ Developing the user interface
- ✔ Understanding what Linux code can do

You may think that understanding how to program a computer requires you to take technical courses in abstract mathematics at your local college, but you're wrong. The purpose of this book is to walk you through all the steps you need to know to write a Linux program so that you can leave the pain behind.

How to Use This Book

In this book, you read the procedures for creating a user interface for your programs and then begin writing the Linux code that tells the computer how to respond to someone who uses your programs.

All the code in this book is set in monospace type as in the following example:

```
declare variable name
```

You want to type, character for character, anything that appears. I tell you if you need to make substitutions, such as using a real variable name in place of `variable name`. Linux cares about whether you use uppercase, lowercase, or a mixture of uppercase and lowercase letters, so look closely at any code that you see in these pages.

Because of the width of the margins in this book, some long lines of code may wrap to the next line. On your computer, however, these wrapped lines appear as a single line of code; make sure that you don't insert a hard return in one of them on-screen.

I sprinkle tests throughout this book. Don't concern yourself too much about them — just use them to test your knowledge (no grades are given). You know immediately how you're doing because I also give you the answers and references to the sections of the chapter that fully explain the answer.

You can also download the larger code samples from the chapters of this book by visiting `www.dummies.com/extras/linuxprog.html`, so that you can just copy and paste the code into your favorite compiler.

Foolish Assumptions

Following are some things that you must know how to do before you read this book:

- Turn your computer on and off.
- Type words on the keyboard.
- Read.

But, seriously, remember that this book is about Linux programming. You probably already know what a bug is, what a command line is, and so on. I don't think that you're someone who's never even touched a computer. I bet you may have read *Windows For Dummies* — maybe even *Linux For Dummies* (both from IDG Books Worldwide, Inc.). You may even be a programmer who wants to know about Linux programming.

Even if you have no previous knowledge, however, you can still follow along. You don't need to know how a computer works, and you don't need a high SAT score. A little common sense is the only requirement to understand what's in this book. Of course, you also need a computer that's running Linux. And I wrote this book with the bash shell in mind, which is just one of the many shells available for Linux. (I discuss the bash shell in Chapter 3.) But even if you're using the C shell, another popular Linux shell, don't despair: In Appendix C, I give you a table of equivalent commands.

If you qualify and possess the guts to continue, get ready for an interesting and fun adventure into the creation of Linux programs for your computer.

How This Book Is Organized

This book consists of ten parts, and each part usually consists of several chapters. If you have no programming experience, a lot of the material in this book makes more sense to you if you read the chapters in order. But if you have a little previous knowledge and can figure some things out, feel free to just pick up this book and start anywhere.

The following sections provide a breakdown of the parts and what you find in them.

Part I: A Beginner's Introduction to Linux Programming

Part I is a brief introduction to all the major features of Linux programming. This part of the book is the place to begin to help relieve your fears about programming a computer.

Part II: The Basics of Writing Code

To find out how to write a Linux program that tells the computer to do something, read Part II. It helps you understand how to use the Linux shell script language to give instructions to the computer.

Part III: Making Decisions

Part III tells you how to instruct your computer to make up its own mind about performing a task and then do something special without asking for additional directions. Your instructions, in effect, enable your computer to become self-reliant.

Part IV: Loops and Loops

Loops are another way of telling your computer to continue doing something until it gets it right. In Part IV, you read about different ways to make your computer repeat itself.

Part V: Writing Subprograms

Just the thought of writing a large computer program is enough to make any sane person run far away. Part V shows you the tricks of how to break down a large program into many smaller programs, known as subprograms.

Part VI: Database Programs and Printing

Database programs are special programs that your computer uses to store and retrieve information in a file on your hard disk. In Part VI, you discover how a computer handles that information. You also find out how to print any information on paper.

Part VII: Debugging Your Program

In this small part, you find out the tried-and-true ways of tracking down a problem in your Linux program. (It's not as complex as it sounds!)

Part VIII: Automating E-Mail

This part shows you step by step how to how to incorporate e-mail into your programs. You discover, for example, how to set your program to automatically send e-mail to your friends, relatives, and anyone else with an e-mail address.

Part IX: The Part of Tens

Part IX contains several chapters of miscellaneous information that you may find useful and interesting, including tips about Linux utilities you can use with your programs.

Part X: Appendixes

This part contains some helpful appendixes. Here you can find a glossary of terms, a primer on using the vi text editor, and information on the differences in writing scripts in other Linux shells. I also include an appendix containing plenty of Linux programming exercises — with answers!

Icons Used in This Book

Denotes technical details that are informative (and sometimes interesting) but not necessary to know about. Skip these areas if you want.

Flags useful or helpful information that makes programming even less complex.

Indicates important information — don't pass up these gentle reminders!

Alerts you to something you don't want to do. Proceed cautiously whenever you encounter this icon.

Points out places where you test your newfound knowledge. Relax — I guarantee that you can pass these tests if you read the chapter.

Where to Go from Here

Now's the time to launch your exploration into the world of Linux programming. Grab a comfortable chair, sit back, and get ready to have some fun.

Part I

A Beginner's Introduction to Linux Programming

The 5th Wave   By Rich Tennant

"I'LL BE WITH YOU AS SOON AS I EXECUTE A FEW MORE COMMANDS."

In this part . . .

*I*f you think that the great-paying jobs go to computer programmers and you're not one because computer programming seems too complicated, this book is for you.

You hear about computer programming at work or on television, and you hear that the kids in your old high school know how to do it. You'd like to give it a try, but you don't know where to begin.

Guess what? You already started as you opened this book. You don't find pages of technical computer jargon here. You do find the first steps that you need to begin programming a computer.

Chapter 1

Checking Out How Linux Programming Works

*T*he primary reason for writing a computer program is to make a computer do something useful. To begin writing a Linux program, you first want to turn off your computer and then use some paper and a pencil to plan exactly what you want to make the computer do.

You can make a computer do virtually anything that you can imagine, short of making it take your driver's test or using it to print money to pay your bills (although some people *do* use computers illegally to print money). A computer program can perform such basic tasks as displaying a few words on-screen or more complicated tasks, such as tracking an airplane flight across the country.

After you determine what you want the computer to do, you must write down step-by-step instructions in a programming language to tell the computer how to do what you want.

Writing a Linux Program

Just as millions of ways exist to earn money, millions of ways also exist to write a computer program correctly. Some people work with their hands to make buildings; others draw up construction plans; and some folks spend their time trying to figure out how to marry into a wealthy family. Similarly, you can write the same computer program in an unlimited number of ways; no matter which way you write it, however, the result is always the same — a *program*.

Your job is that of a *programmer*, or the person who writes a computer program. You want to write programs that are easy to use, of course, and that correctly tell a computer what to do. No one can use a program that doesn't work correctly (although that doesn't stop you from selling your programs before you're run out of town), and a program that's difficult to use frustrates anyone who uses it — and people often toss it in the garbage, even if it works fine.

To make sure that each program you write gets the job done, you need to test it to make sure that you're on target. If you design a program to display names and addresses on-screen but it prints names and addresses instead, the program obviously doesn't work (unless, of course, you change the program's intent to printing names and addresses).

Deciding whether your program is easy to use, however, is a difficult job. What you may think is easy can prove an insurmountable task for someone else. Everyone knows, for example, how to board a bus, pay the fare, find a seat, and get off the bus at the right bus stop, even if she's never traveled on that particular bus line. The same concept applies whenever someone uses your Linux program (if you make it easy to use, of course). Users expect to start your program by typing the name of the program into the computer or choosing your program from a menu that appears on-screen. After your program is running, users expect menus that walk them through each step and screens that demonstrate a logical flow. The structure of your program should be similar to other programs and familiar to anyone who uses it.

Understanding the Linux programming development cycle

The following nine steps are necessary to create a Linux program (the same number of innings necessary for a no-hitter in baseball — unless it's a rain-shortened game), with the first eight steps being the *development cycle:*

1. **Decide what you want the computer to do.**

2. **Decide how your program is to look on-screen (the *user interface*).**

3. **Create the user interface by using common objects such as text and areas in which users can enter information.**

4. **Arrange these common objects into a logical flow on one or more screens.**

5. **Write instructions in Linux to make each part of the program do something.**

6. **Run the program to see whether it works.**

7. **If your program doesn't work, say out loud, "I hate computers!" (and then remember that computers do only what you tell them to do).**

8. **Look for errors (known as *bugs*) in your program.**

9. **Start over (not optional).**

Don't plan to memorize these nine steps. Plan to follow them, however, every time that you write a computer program. No shortcuts are available, and you can't skip any steps. Skipping a step is similar to trying to run before you get out of bed, get dressed, and jump out on the sidewalk: You can move your legs as fast as they can move, but you don't get anywhere. (If you tire of this fruitless effort, you can always just stop, roll over, and pull the covers over your head.)

Guess which step is the most difficult? The first step! After you know what you want a computer to do, you must find a way to give the computer the correct instructions. The trick to completing this step is to lock yourself in a room with plenty of junk food and caffeine sources and keep plugging away until you succeed.

Developing the user interface

A *user interface* is simply the method that you use for giving commands to a computer as a program's running, enabling the computer to respond. This interface is what a program displays on-screen and includes which keyboard keys users must press to use the program.

The user interface in a Linux program doesn't feature the exploding screen or rainbow-colored windows that you see in Microsoft Windows programs. Your creativity alone must create excitement from the sparse screens that you can build in Linux.

But don't use this limitation as a crutch! You still can create easy-to-use Linux programs, even if you can't use all the bells and whistles that a Windows program can offer.

A quick (and incomplete) history of Linux

Before you begin to write Linux programs, you may find the story of Linux programming's origins of interest.

Back in 1991, Linus Torvalds was a University of Helsinki undergraduate student who wanted to run the Unix operating system on his PC. Unix cost more than what Torvalds could afford, so he got together with fellow student programmers, and they created their own version of Unix, naming it Linux. (*Lin* comes from *Linus* and *ux* from *Unix.*)

Three years passed before the first version of Linux was introduced to the public. About 125,000 people were the first to use Linux. The number of Linux users stands at about 10 million today. Version 2.2 of Linux enjoyed the following key advantages over its chief rival DOS:

- Linux uses *demand-page virtual memory*, which is a fancy way of saying that Linux stores the portion of a program that it doesn't use on disk if insufficient space remains to store the program in memory. This feature enables you to run large programs.

- Linux is multitasking and can run more than one program at the same time.

- Linux works with more than one user at a time, which is perfect for network servers that require more than one person to access the server at the same time.

- Linux is free!

Before Linux came Unix. Back in the 1960s, some Bell Labs employees set out to build a program that enabled a computer to become a *multitasking operating system*, or an operating system that runs more than one program at the same time. They used the same clever program to enable more than one person to use the same computer at the same time, which is known as a *multiuser operating system*.

The name given to this brilliant program was Unix. Unix is more than one program, however; it's a group of programs divided into the following three parts:

Kernel: Controls the parts of the computer, such as the hard disk, memory, and other stuff that makes the computer work.

File system: Makes sure that you don't lose your information.

Shell: Controls how the computer works.

The Bell Labs folks also tried to make controlling a computer easy. They built many programs into Unix, each of which does something well. These programs, known as *utilities,* can sort information, search for information in a file, and perform a variety of other tasks. You can find out more about utilities in the section "Linux utilities already exist," later in this chapter.

Those computer whiz kids came up with a way to make building a program much easier than ever. Now programmers can combine just the utilities you need into a Unix program called a *shell script.* This script enables you to write complex, sophisticated Unix programs in just a short time. All the tricky stuff is already programmed into the utilities. You just need to choose the right ones and combine them into the programs that you write.

By the 1980s, these Unix features, in addition to the rapid creation of powerful and low-cost computers, brought Unix from the halls of universities and the Department of Defense (DoD) into industry.

Today all the development that went into the creation of Unix is carried over to the version of Linux that you're using to write and run your programs.

Examining user-interface objects

A user interface in a Linux program consists of two objects: the text and the cursor (where the user actually types something in), as the following example shows (except that you need to imagine the cursor appearing after `Enter your selection:` because I can't print the blinking cursor in the book.):

```
The Telephone Directory

1. Find a telephone number
2. Modify an existing telephone number
3. Add a new telephone number

Q Quit

Enter your selection:
```

Unlike Windows and the Mac's OS, which are graphical-based environments, Linux is a character-based environment.

Linux displays only characters on-screen unless a fancy Motif program is running on the computer. (A *Motif program* makes the Linux interface look like that of Windows.) And in your Linux programs, you can't create any of the push buttons, drop-down list boxes, or other objects that Windows and the Mac use.

Its developers were concerned only with making Linux easier for programmers, not ultra easy for someone to use the program. Remember, however, that because *you* are the Linux programmer, you do want to make your Linux programs easier for the user.

More about pictures and characters (if you really must know)

In the olden days (do I sound like one of your grandparents?), when computers ran very slowly, computers could display characters on-screen fast in only one way: A program simply told the computer to display a letter on-screen. ("Give me an E! Give me a Y!") The computer was smart enough to display the letter at the spot where the cursor was sitting.

Your computer screen consists of tiny "light-bulb" dots known as *pixels*. If you turn on the appropriate pixels, the letter *e*, for example, appears on-screen.

A *character-based* system divides the screen into blocks of pixels known as *character blocks.* A character block typically contains 45 pixels. (That's nine rows and five columns, but who's counting?) Your computer, not your program, controls which of the 45 pixels in a block light up.

A *graphics-based* system, on the other hand, includes no character blocks in it. Your program must light each pixel individually to form letters or any other image that you want to appear on-screen.

Writing Linux code

After you plan what you want your programs to do and how to make them easy for someone to use, you must write down your ideas in such a way that a computer can understand what you want it to do. You must use instructions (also known as *code*) that you write in a computer language. You can use C++, Java, or a Linux shell-script language (why else would you be reading this book?) to direct the computer to do what you have in mind. You may want to organize your thoughts in the following order:

1. **Decide which tasks you want the computer to perform.**

2. **Determine the order in which you want the computer to perform each task.**

   Think of this step as similar to knowing that you must stand upright before you begin running.

3. **Find the correct commands in the shell-script language that tell the computer which task you want it to perform.**

4. **Use a Linux editor program (sort of an old word-processing program without the fancy features) to type all the commands into the shell-script file in the order in which you want the computer to follow them.**

   I give you my recommendations for a text editor in Chapter 3.

Stuff you probably don't want to know about programming languages

Your computer doesn't understand English — or Spanish or any other spoken language, for that matter. The only language that it understands is *binary code* (or *machine language*), which consists of a bunch of zeros and ones. Try writing a program by using this method, and you quickly head directly for the loony bin. Programmers are different from the average Joe, but they're not crazy, so some scientists created an "easier" programming language known as an *assembly language*.

Before your computer can run the assembly-language program, you must call in the translator.

Another program must interpret the assembly language into the zeros and ones that your computer can read.

As with any translation, problems can arise. Saying certain things in one language, for example, sometimes takes longer than saying the same things in another language. And a computer language is no different. Saying the same thing takes longer in assembly language than it does in machine language. Assembly-language programs, therefore, end up larger and slower than do the same programs that you write in machine language.

Because many programmers found assembly language difficult to use, the scientists went back to the drawing board and created new and improved languages, such as C, C++, Java, and Visual Basic. (The scientists created a number of other languages, but who cares?) The creators of each of these newfangled languages set out to make writing instructions to a computer as easy as writing instructions to a friend.

Although no computer language is as simple to use as your own mother language (English, Spanish, or whatever), the best computer language is the one that enables you to create a program in the shortest amount of time and with the fewest number of mistakes. Remember that, because you must translate each of these fancy programming languages into machine language, you may as well just avoid arguments over which is the better computer language to use.

The computer language that your programs use isn't what makes the difference in their performance over similar programs anyway. The competitive edge lies in the design of the programs and the efficiency of the program that performs the translation into machine language.

Many programmers forget that the translator program is the "programmer" that writes the actual instructions that your computer executes. You have no say over which translator program your program uses: If a translator isn't already installed on your computer, it comes with the computer language that you use.

If you want to create an ultra-fast program (and you're willing to go through the torture of writing it), learn how to use assembly language. Otherwise, stick with a language that's easier to use, such as Visual Basic or Linux shell scripts. You can read more about shell scripts in the sidebar "A quick (and incomplete) history of Linux," earlier in this chapter.

Giving a Linux Program an Appropriate Name

You can save a Linux program in one file or in more than one file, depending on how many commands you need to tell the computer what you want it to do. You always need at least one file for any Linux program.

Some computer languages, such as C++, Java, and Visual Basic, require a project file that helps you keep track of your programs. Linux programs, however, don't require any special file. Nothing's special, in fact, about the file that contains your Linux program except how you name your program files.

Following are some guidelines and rules for choosing a filename:

✔ You can call the program file virtually any name that you can imagine (although MoeLarryCurly is a little less than creative). Use some common sense and make the name reflect the contents of the file (TelephoneList, JanBudget, or FamilyTree, for example).

✔ The filename can have an unlimited number of characters. You can use just one character if you want, but you're better off if you make your filenames a little more descriptive than that. (How can you ever remember what's in a file that you name simply X?)

✔ Feel free to use a combination of upper- and lowercase letters in your filenames. Linux doesn't change filenames into all uppercase letters.

✔ Don't use spaces or the following characters in your filenames (because your computer doesn't like you if you do):

$! & ; | \ /

The following list shows variations for naming your files (and although the names are similar, each file is actually different because Linux is case sensitive):

✔ AddressList

✔ addresslist

✔ addressList

✔ Addresslist

✔ Address__List

Running a Linux Program

You can run your Linux program *almost* right away. You don't need to use another program to convert your Linux program to machine language before you can use your program. (I describe machine language in the sidebar "Stuff you probably don't want to know about programming languages," earlier in this chapter.) You get either instant gratification or pain (if the program doesn't work correctly).

Keep running your program over and over again until you stamp out those confounded bugs. In other words, fix all the problems with your program. Only then do you want to call all your coworkers over to see your new creation.

Making a file executable by using the chmod utility

Your Linux program files don't need any extensions, such as EXE, BAT, or COM. (You can leave extensions to the Windows programs you write.) You must, however, tell the computer that the file is an *executable* file — that is, a file containing instructions for the computer to follow. You use the chmod utility to tell your computer which files are executable. Type, for example, the following command at the prompt (replacing *myfile* with the name of your file, of course!):

```
chmod 711 myfile
```

If you don't make a file executable by using the chmod utility, Linux doesn't recognize it as such. After you make a file executable, you can run the program by simply typing the name of the program at the command prompt.

What chmod 711 actually means

Your computer knows whether a file is a program by the permissions that you grant to users of the file. A permission limits the accessibility to the file. You can grant three kinds of permissions to any file: *read*, *write*, and *executable*.

First, decide who can use your program: the *owner* (you); the *group* (such as your friends who work with you); and *others* (everyone else in the world). You can grant individual permissions by placing the sum of permissions (which you derive from the level of permission that you grant to each category of user) in the correct order within the chmod utility, as the following example shows:

    owner   group   others

The first of the three numbers that you use with the chmod utility refers to the permission that you grant to the owner of the file (that's you). The second number identifies the permissions that you grant for the group. The third number tells the utility how to set the permissions for everyone else.

To grant the permissions that you need for a program, you use the sum of the following numbers for each category of user. Each level of permission corresponds to one of these numbers, as the following list shows:

- ✔ Read: 4
- ✔ Write: 2
- ✔ Executable: 1

You add these numbers together to determine the permission level for each category of user and then use those three sums with the chmod utility. Say, for example, that you want to make the file an executable file (a program file), but you also want to read the file on-screen and change whatever you see; you need read and write permissions to do this stuff.

Add together the numbers for each permission level that you want to grant yourself (4 + 2 + 1 = 7). The sum, 7, is the first of the three numbers that you use with the chmod utility. If you just want to grant yourself read and write permissions without making the file an executable file, however, you use the number 6 (4 + 2 = 6) with the chmod utility for your own level of permission.

So chmod 711 *myfile* (where *myfile* is the name of the file to which you're assigning permissions) means that the owner (you) has read, write, and executable permissions and that both the group and others can only execute your program.

Linux Shell-Script Languages versus Other Languages

Because writing a program in Linux requires a different way of thinking than does programming in other computer languages, this section gives you some important features that are easy to overlook. They're here, at your fingertips, whenever you feel a lapse of memory coming on.

Linux utilities already exist

In most programming languages, you first plan what you want the computer to do and then decide which instructions to give it to make that happen. Linux programming is a little different. You still must plan the task to get the job done, but most of the instructions already exist in the form of a Linux utility. So you need only to divide your program into the tasks that you want the computer to perform and then find the appropriate Linux utility to carry them out. (Bell Labs created Unix so that programmers can quickly assemble their programs from well-tested utilities. All you need to do is to choose the right utilities and put them in your program.)

Each utility requires input (that you supply). After the utility finishes working, it delivers output that you can use as input for another utility. As an example, a text-editor utility creates a file that you can use as input for the spell-check utility.

Learning how to use a Linux utility could become a nightmare if not for this clever little trick: Most utilities include a how-to manual, known as a *man page*, that's installed on any computer running Linux. (And, no, it's not a list of eligible men.) *Man* is short for *man*ual. To display the manual on-screen, just type the following line (replacing *utility* with the utility name!) and press Enter:

```
man utility
```

After you find a utility you want to use, test it out before you make it part of your program. (Each utility, by the way, is itself a program.) Enter the name of the utility on the Linux command line along with the input that it needs. After you press the Enter key, the utility crunches away, and the output appears on-screen (unless, of course, the utility's job is to send the output to a printer or modem).

Linux reads, converts, and executes one line at a time

Most programs that you use on a PC have the EXE extension. These letters in a filename tell Windows that the file is a program that's in machine language. (You can save any file with an EXE extension, of course, but saving anything other than a program this way only confuses your computer.) The computer can jump right into the program and follow your instructions as fast as a speeding bullet.

You don't get this same performance with Linux programs. Programs that you write in most other computer languages are *compiled* (already in machine language before the program is run), but that's not the case for Linux. A *compiler* is a program that translates your program into machine language and then saves the translation in a file (the EXE file in Windows). You also must translate your Linux programs into machine language, but this translation takes place as a user runs an executable program rather than as you create the program.

The translation takes place one line at a time. Your computer reads one line of the Linux shell script, converts the line into machine language, and then executes the instruction. Your computer then goes back to your Linux shell script, reads the next line, and follows the same steps for that line. This process continues until your program ends. Translating your program line by line as you run the program can, unfortunately, slow things down a little.

Linux can run quietly in the background

Whenever you run a computer program, it takes over your computer: The program determines what appears on-screen and when you can use your keyboard.

Your Linux program isn't a hog — it's willing to share your computer with other programs, because Linux is a multiprocessing operating system. Someone who needs to run another program in addition to your program can tell the computer to run your program and then to run the other programs. Because your program just does its thing in the background, this process is known as *background processing.*

The program that you're currently using, in what's know as the *foreground process,* takes charge of everything that you see on-screen. Any program that runs in Linux is a *process* because Linux is processing the instructions and data that associate with the program. A *daemon* — any program that's running in the background — is out there somewhere, too. If you launch your program as a daemon, it runs quietly somewhere in your computer's memory, where only your computer can find it. Forgetting that the program is even running is easy to do.

Any program can become a daemon if you type **&** (an ampersand) after the name of your program on the command line — which is the line on which the cursor rests, patiently waiting for you to enter the next command or program name.

A daemon continues to run until you log off your computer, unless you start that program in a special way. (The only way to stop a daemon for good is to use the `kill` command.) You can, however, also run your Linux program by using the `nohup` command, which tells your computer to continue to run the program even after you log off. To run a program this way, type the following at the command prompt (but replace *myprogram* with your program's name!):

```
nohup myprogram
```

Linux uses subprograms

Whenever you write any type of program, you want to break up what you need the computer to do into a series of tasks. Each task then becomes an individual part of the entire program. You can divide an address-book program, for example, into segments that enable you to perform the following separate tasks:

- ✔ Enter a new address.

- ✔ Find an existing address.

- ✔ Modify an existing address.

In other programming languages, you build each segment of a program separately from the other segments and then assemble them into the final program. You can't execute any individual program segment (known variously as *procedures*, *functions*, *methods*, and *subroutines* in languages such as Java, Visual Basic, and C++) by itself.

The drawbacks of Linux programming

All the good parts of Linux programming are balanced by factors that some Linux programmers wish would change for the better. (Don't hold your breath, however.) The Linux environment is ideal for hackers and people who don't like the limitations of Microsoft Windows and the Mac (where the command line is hidden from you). For the rest of us, however, Linux is a step backward.

Some people (such as Bill Gates) try to hide all the complicated stuff behind fancy windows. The folks at Bell Labs, however, designed Unix so that you must get hip-deep into the mess. Rather than just press buttons and choose items from drop-down menus as in Windows, anyone using a Linux program (including yours) must type commands on the command line to get the program rolling. (Sort of takes you back to the days of DOS and the Apple IIe in the 1970s and '80s, doesn't it?)

To create the fancy screens that users expect from professional programs, you must go beyond Linux programming and learn how to program *X-Windows* (which provides multiple windows on-screen) and *Motif* (which supplies push buttons and scroll bars). X-Windows and Motif are programs that are available in most recent releases of Linux.

Another drawback of Linux programming is the shell-script language that you use to create programs. The words that you use to tell a computer what to do are different in each computer language. You use different words in the C++ and Java programming languages to display your name on-screen, for example, than you use to perform the same task in Visual Basic. In Linux programming, however, you use different words for the *same* instruction. The exact words that you use in your Linux program depend on the shell that interprets your script.

The *shell* is the program that translates the commands that someone enters at the command line into instructions the computer can understand. Entering a command can be as simple as clearing the screen or translating each line of your program. Linux has many shells: the *Bourne shell*, bash shell, *C shell*, and *Korn shell* are just a few — whiz kids are creating new ones every day. (See Chapter 3 for more information on these five main shells.)

Because each shell uses its own language, as you set out to write a Linux program, you must first decide which shell language to use. This problem doesn't exist in other operating systems, because they use only *one* shell.

Linux programming is somewhat different. You still divide the program into segments, but the segments are really smaller programs (known as *subprograms*). Unlike the procedures, functions, and subroutines in other languages, you can run each segment in Linux by itself, or another program can call each individual segment.

You can use a subprogram a number of times within a program simply by calling the subprogram. You can save countless hours of programming time by reusing instructions in a subprogram. Then you don't need to write the instructions over again or spend time debugging. You write and debug instructions one time as you create the subprogram and then you call the subprogram whenever you need it in your program.

You must set the permissions for the subprograms that you create as executable so that you can run them as part of your program. To find out about permissions, see the section "Running a Linux Program," earlier in this chapter.

Testing your programming knowledge

1. What's an illegal name to give a file for a Linux program?

   a. A cuddly animal name.

   b. A name with spaces or characters such as $ and !.

   c. A name that's hard for Linux to pronounce.

   d. One you don't know how to spell.

2. How do you make a file executable for Linux?

   a. Accuse it of treason.

   b. Tell everyone its secret name.

   c. Use the chmod utility.

   d. Use the keyboard.

   Answers: 1) b. See "Giving a Linux Program an Appropriate Name." *2) c. See* "Making a file executable by using the chmod utility."

Chapter 2

Designing Your First User Interface

. . . .

In This Chapter

▶ Deciding how to tell users what to do in a Linux program

▶ Creating a plan for your Linux program to follow

▶ Mapping out your program's on-screen elements

. . . .

*B*efore you can write your first Linux program, you must know how to make your program easy for someone else to use. You must decide how users are to interface with your program, choose which words to display on-screen, define the list of menu options, and then write the Linux code.

Although programs are different from each other, most tend to work the same way because they include similar features. Programs display a menu, ask the user to make a selection, and then respond to the request. Every user interface, for example, shows information on-screen. Windows and Mac programs use a graphical user interface to display information, and Linux programs use character blocks to display information. Both types of programs can display practically the same information on-screen.

After a user starts a program, the program displays options from which the user can choose to tell the computer what to do next (pick tomorrow's winning lottery number, for example). Windows and Mac programs present these options as *icons* (little pictures that a user clicks with the mouse to issue a command), menu-bar items, and other fancy techniques. Linux programs display options in text format and simply ask you to press a corresponding key on your keyboard.

Instructions in a Linux program appear on-screen to tell users what the program expects them to do next. The program is saying, in effect, "Come on — press one of those confounded keys!"

A short history of user interfaces

A long time ago, back when the '57 Chevy was new, computers weren't friendly. Programming a computer to do *anything*, in fact, was a downright dreadful task. You sat in front of a bunch of cables and a computer full of holes and then plugged the correct cable into the correct hole, in much the same way as telephone operators do in those old movies.

Someone must have gotten electrocuted somewhere along the line, because by the time that Eisenhower was moving out of the White House (during the 1960s, for those of you who weren't born yet), computer technicians eliminated the task of plugging in wires. Paper, in the form of cards that resembled index cards, took the place of cables. Each task that you wanted the computer to perform you represented by marking one of these *punch cards* with a series of holes. (You could indicate only one task per card.) In the final step, someone needed to stack thousands of the punch cards in a precise order and then feed them into the computer.

By the time the Nixon era was winding down (during the 1970s — yes, this sidebar is a history quiz in disguise), someone came up with a bright idea: Get rid of punch cards! At the moment that this brilliant person decided to use a keyboard and a television monitor to teach the computer to perform tasks, the modern-day user interface was born. After you turned on a computer, a blinking dot (and nothing else) appeared on-screen. The dot implied that the computer was ready for its first command — no menus or instructions appeared on-screen. You had to know that the appearance of the blinking dot meant that it was time to type a computer instruction on the keyboard. This command-line interface appeared whenever the DOS prompt came on-screen. To get a computer to do anything, however, you needed to know the correct command to give to the computer (and how to spell the command correctly as well).

During the 1980s (the history quiz is over), as programmers transformed sparse screens into groups of choices that users needed to make, programs became *menu driven.* Some smart people (and you can soon join their ranks) developed programs that seemed to demonstrate the best way to show menus on-screen.

Great! An easy way for anyone to use a program — except that no two programs worked the same way. Some brighter programmers set out to fix this problem (and made about a billion dollars) by throwing away the old computer manuals and making way for the *GUI,* or *graphical user interface.*

No, Bill Gates didn't invent the GUI. Many programmers and companies, including Xerox and Apple Computer, had a hand in creating it. Gates just had the marketing clout to make the GUI popular.

Linux's basic user interface hasn't progressed much beyond the command-line interface, because most Linux whiz kids are hackers who are comfortable with working with the command line.

Linux has the GUI world look, through add-on software such as X Windows and Motif, which are the forerunners of Windows.

The Linux shell-script language provides all the commonly used parts of a typical Linux program — display information, read the keyboard, and do something with the information read from the keyboard. A user just must use the right words in the shell-script language to provide the correct instructions to the computer.

You can perform in your Linux programs virtually any task that one of those fancy Windows or Mac user interfaces can do. Linux doesn't use *fancy* menus, but it does use menus. It displays no fancy scroll lists, for example, but it can display a list of on-screen options from which users can make selections. (Who needs all that window dressing anyway? Most users just want to get the job done.)

Planning What You Want Users to Do

Ah, where to begin? Start with the old-style computer if you want — paper and pencil. (You never need to upgrade it, and it works even without electricity.) Then draw a picture of what you want users to see and do as they use the Linux program that you create.

Here are the steps to follow:

1. **Know what you want the program to do before you set out to design the user interface.**

2. **Pretend to be a person who's going to use your program.**

   Pretend that you have no information about the program except perhaps its name and a general idea of how the program can help you.

3. **List on paper the menu selections that you want to enable users to make after your program begins.**

4. **For each possible user selection, list what you want the computer to do after a user chooses that option.**

This following list, for example, shows the first task (and related subtasks) that a user must perform:

1. *Opening screen*

   a. *Locate telephone number*

      Enter telephone number

      Display telephone number

      Change telephone number

      Return to preceding menu

      Exit

   b. *Change entry*

      Enter telephone number

      Display telephone number

      Change telephone number

> *Cancel preceding change*
>
> *Return to preceding menu*
>
> *Exit*
>
> c. *Add new entry*
>
> > *Enter new information*
> >
> > *Cancel new information*
> >
> > *Return to preceding menu*
> >
> > *Exit*

Don't be afraid to make a mistake. (That's why they make pencil erasers.) The only way that you can perfect your programming skills is by trial-and-error (and you may end up on *Court TV*).

The more that you use paper and pencil to create a plan, the easier translating your perfect set of planning notes into a full-scale Linux program becomes. After you finish your plan, you can concentrate on getting the computer to do what you want.

Planning What You Want the Computer to Do

The whole purpose of a computer is to do more than anyone who uses the computer must do. (That's to say that users, ideally, are to do little to perform a task, while computers do most of the work!) That's the concept behind computer automation: Your program displays options on-screen and asks users simply to press the corresponding key on the keyboard for whatever task they want the computer to perform.

A computer must know what to do both before and after users of a Linux program make menu selections from the keyboard. The following list shows just some of the tasks that you, as a programmer, must consider ahead of time for any computer that runs one of your programs. Your Linux program must be capable of performing the following tasks:

- ✔ **Run the correct shell for your program:** Because you write Linux programs in a shell language (the C shell, for example — but no seashore jokes, please), the computer must have the correct shell running so that your program can work.

- ✔ **Do a little "housekeeping":** The computer needs to clear the screen of any text that appears on-screen so that it doesn't confuse the user of your program.

✔ **Display text on-screen:** The computer must display each line of text on-screen in the correct order. (The text is a combination of labels, choices, and instructions.)

✔ **Take a breather:** The computer simply waits until the user presses a key on the keyboard.

✔ **Decide what to do after the user presses any key.** (Don't go looking for the *"any"* key on your keyboard — you don't have one.)

✔ **Determine which keyboard keys to respond to and what to do after the user presses those keys.**

✔ **Ignore some keys if they aren't the valid keys that the user can press to make a selection.**

✔ **Decide whether to erase what's on-screen after the user presses one of the allowable keys.**

✔ **Do something special:** Show other choices on-screen, for example, or find some information and display it.

✔ **Remove all the text that the user places on-screen:** Clean up your mess so that another program (or someone's mother) doesn't need to do it for you.

Designing the Screen Layout

After you plan what you want your Linux program to do (as I describe in the preceding section), you need to decide how the screens for your programs are to look. I suggest that you sketch out each screen that you want your program to display to users.

First, come up with a title or some words that generally describe the screen. A single line of text at the top of the screen is sufficient.

The content of the rest of the screen depends on what the computer is doing as it's showing the screen. Following are some common uses for screen displays:

✔ Display an appropriate message to users.

✔ List menu options.

✔ Provide information, such as names and addresses in a file.

✔ Collect user information.

Understanding what menus do

All of us, at some point, have chosen items from menus, regardless of whether those menus were part of those frustrating telephone-answering systems ("Press 1 if you want the sales department; press 2 if you want the complaint department") or appeared on a computer screen.

Some reasons for using menus in computer programs are obvious, as the following list shows:

- Menus offer an easy way for users to tell a computer what they want it to do.
- Menus restrict a user to a specific task so that the programmer (you) can focus on giving the computer the correct instructions necessary to carry out a task.
- Menus show only tasks that the user can perform immediately. Tasks not appropriate for the current activity aren't available. You can't ask a computer program to change a telephone number, for example, until you first tell it to find the number in a telephone directory.

Maintaining consistency

All of us are creatures of habit. We wake up at approximately the same time every day, arrive at work on schedule, grab a cup of coffee, and then arrive at home like clockwork to get ready for a repeat performance the following day. (Some of us also need to get a life!)

Each of us is generally consistent, and so are all the other people we depend on, such as spouses, the people who make our coffee, the local dry cleaner who makes sure that our clothes look sharp, and so on.

Just as people are usually consistent, they usually want the programs they use after arriving at their workplace to be consistent, too. Most people like to jump right into a program and put the computer through its paces — no one usually can spare the time to learn how to use a program. Such quick starts are possible only if the way that someone uses one program is the same way as that person uses all other programs.

If users must ponder for more than a few minutes about how to use a computer program, they usually give up and decide that the program is junky (but they normally use words that I can't repeat in a family book).

How do you prevent users from tossing your programs into the garbage can? You must make the user interface in your programs consistent with those of similar programs. Don't get too creative, or you may confuse someone who's using your program for the first time.

Choosing your words carefully

The words that you use on-screen in your programs are critical to the design of a quality user interface. If users don't understand the terms you use, they can't use your program.

Following are some tips you may find useful in making your programs communicate effectively with the people who use them:

> ✔ **Avoid using abbreviations and acronyms (words that you form from the first letter of multiple-word phrases).** Don't, for example, tell users to "Take the EXE and send it via FTP so that your OS can take it from there."
>
> ✔ **Make sure that the words you use to describe an option reflect precisely what happens after a user chooses that option.** Don't name an option *Edit*, for example, if *Edit An Address* more accurately describes what the option does.
>
> ✔ **Use simple words that are easy to understand.** Don't show off your vocabulary in designing a computer program.

The following example demonstrates a typical opening menu for a personnel database program:

```
FOR OFFICIAL USE ONLY

Personnel database

1. Display information about an employee
2. Add information about a new employee

Q Quit

Enter your selection:
```

The first line specifies that only authorized staff members can use the program. The second line simply tells users that this program is a personnel program.

The first user option, Display information about an employee, starts the user down the path toward locating and changing information about an employee. The screen that appears if users choose this option displays the employee information and asks whether they want to edit the information or delete the employee's name from the database, as shown in the following example:

```
Confidential Personnel Information

Bob Smith        Social Security #.: 555-55-5555
555 Any Street   Title: Office Manager
Anywhere, USA 55555  Start Date: 1/2/89

Department: Administration   Salary: $75,000

  1. Edit information
  2. Delete information
  Q Quit

Enter your selection:
```

The second option from the original example, Add information about a new employee, sends users down a different path, from which they can enter into the database some information about a new employee.

The last user option is the escape hatch: If users don't want to continue with the program, they can just press *Q* to quit the program.

Finally, a single line of instruction tells the user to make a selection.

Keeping your menu tree pruned

Don't you hate spending more time choosing items from menus than actually using a program? Now you get the opportunity to fix that problem in the programs that you create by minimizing your program's *menu tree,* or list of menus.

No magic number exists for the number of menus to put in a program. Try using just a few menus and then asking a friend to test your program. If that person becomes discouraged trying to navigate through your menus, you know that you have too many. Take out your tree pruner and trim some of the branches on your menu tree.

Because someone who uses your Linux program wants to do something other than just respond to your perfectly designed menus, each menu must address all possible tasks that a user may want to accomplish. After your program finds an address and displays it on-screen, for example, a user can modify the address, delete the address from the file, return to the preceding menu, or just leave your program.

If users decide to modify the information that's on-screen, you don't need to ask which piece of information they want to edit — that's obvious. A better idea is to enable *the user* to change the information.

Testing your programming knowledge

1. What are the two common parts of a user interface?

a. Pizza and a Coke.

b. Menus that everyone can understand and instructions to help someone out in a pinch.

c. The telephone and telephone numbers.

d. A computer manual close at hand and a lot of patience.

2. What's the most commonly available tool to use in designing a user interface?

a. A jigsaw.

b. Someone else's idea that you can copy.

c. A pencil and some paper.

d. A jackhammer (not for use at night).

Answers: 1) b. See "Designing the Screen Layout." *2) c. See* "Planning What You Want the Computer to Do."

As you plan your Linux program menus, keep in mind all the times that you've needed to step your way through one of those telephone menus (for example, "Press 1 if you want to shoot the person who designed this system. . . ."). You're the programmer who can make someone happy by guaranteeing that your menus are easier to use than those telephone menus.

Remembering that flexibility lowers frustration

The best type of program is one that works the same way that the user works. Because each user works a little differently from every other user, you must keep your Linux programs flexible so that they don't cramp anyone's style. This task is *not* an easy one. Try putting yourself in the place of someone who may use your program and then ask yourself the following questions:

  ✔ Am I backtracking through the menus too much?

  ✔ Does this program flow naturally?

  ✔ Can I move quickly from one task to another?

If you find yourself experiencing a problem in using your program, you can expect that someone else who uses your program is also likely to encounter the same problem. Make sure that you resolve any such problems and that your program works effortlessly — before the user gets it.

Avoiding dead ends

A good program enables users to move around the program quickly without needing to retrace their steps. Nothing's more frustrating than following a long menu trail only to discover that you end up in the wrong place. The only way out is to turn around and follow the trail back to your starting point.

You can avoid these dead ends by always enabling users to jump to key positions in your program. (You're in effect giving users the chance to say, "Beam me home, Scotty.") Decide which menus in your program are the important ones (the ones that start the program or perform another major task, such as displaying the screen that enables a user to locate information). Then include the important menus on other menus in your program so that users can jump to them quickly.

Always make sure that each menu contains an option for exiting the program. This option is an escape hatch in case a user panics and wants to stop using your program.

Making your program the teacher

Few computer users ever take the time to read the documentation that comes with their programs. Most people just start a program right up, confident that they can zip through the screens in a flash. They apparently believe that any program that requires reading those manuals just isn't worth owning. Not all the features of a program are obvious, however — some require the user to read the instruction manual or go to a class to fully utilize the features of the program.

If this situation sounds all too familiar to you, you're in the majority. As a programmer, you must deal with the problem of knowing that few users are likely to read any of the documentation that you write to show them how to use your program. Without reading the documentation, most users probably can't even use your program.

Following are a few ways to handle this situation:

- Make sure that you provide clear on-screen instructions whenever you expect a user to respond to your program.
- Include a single line of text to describe what a user needs to do next.
- Provide detailed instructions on a Help screen that users can open by pressing the Help option on any menu in your program.
- Always define, on the Help screen, any technical term that you use in the program.

Chapter 3

Writing Your First Linux Program

● ●

In This Chapter

▶ Outlining your program

▶ Choosing a shell language to use

▶ Choosing a text editor

▶ Writing Linux code for your program

● ●

To have your computer do something, you must clearly state each thing that you want it to do. Computers *always* do what you tell them to do (and only what you tell them). So even if you give your computer instructions that are unclear or out of order, your computer follows those directions without out question.

Before you can speak the language of programmers (*nerdish*, they sometimes call it), you need to learn programming etiquette.

✔ A single instruction to your computer is known as a *command*.

✔ Several commands together are known as *code*.

✔ All the instructions that you need to complete the task are collectively known as a *program*.

According to programming etiquette, programmers never write a program. They write code. And only uncool programmers ever ask to see your series of commands. "Can I see your code" is the correct way to ask permission to snoop into someone else's program. (But who asks before taking a peek?)

Starting Out: Before You Write a Linux Program

You must write instructions in a language that your computer understands; otherwise, your computer can't do anything. Before you write an instruction, you must choose a computer language. In using Linux, that language is a *shell language.* A shell language contains special commands known as *reserved words.* These words convey a special meaning to Linux, so you must be careful whenever you use them in your program. Following are a few such reserved words that are part of the bash shell language:

case	elif	let
clear	else	read
continue	if	then
echo	for in	while

Linux code is a bunch of shell-language reserved words that you join together to form a program. Whenever your computer reads a reserved word, it says to itself, "I remember how to do that." This situation is similar to how your dog knows what to do if you say, "Sit." (That is, if your dog is well-trained! My dog just sits there ignoring me, but at least my computer follows my commands.)

Your Linux program can consist of only one reserved word or of hundreds of reserved words strung together. One-word programs usually perform one task. A program that consists solely of the command ls — which is short for *list* — displays the current directory on-screen . . . and does nothing else. Longer programs, on the other hand, can do many things.

No one in his right mind would write one long program that contains hundreds and hundreds of reserved words. Your computer can easily read all those words, but you'd become so confused that changing the program or finding an error in it becomes unmanageable.

Outlining your program

If you were going to build your dream house, you wouldn't start by hammering lumber together. Instead you'd sit down with your paper and pencil to sketch out your ideas.

If you want to write a Linux program, follow the same procedure for building your dream house. Sit down and write in English (or another language, if you prefer) all the steps that your computer must do to complete the task.

As you compose your outline, you write a mixture consisting of both our everyday language and certain reserved words. This combination is known as *pseudo code.* Your outline may contain an element that reads similar to that of the following example: "if I press the letter Q, then end the program." The words if and then are reserved words, but the other words aren't. Don't worry; you quickly discover how to distinguish reserved words from everything else. The following outline's a typical example of pseudo code that shows you how to mix reserved words with regular language as you outline your program. I put the reserved words in monofont so that you can pick them out. The program is something that's probably familiar to you if you've ever started a program that first asks you to enter your user identification and a special password. The following outline shows all the steps that your computer must take to check your identification (with reserved words appearing in **bold** this time):

1. Start `bash`.
2. Clear the screen.
3. Show the title.
4. Tell the user to enter a user ID.
5. Wait for the user to enter a user ID.
6. Save the user ID in memory.
7. Tell the user to enter a password.
8. Remember not to display the password on-screen.
9. Wait for the user to enter a password.
10. Compare the user ID with known user IDs.
11. **if** you find the user ID **then**
12. Compare the password with the user ID's password.
13. **if** the password matches **then**
14. Show the opening menu.
15. **else** tell the user the wrong password was entered.
16. Clear the screen.
17. End the program.
18. **endif (end** the block of instructions, Steps 14 – 17, under the **if** statement).
19. **else** tell the user that he entered the wrong user ID.
20. Clear the screen.
21. End the program.
22. **endif (end** the block of instructions, Steps 18 – 21, under the **if** statement).

Being logical

Each line in your program plan must appear in the order in which you want the computer to perform the task. Think of how you'd do what you want the computer to do. Write down those steps on your paper.

The following steps, for example, are what you need to tell someone to do to enter a menu choice at the keyboard:

1. Clear the screen of any text.

2. Show the menu on-screen.

3. Tell the users to enter the letter that corresponds to the menu option that they want.

4. Wait for keyboard input.

Just think what the computer would do if you told it to "show the menu on-screen" and then to "clear the screen of any text." (Unless, of course, you want to elicit the reaction "Something's wrong with my monitor!" from your users.)

Most errors in your program, which are known as *bugs*, occur because the computer follows an instruction that's out of the correct order. (See Chapter 19 for information about bugs and debugging.) Instructions that are out of order are the hardest errors to find, especially if your program contains hundreds of lines of code.

Keeping track of loose ends

Your plan for your program can easily become confusing, especially if you want your computer to do a lot of stuff. Even a task that's very simple for you to perform takes a lot of instructions for the computer to follow.

A basic task such as checking your user ID and password takes 24 lines in Linux code. Imagine then how many lines you'd need for even the simplest program that you have in mind.

Following are a few ways to avoid losing your way through your plan:

 ✔ Place each instruction on its own line in your plan.

 ✔ Assign numbers to each line.

 ✔ Indent instructions that you're associating with the preceding instruction (such as whenever you use the `if` reserved word).

Breaking down large programs into parts

Before you actually write a program, I want to steer you toward some good programming habits. You can make your large program easier to work with by breaking it down into several smaller programs. After you complete each of these small programs, you can call each one from other programs as you need them.

Each small program that's part of a larger program is known as a *subprogram*. (In other computer languages, these subprograms are known as *functions*, *procedures*, and *subroutines*.) A subprogram contains all the reserved words necessary to perform one particular task. Each time that you want your computer to carry out this task, you call the subprogram.

One subprogram may instruct the computer to display a menu on-screen. Another subprogram may tell the computer to read what someone enters at the keyboard and compare it with menu options. But not every program needs subprograms. If you experience no problems reading the code in your program, you probably don't need to create subprograms. (I explain more about subprograms in Chapter 14.)

Finding repeated code

Don't be surprised if your plan for your program grows rapidly. It's like sketching the layout of your new home and then adding a formal dining room, a formal living room, and the family dining room, and an informal living room. . . .

At some point, you must sit back and ask yourself whether you really need all these rooms in your house. Then you review the plans for economy. Is anything duplicated in the plans? Can you use one thing for another purpose? Do you really need a water fountain in the doghouse?

The following steps describe a way to reduce the size of your program:

1. **Look for instructions that repeat in your plans.**

   How many times, for example, does the computer display the same menu?

2. **Place instructions that repeat into a subprogram and then plan for your computer to call the subprogram each time that you need it.**

   See Chapter 14 for more information on subprograms.

3. **Give the subprogram a name that reflects the task that it performs.**

   The name *opening menu*, for example, is a good name for a subprogram that displays the opening menu. (Did anyone really go to MIT for that?)

Testing your programming knowledge

1. What are reserved words?

a. Words that shy people use.

b. Special instructions that every program-ming language has.

c. Words to get you into an expensive restaurant.

d. Words that you use in an emergency.

2. How can you design a large program without getting lost?

a. Have a team of programmers write your program for you.

b. Copy someone else's idea.

c. You'd never attempt such a project.

d. Outline your program before writing Linux code.

Answers: 1) b. See "Starting Out: Before You Write a Linux Program." *2) d. See* "Outlining your program."

Dividing your program into subprograms helps a lot as you make changes to the program. Say, for example, that in five places in your program, the com-puter displays the opening menu. If you modify the opening menu, you must make those changes in five places. But if the opening menu is a subprogram, you make only one change.

Translating Your Program into Linux Code

After you spend days fine-tuning your plan for your Linux program, you can turn your attention to translating your plan into Linux code. Don't rush into writing code. Many programmers make this common mistake. You have plenty of time to write your program.

Concentrate on following the logic of your plan. Keep an eye peeled for wrong turns and places where you give the correct instruction at the wrong time. Even the best programmers make mistakes in logic.

You're sure to find that tracking down those bugs in your plan is easier if you do it *before* you actually begin building your program. It's like finding out that the doorway in the plans for your dream house is too small before the con-tractor begins building the front of your house.

Understanding what Linux code can do

You can make your computer do all sorts of things by giving it the correct instructions. And you write the instructions that you give the computer in Linux code. You can, for example, use Linux code to make your computer perform the following tasks:

✔ Calculate a result.

✔ Show the result on-screen.

✔ Store information in a file.

✔ Retrieve information from a file.

✔ Read characters from the keyboard.

If you want to calculate the number of stocks that you own that are worth the money you paid for them, a Linux program can perform the calculation. (You must provide the necessary information, of course.)

After your computer completes the calculations, you probably want it to display the results on-screen. To make it do so, you need to use the echo reserved word and follow that word with the results of the calculation.

You can enter the number of stocks that you own directly into your program. You call this method *hard* coding, and you generally want to avoid it, because you'd then need to change the program each time that a value changes. (What a waste of time!) Another way is to set up your program to ask you to enter each stock price.

Either way, the program typically stores the result of the calculation in a part of your computer's memory that it identifies by a name that you give it. The part of the computer's memory that now contains the results of the calculation is known as a *variable*. Whenever you want the computer to use the result, you use the name of the variable, preceding it with a dollar sign ($). (I explain variables in Chapter 4.)

In the following example, you're telling the computer to display on-screen the value that the memory location by the name of BestStocks contains (BestStocks is also the name of the variable):

```
echo $BestStocks
```

Of course, your Linux program can do a lot more than simply turn your computer into the world's most expensive calculator.

In fact, your computer can perform nearly any task that you can imagine (except finding you a rich spouse) if you give it the correct shell-language instructions.

Outlining — line by line

Begin translating your program plan into Linux code a line at a time. Each line of your plan eventually becomes one or more lines of the program depending on the task that you want your computer to perform. You can perform some tasks with one reserved word; others require several reserved words.

You don't need to worry about the Linux jargon yet, although I do want to give you an example. The following steps describe what you need to do if you want to translate your outline into Linux code. In any case, you want your outline to look something like the following example:

1. Start the bash shell.
2. Clear the screen.
3. Show the title.
4. Ask the user to enter his first name.
5. Wait for the user to enter the name.
6. Display a hello message using the user's name.
7. End the program.

Make note of the reserved words that you use in your outline. Avoid guessing. Feel free to look up the reserved words in this book. (I love an open book test, don't you?)

By the way, many programmers use an editor to create their outlines instead of paper and pencil. (An *editor* is a simple word processor, and I talk about editors in the section "Considering Your Options for Text Editors," later in this chapter.)

Making your outline correspond to Linux code

Now you want to number each part of your Linux program to correspond to the line numbers on your program plan as you write your code. These numbers help you make sure that you don't skip a part of the program. But don't think that you need to know this code now. The following code section is just an example of how your code is going to look as you translate your outline into Linux code. Step 7 seems to be missing in this example. This step is the one that ends the program. You don't need to tell the computer when to end the program, however, because it knows to stop if it finds no more instructions.

```
1. #!/bin/bash
2. clear
3. echo "Welcome To My First Linux Program"
4. echo "Enter your first name: "
5. read response
6. echo "Hello, $response"
```

You want to remove the numbers from your program whenever you're ready to run the program. (Linux programs don't use line numbers.)

The following sample shows you how your program looks, ready to run:

```
#!/bin/bash
clear
echo "Welcome To My First Linux Program"
echo "Enter your first name: "
read response
echo "Hello, $response "
```

Don't become upset if you find yourself unable to translate your program out-line line by line into your program, as in the example I'm using. Just as in translating English to Spanish, such a translation isn't always so direct.

This sample program probably contains reserved words that are confusing to you. You find out about them throughout this book, but I want to give a brief explanation here just in case you can't wait:

✔ The #! /bin/bash tells your computer to start the bash shell.

✔ The clear reserved word clears the screen.

✔ The echo reserved word tells the computer to show the text.

✔ The read reserved word takes the characters someone enters at the keyboard and saves them in your computer's memory in a location with the name of response.

✔ You use the dollar sign ($) in front of the word response to display on-screen the characters that the program stores at that memory location.

So does that explanation keep you happy for now?

Choosing a Linux Shell

A *shell* is the program that sits between you and the Linux kernel. The *kernel* is the program that talks to your computer. The shell program reads your instructions, translates those instructions into something that your com-puter understands, and sends the translated instructions to your computer.

Many shell programs are available. Each one may speak a different language. This situation can become a problem for you. The shell program that runs your program may not be the same shell program that's on the computer of the person who uses your program.

You hope that many people are going to use your program. (How else can you become rich?) So how can you be sure that all of them are running the shell program that you use? You can't. But you can maximize your chances of exposure if you follow some basic guidelines and are familiar with what a shell can do. I explain a little about several of the main shells in the following sections.

The bash shell

The bash shell is probably the most popular shell in existence, as well as the default shell for most Linux installations (including Red Hat and Debian GNU/Linux, just to name a couple), and for these reasons I cover bash exclusively in this book. You start the bash shell by typing **bash** into your computer at the command line; then press the Enter key.

The bash shell has had a pretty diverse history, starting back in 1979 when a man named Stephen Bourne created the first major shell program for Unix. And guess what he called it? The *Bourne shell*, of course! Nearly every copy of Unix comes with the Bourne shell. (You start the Bourne shell by typing **sh** into your computer at the command line and then pressing the Enter key, if you want to check out this ancestor of bash, but again, I cover only bash shell programming in this book.)

The Bourne shell eventually grew up and gave birth to a new and enhanced generation shell that's formally known as the *Bourne Again shell* but is by far more commonly known as bash. Most people consider Brian Fox as the father of bash and Chet Ramey as the stepfather because Chet's taken over the job of maintaining bash. You can say that this new incarnation of the Bourne shell has the same genes as its dad — and some new tricks that the "old man" only wishes that it could perform, such as increased flexibility to reuse code.

The C shell

Well, just when Bourne thought he'd built the invention of the century, along came some guy with a better idea — Bill Joy from the University of California at Berkeley. He's the guy who came up with the idea for the *C shell*. Joy capitalized on the weaknesses in the Bourne shell. The C shell uses reserved words that the C programming language uses. (C is the language that some programmers love and the rest of us can live without.)

Bourne-shell programs can't run in the background. They always must take control of the screen and keyboard. You can't just tell your computer to go do something and then come back after it finishes. By using Joy's C shell, however, you *can* give it such a command, and so the C shell soon became the shell program of choice on many computers running Linux.

You can start the C shell by typing **csh** and then pressing the Enter key.

Other programming languages for Linux

I tell you a lot about Linux shells in the accompanying sections — so much so that you probably think you're walking along the beach with a marine biologist. You can, however, also use more sophisticated programming languages to tell Linux what to do. The most popular for such use are C, C++, and the caffeine-filled Java.

A *programming language* contains a group of words similar to those of the bash shell that I describe in this book. Programming languages, however, enable you to perform complex and fancy tasks on almost any computer, such as creating a stock ticker that moves across the screen and building a graphical user interface (GUI) with all the buttons and other options that you find in Windows and on the Mac.

The *C programming language* is a senior member of the community and was involved in the birth of Unix at Bell Laboratories. Programmers used the C programming language to write Unix. You can find out more about the C programming language by reading *C For Dummies*, by Dan Gookin (published by IDG Books Worldwide, Inc.).

The *C++ programming language* is an enhanced version of the C programming language. That's why the two plus signs (++) follow the C. The C++ programming language uses all the words in the C programming language, plus it adds a few of its own. Programmers use the C++ programming language to develop object-oriented programs. I don't have enough room in this book to explain

object-oriented programming, so you need to pick up a copy of *C++ For Dummies, 4th Edition*, by Stephen R. Davis (also published by IDG Books Worldwide, Inc.), if you really want to know more about the C++ programming language.

Java is the new kid on the block that's specifically designed for Web applications, although you can use Java to write the same types of programs that you use C and C++ for. Java's roots lie in C++, so you can say that Java is an enhanced version of the C++ programming language. Instead of calling it C++++, however, its developers named it Java. (I guess C++++ is too much of a mouthful to say.) Java's claim to fame is that you can run the programs that you write in Java on any computer with the Java engine, which you find on most computers. Linux shell programs, on the other hand, can run only on computers that actually use Linux and Unix. You must rebuild programs in the C programming language and the C++ programming language for each type of computer that you run them on (such as Linux/Unix computers, Windows machines, and Macs). You can run a Java program on many computers, however, without the programmer needing to change anything in the program. You can read more about Java in *Java For Dummies, 3rd Edition*, by Aaron E. Walsh (you guessed it — published by IDG Books Worldwide, Inc.).

The Korn shell

Just when Joy seemed to be on the top of the heap, along came David Korn, one of those whiz kids at Bell Labs. He created a shell that overcame the weaknesses of the C shell. The Korn shell can run Bourne-shell scripts without changing the script. And newer versions of the Korn shell offer windowing capabilities. You don't, however, find the Korn shell on every computer that runs Linux.

Start the Korn shell by typing **ksh** and then pressing the Enter key.

Sometimes you may not have Linux set up to run a shell just by your typing the name of the shell at the prompt. If you can't start a shell this way, your copy of Linux needs a bit of tweaking. *Linux For Dummies*, by Jon Hall (published by IDG Books Worldwide, Inc.), can show you how to tweak Linux. You can, however, also run a shell by specifying the location of the shell. Shells reside in the /bin directory. I use the pathname to run the bash shell by typing at the prompt **/bin/bash** and then leaving a space, which I follow by typing the name of the program that I want to run. Then I press Enter to run the program.

The Perl shell

I consider another popular shell language the "pearl" of Linux — mainly because its name *is* Perl. *Perl* (*P*ractical *E*xtraction and *R*eport *L*anguage) is a shell language that programmers commonly use to create *Common Gateway Interface* (*CGI*) programs for Web applications. You run a CGI program by using Perl many times without knowing it if you ever enter information on a Web page, such as giving the Web site your e-mail address or credit card number. By clicking the Submit button on the Web page, you're telling the Web site to run a CGI program, which is probably a Perl-shell script program. Pick up a copy of *Perl for Dummies*, by Paul Hoffman (published by IDG Books Worldwide, Inc.), if you want to find out more about Perl.

Considering Your Shell Options

The difficulty you experience in picking the exact Linux shell to use for your program is unique to Unix-based operating systems such as Linux. You don't encounter this problem if you write a program for Windows machines or for the Mac. In each case, Bill Gates or the guys at Apple Computers decide for you which shell you use.

Following are a few points to consider in choosing a shell language:

- ✔ **Anticipate who's going to use your program.** If the program's going to run only on your computer, whatever shell you pick is fine.

- ✔ **Decide how someone's going to use your program.** If you design your program to go off and do something in the background while you do something else (such as copying a large file), the bash shell, C shell, Perl shell, and Korn shell are all good candidates — but not the Bourne shell.

> ✔ **Look for the common shell that's on all the computers running your program.** If you're writing your program for a bunch of friends who're using a fancy new shell program that hit the Internet, you, too, want to use that shell program.

Choosing the bash Shell

I'm going to just cut to the chase. My choice for the shell program to use for your Linux programs is bash. Some programmers may disagree, but here's why I make this pick.

The bash shell is an old standby and is available on nearly all the computers that are likely to run your program.

The suppliers of all the versions of the Unix operating system, including Linux, support most versions of the bash shell. So if you run into trouble, you can find someone to call (even if you must pay a support fee).

Considering Your Options for Text Editors

You must eventually write your program in an electronic form and save it to a file. Although nothing's stopping you from using a word processor to write your program, most Linux programmers prefer to use a special kind of word processor known as a *text editor*. A text editor is a plain-Jane word processor. You don't find any fancy features in it.

A number of text editors are available in Linux that you can use to create your program. Each editor has its fans and detractors.

Choosing vi because it's nifty

The choice of which text editor to use depends on how simple and powerful a tool you want. And, probably more important, your choice may depend on which text editor is available on your computer.

Linux comes with a few text editors that you can use to write your programs. Each has advantages and disadvantages. Consider the following options:

> ✔ The old standby is *ed*. This text editor enables you to write or change a program one line at a time. Because ed isn't a full-screen text editor, most programmers simply skip this choice.

✔ Another old standby is *vi*. You can find *vi* on most computers that run Linux. This program is a full-screen text editor — that's to say that you can work on one full screen at a time instead of working just line by line. But *vi* is a little tricky to use.

✔ A more powerful text editor is *emacs*. This text editor is available on some releases of Linux and can work on several files at the same time.

And the envelope, please. The winner for the title of text editor that I use in *Linux Programming For Dummies* is . . . *vi*! I make this selection only because *vi* is the full-screen text editor that you're most likely to find on your release of Linux. And guess what? Although I explain a little bit about *vi* in the following sections, I also include more details about the program in Appendix B.

Giving vi a try

I'm now assuming that you're using *vi* as your text editor in this and the following section. (If you're using another text editor, you're on your own.) At the command line, type **vi** into your computer and press the Enter key. A full screen of *tildes* (~) appears. Each tilde is a blank line in your program, so this means that you have a full screen of empty lines, which is the meaning of a full-screen editor. You move around your program by performing keyboard gymnastics with your fingers. Don't bother trying the arrow keys; they don't work.

The *vi* text editor works in the following three modes, which you need to know about:

✔ *Command mode* enables you to move about your program without changing the text itself — you just enter commands. You're in the command mode after you first start *vi*. You can tell *vi* to enter the command mode at any time by pressing the Esc key.

✔ *Insert mode* enables you to enter or edit text. From the command mode, press the letter **i** or letter **a** (make sure that you type in lowercase!) on your keyboard to enter the insert mode. After choosing the insert mode by using the letter *i,* you can insert text before the cursor. If you use the letter *a,* you add text after the cursor.

✔ *Last line mode* is what you use to save your program, load another program, or quit *vi*. Press the Esc key to enter the command mode (unless you're already in it) and then type the colon (:) on-screen, following it with the last-line command that you want.

Many programmers find *vi* a little awkward to use, especially as much better text editors are available for Windows and the Mac. After you accustom yourself to working with *vi*, however, you don't give it a second thought. It's like driving with a stick shift. After you drive with a stick shift for a while, it becomes easy. See Table 3-1 for a summary of the most useful commands in *vi*.

Note: You must be in the command mode to use these commands — and keep in mind that Linux is case-sensitive, so type the command exactly as I give it. Commands don't appear on-screen.

Table 3-1	vi Commands
Command	*What It Does*
Moving the cursor	
j	Down one line
k	Up one line
h	Left one character
l	Right one character
$	To the end of the current line
0	To the beginning of the current line
+	To the beginning of the next line
−	To the beginning of the preceding line
Deleting	
dd	Entire line
x	Character under the cursor
X	Character to the left of the cursor
5dd	Delete the current line plus the next four lines
Undeleting	
u	Last change
U	All changes to the line
Inserting text	
i	In front of the cursor
I	At the beginning of the line
a	After the cursor
A	At the end of the current line

(continued)

Table 3-1 *(continued)*

Command	What It Does
Copying and pasting text	
yy	Copies line to the computer's memory
p	Pastes text from the computer's memory to the screen after cursor
Scrolling the screen	
Ctrl+F	Forward one screen
Ctrl+B	Back one screen
Ending vi and saving changes	
ZZ	Quits vi and saves changes
:w	Saves changes without exiting vi
:q	Quits vi
:q!	Quits vi without saving changes
Changing modes	
i	From command mode to insert mode
a	From command mode to insert mode (append)
:	From command mode to last line mode
Searching text	
/text	Searches from cursor to end of file for text you indicate
/	Repeats preceding search
?	Repeats preceding search from cursor to beginning of file
:n	Finds line number in which n is the line number you want to locate

Avoiding common vi mistakes

Whenever you use an unfamiliar text editor, you're bound to make a few errors. You join the ranks of many professional programmers whenever some of vi's common traps trip you up. Following are a few mistakes that anyone can make:

✔ **You forget about the** vi **modes.** After vi shows you an empty page, you begin typing. Only a portion of what you type appears on the page. That's because you're not in the insert mode . . . until you inadvertently type the letter i in your text. From that point forward, you're inserting text — but not before.

✔ **You try to move to a blank line.** Because vi starts each line on the page with a tilde (~) to symbolize a blank line, you assume that you can move the cursor anywhere on the page. Blank lines, however, are not really there in vi. You must open each line by pressing the Enter key or by using the o key in the command mode.

✔ **You forget to specify a name for the file after you start** vi **and** vi **is unable to save the file.** This situation occurs all the time if you're in a rush to write your program. The solution is to name the file as you write by using the last-line mode (substituting the name of the file for filename), as in the following example:

    :w filename

You can bet that you soon find your *own* common mistakes. But as long as you try not to repeat them, you're going to do all right.

Stopping vi and saving changes

Starting vi and entering text on the page is easy. Getting *out* of vi is a little tricky. You can eject yourself from vi in the following several ways if you're in command mode:

✔ Type :q to stop vi.

   If you haven't saved your file, vi prompts you to do so.

✔ Type ZZ to save your changes and to stop vi.

✔ Type :wq to save your changes and to stop vi.

✔ Type :q! to stop vi without saving your changes.

Writing Your First Linux Program

In this section, you finally get to sit down in front of your computer and write your first Linux program. You begin with a simple menu program. The program displays a list of things that the user can do with your program. The program also reads the selection that the user makes on the keyboard. You can build on this program throughout all other chapters in this book, making your program do something after someone chooses an option.

Writing a program to display a menu

The purpose of this program is to display a simple menu on-screen. For this example, you're going to make a telephone book menu that looks as follows as your program runs:

```
The Telephone Book

1. Display A Telephone Number
2. Add A New Telephone Number

Q Quit

Enter your selection:
```

Follow these steps to create your program:

1. **Type** vi mymenu **at the command prompt.**

   This command starts vi and names your program *mymenu*.

2. **Type** i **after the blank (except for the tildes) page appears on-screen.**

   This command takes you to the insert mode.

   If you choose to use another text editor besides vi, you don't start the text editor by using the commands shown here. You probably can find how to use the text editor by typing man *text editor name* at the command prompt. (Of course, use the name of your text editor instead of typing ***text editor name***. If you're using emacs, for example, you type man emacs.) The manual pages for your text editor should then appear on-screen. If they don't, the manual pages aren't on your computer. Call the person who's responsible for your computer and ask that he install these pages.

3. **Type the Linux code that follows on the blank page:**

```
#!/bin/bash
clear
echo " "
echo "The Telephone Book "
echo " "
echo "1. Display A Telephone Number "
echo "2. Add A New Telephone Number "
echo " "
echo "Q Quit "
echo " "
echo "Enter your selection: "
```

Here's what you're doing!

You're starting the bash shell script by using #!/bin/bash as the first command of your program.

Next, you're using the `clear` reserved word to tell your computer to erase any text that may already appear on-screen.

You're then using the `echo` reserved word to display text as well as blank lines on-screen. All the characters between the quotation marks appear on-screen.

Of course, you don't need to copy this program exactly. Become a little adventurous and experiment. Change the text, change the spacing — go a little crazy. This kind of experimentation is the only way that you really discover how to create a Linux program.

Saving your program

After you're satisfied that all the instructions in your program are in the correct order and that you're using the correct words to tell the computer what to do, you're ready to save your file.

Following are several ways to save your file by using the `vi` text editor (some of which are familiar to you if you first read the section "Stopping vi and saving changes," earlier in this chapter):

- `ZZ`: Saves your file and exits `vi`.
- `:w`: Saves your file without exiting `vi`.
- `:wq`: Saves your file and exits `vi`.
- `:w filename`: Saves your file under a new name that you specify (so that `:w mymenu2`: for example, saves your file as *mymenu2*).

Always save your program while you're still writing your program in `vi`. Until you save your program in a file, everything that you type exists only in your computer's memory. If you turn off your computer (or the power company does it for you), you lose all your hard work!

Making your program work

Your program is almost ready to run . . . but not just yet. You still must tell your computer that your file is an executable file. An *executable file* is a file that contains instructions for your computer to follow.

Follow these steps to tell your computer that your file is executable:

1. **Move to the directory that contains your file if you're not already in that directory by typing the following command at the prompt:**

   cd /*mydirectory*

   Remember to replace mydirectory with the directory name on your computer that contains your program file.

2. **Make the file an executable file by using the chmod utility, typing the following at the command prompt:**

   chmod 711 mymenu

   This command enables everyone to run your *mymenu* program — but only you can see the file itself. (Refer to Chapter 1, where I explain a little about the chmod utility.)

3. **You can run your program by typing the name of the program at the command line as follows and then pressing Enter:**

   mymenu

   If you have problems running your mymenu program, try running the program as ./mymenu.

   The program displays the menu on-screen and prompts you to enter a selection from the menu. After you enter your selection, the program ends.

Making changes to your program

You can change your program at any time by recalling your program to the screen by using the vi text editor or the text editor of your choice.

Using vi as my model, for example, I simply type **vi mymenu** at the command prompt. Here I can start vi again and use the name of the program file. Remember that, after you first start vi, you're in the command mode.

Expect to edit your programs frequently. Always make another copy of your program under a different name before you begin changing your program. You can use this backup copy of your program in case you accidentally destroy your program during editing.

Part II

The Basics of Writing Code

The 5th Wave   By Rich Tennant

THAT IT! TARZAN TAKE NO MORE! KEEP GET BAD MESSAGE! WHAT MEAN?! TARZAN TRY EVERYTHING! MAKE TARZAN MAD LIKE CHEETAH! WANT PUT ROLODEX THROUGH SCREEN!

In this part . . .

Great! You've reached the point where you actually start writing Linux code to make your computer do something worthwhile. So far, you've discovered the finer points of building a user interface (with an occasional Linux command sprinkled here and there).

What matters to those who use your program is what your program can do for them. Just because you design the perfect plan for your program doesn't mean that your work is done.

Writing instructions for a computer can intimidate even the hearty adventurer, but you have nothing to fear. Writing Linux code is as simple as giving someone step-by-step instructions: You've done that most of your life.

Caution: Programming is addictive and a whole lot of fun after you get started. So don't waste any more time: Start to code.

Chapter 4

Getting Indecisive with Variables

● ●

In This Chapter

▶ Understanding data

▶ Understanding variables and values

▶ Assigning numbers and strings to variables

▶ Declaring data types

▶ Making a string array

● ●

*A*fter you know what you want your computer to do, the time is right to write Linux code. The place where you begin to write your Linux code is in a text editor file (as I explain in Chapter 3).

Your text editor file that contains your program just tells your computer to do something. The simplest program that you can write tells your computer to stop running your program. You use only the reserved word `exit` in this program, as shown here:

```
exit
```

You want your programs to do more, however, than just this task. You can, for example, design a program to ask someone for a name and address. You also need to write instructions into your program to tell the computer to read this information and do something with it.

In this chapter, I tell you all about how to store and use information in your program: You create a storage space inside your computer's memory and then place your information into that space. Of course, I also tell you how to retrieve the information for use by your program.

Understanding Data

Information that your program receives from someone who uses it is known as *data* — now you also know where the character on *Star Trek: The Next Generation* got his name. Good programs follow these three simple steps:

1. They get data from the keyboard or a file.

2. They do something with the data.

3. They show the data on-screen or in a report.

The reason for writing your program is to turn your computer into an electronic factory. In one end goes all the data that the computer needs to do something. And out the other end comes useful information. This information processing is all that a word processor, a spreadsheet, and a database program actually do. And the data that all these programs use manipulates only two things: *strings* and *numbers,* as the following sections describe.

Strings

A *string* is usually a bunch of letters or characters that you . . . well, *string* together. A character can be a hyphen or any character that you find on the keyboard. A string can consist of just a *single* letter or character, too. An entire sentence can also be a string. And this entire chapter can be a string as well. In fact, any group of letters, spaces — and even numbers — can act as a string (as you see in the section "Variables 101," later in this chapter).

Numbers

A *number* can consist of any type of number, such as amounts of money, someone's age or height, the number of friends who come over to your cookout (and don't invite you to their cookouts), and so on. This category includes positive and negative numbers as well as whole and fractional numbers.

And, to complicate matters, numbers are also characters! This dual-identity situation may seem a little confusing to you, at least at first, but it isn't so confusing to your computer. If you tell the computer that the number is part of an address or telephone number, the computer treats the number as a letter or character. If you tell the computer to add (or perform any mathematical operation) using numbers, however, the computer treats these numbers as numbers (and not as characters). Clear? Well, keep reading.

A Gentle Introduction to Variables and Values

That your computer knows how to keep track of the numbers and strings that someone enters into your program may seem like magic to you. Knowing that 555-55-5555 is someone's Social Security number is easy for you. Your computer, however, just recognizes it as a number or a string.

Your program must tell your computer the following: "If someone enters 555-55-5555, give this number the name SSNum and then put it someplace. But don't forget where you put it. I'm going to call for it later."

Your program must also tell your computer when to use the Social Security number: "Time for the Social Security number. You remember where you put it, don't you? It's under the variable name SSNum."

Your program then finds the variable SSNum and copies the number so that your program can do something with it.

A *variable* is a place in your computer that holds a *value* of a particular number, such as a Social Security number. The Social Security number that you give the variable name SSNum is a value. (In fact, it's the key to all your financial, medical, and employment history!)

You can think of a variable as an empty box. You can print a name on the side of the box to remember what you put into the box. The name on the box is like the name of the variable (SSNum). You can store something (a real Social Security number) inside the box, which is like assigning a value to the variable.

Variables 101

Linux uses the following two kinds of variables:

- ✔ Those you create that only your program uses: *local variables*.
- ✔ Those that you or someone else creates that your program and other programs can use: *environment variables*.

Whenever your program needs to save data, you create (or *declare*) a *local variable*. Only your own program can use this variable.

Every time that you log into Linux, a whole bunch of variables are already available. These are *environment variables*. Environment variables contain information that tells your computer information about you and about the computer. A common environment variable, for example, is EDITOR. The value that you assign to this variable is the name of the text editor that's on your computer.

Declaring variables

You can create a variable by using the reserved words declare and export, following them with the variable's name. Here's an example:

```
declare FirstName
export editor
```

In this example, you can see the creation of the following variable:

- ✔ The reserved word declare declares an environment variable.
- ✔ The reserved word export makes the variable available to the environment.

Placing variables

Although you find no special place in your Linux program to declare a variable, you can, in fact, declare a variable anywhere in your program. Placing a variable just anywhere, however, isn't what most programmers consider a good programming practice. If you do, you're likely to end up hunting for those variables the next time that you read your program.

A preferred programming practice is to declare all the variables at the beginning of your program. That way, they're all in the same place whenever you need to find them.

Combining your variables

You can declare variables of the same kind (such as two string variables) on the same line at the beginning of your program. The following example shows you how to do so:

```
declare FirstName LastName
```

You can type as many variable names as you can fit on the line. Notice that a space separates each variable.

See how easily you can locate the variables that you use in your program? You don't need to search every line of the program. Simply look at the first few lines of your program to examine all the variables.

Naming variables

You can name a variable anything that you want (and you can store anything imaginable in it). Naming a variable SSNum and then shoving some telephone number in it, however, just doesn't make much sense.

Make programming Linux easy for yourself: Give names to your variables that tell someone (you, for example) exactly what kind of data you're stuffing in them. Naming a variable SSNum seems right only if you intend to place a Social Security number in the variable — just as you want a variable that you designate FirstName to hold the characters in someone's first name.

Following are some rules to keep in mind as you name your variables. All variable names must . . .

- ✔ Begin with a letter.
- ✔ Consist of only letters (upper- or lowercase), numbers, and the underscore character (_).
- ✔ Have no spaces.

Of course, you can't use a reserved word as a variable.

Linux gives you no problems at all if you follow these rules in naming variables. (Although you may find that it doesn't like other parts of your program!) Following are some examples of variable names that make Linux happy:

- ✔ DeptNo
- ✔ Fax_Num
- ✔ Acct573

Following are some examples of variable names that make Linux choke:

- ✔ First Name (Spaces are forbidden.)
- ✔ 573Acct (The first character must be a letter.)
- ✔ exit (Reserved words also are forbidden.)

Testing your programming knowledge

1. What does the following Linux command do?

```
declare street city state zip
```

a. Gives words to the quarterback to shout before he hikes the ball.

b. Declares four variables.

c. Tells the computer where the user lives.

d. Stuffs the entire set's address into variables.

2. What's the purpose for declaring variables?

a. So that you can keep your data secret from hackers.

b. To add a touch of royalty to your program: I declare you a variable!

c. To tell the computer to reserve space to store a certain type of data.

d. To make sure that your program has data it can use.

Answers: 1) b. See "Declaring variables." 2) c. See "Declaring variables."

Assigning numbers to variables

After you create a variable by naming it, you probably want to stuff something into the variable. This action is known as *assigning a value* to the variable.

To assign a value to a variable, you must use a super-complex, scientific gizmo that requires you to earn at least a master's degree in computer science from MIT (just joking). All you need to know is how to use the equal (=) sign and the reserved word let, which tells the computer to assign a particular value to a particular variable.

The following example shows you how to stuff a value into a numeric variable that I call MySalary. Instead of yelling at your computer to "Put the number one million in my salary variable," you just write the following:

```
let MySalary=1000000
```

You begin with the reserved word let, following it with a space and the numeric variable. Then you enter the equal sign and the value that you want the variable to possess. (Watch that you don't put any spaces before or after the equal sign.)

A variable can have only one value. You can change this value by assigning another value to the variable. Your computer then throws out the old value and replaces it with the new value. The old value is lost forever.

Imagine that you want to write a program that tells your computer to give you a starting salary of a million dollars. And just because you do such a good job writing this program, you tell your computer to double your salary.

Try this example on your boss:

```
let MySalary=1000000
let MySalary=2000000
```

As your computer is reading your program, it's saying: "Okay, you want me to create a numeric variable MySalary? I can do that. And you want me to put the number one million into this variable. I can do that, too. Then you want me to erase the one million and put the number two million in its place. That doesn't make much sense, but I can do that."

Assigning strings to variables

Assigning strings to variables is just as easy as stuffing numbers into a variable. Following are a few differences between the two procedures:

- ✔ You use the reserved word declare or export to create string variables.
- ✔ Quotation marks must surround the string to tell your computer where the string begins and ends.
- ✔ A dollar sign ($) must precede a variable whenever you refer to the variable in your program.

Now you can assign someone's first name to a string variable, as the following example shows:

```
declare FirstName="Mary"
```

Or you can assign someone's first and last name to a string variable, as in this example:

```
declare Name="Mary Smith"
```

Or assign a whole bunch of words to a string variable, as follows:

```
declare MyGoal="Buy out Bill Gates"
```

Sometimes strings consist of numbers instead of letters, but they're still strings, such as in the following telephone number:

```
declare Telephone="555-5555"
```

Don't forget this rule: Put quotation marks around a string value. Quotation marks tell Linux that characters appearing between the quotation marks belong together and that it's to treat them as a string.

Assigning variables to other variables

You can take data that you stuff into one variable and copy it to another variable. You end up with two copies of the data. Your computer doesn't remove the data from the original variable.

The following example shows you how to copy data from one variable to another by using a string variable:

```
declare MyGoal="Buy out Bill Gates"
declare OurGoal="$MyGoal"
```

In this example, you're telling your computer in the first line to go to the variable MyGoal and copy the data that's there. Next, you're telling your computer to take that data and place it into the variable OurGoal. You're doing so by using the name of the original variable, and you're placing a dollar sign ($) in front of it.

You can perform this same copying procedure by using a numeric variable, as in the following example:

```
let MySalary=1000000
let OurSalaries=$MySalary
```

Your computer takes a copy of the value of your salary and stuffs it into the variable OurSalaries. The value of OurSalaries is now the same as your salary, 1000000. Your own million-dollar salary, however, remains safe in the MySalary variable.

Using Data Types

A Linux variable can store any number or string. You can confuse your computer, however, if you first tell it one thing and then tell it to do something completely opposite (and computers don't like you confusing them).

Say, for example, that you ask your computer to find a place to stuff someone's name (that is, to create a variable). But as the time arrives to do the actual stuffing, you give it the person's salary instead.

Your computer turns around and says something like "Hey — what goes on? First you tell me that you want to store a string. Okay, so I do all this work and find the perfect spot for your string. Now you give me a number. I have no room for the number there." What's more embarrassing is if it's someone else's computer that complains — which means that everyone who uses your program knows that you goofed.

Whenever you declare a variable, you specify the *data type* of the variable. Some computer languages use many data types to handle all sizes of numbers and strings. But don't concern yourself with all these choices. Linux uses just the following two data types:

✔ Numeric data type

✔ String data type

Make sure that you check the data type of the variable in your program before you assign it a value. That way, you don't give your computer a reason to complain about your program.

The Scope of Variables

The *scope* of a variable determines who can use the variable within Linux. You can tell Linux who can access a variable two ways: by using *local* and *environment* variables.

Only the program that creates it can use a *local variable*. This property of a local variable helps you isolate its information from anything else that's running on your computer. The following example shows you how to declare a local variable within your program:

```
declare SSNum
let Salary=1000000
```

But what if you want to share this information with other programs? In that case, you must declare the variable as an *environment variable*. Any program that's running on your computer can read a global variable and change the value of the environment variable.

In many computer languages, such as the Java language, you create a *global variable* by putting it in a special place in your program file. But you don't declare a global variable in Linux that way. Instead, you use the `export` keyword, which creates an environment variable. As is true of a global variable, you can share an environment variable with other programs.

The following example shows you how to declare a global variable within your program (so just follow this example so that the entire world can know your Social Security number):

```
declare SSNum="555-55-5555"
```

You must be very careful whenever you decide to use a global variable in your program for the following reasons:

- ✔ Any program running on the same computer as your program can read and change the value that you store in the global variable.

- ✔ The last value that you assign to the global variable is the one that your computer keeps. So if two programs change the value of the same global variable, one program may not work correctly.

- ✔ Finding a problem resulting from someone assigning a wrong value to a global variable can become a nightmare. You don't know which program changed it.

Chapter 5

Interfacing with the User

• •

In This Chapter

▶ Getting data from the keyboard input

▶ Displaying data that the user enters

▶ Keeping your data in a file

• •

*T*he part of the program that the user sees — the *user interface* — is like window dressing for your program. It makes your program look pretty. A pretty user interface, however, doesn't necessarily help someone do something with your program.

If you want your program to be more useful than just a pretty picture on-screen, you need it to interact with the user. Your program must carry out the following tasks to interact with the user:

✔ Get information from the user (via the keyboard).

✔ Do something with that information.

✔ Show the results of what it does with the information on the user interface.

In this chapter, I show you the command that tells your program to read information that someone enters from the keyboard. Then I show you how to display that information on-screen.

Keyboard Input

The user interface displays messages (known as *prompts*) on-screen, and these messages tell someone to press a key on the keyboard — but your program can't *force* the user to press a key. Your interface is all you have to entice the user into doing what you want.

Pretty Linux

Mr. Gates finally gave DOS a makeover, and it came out looking like Windows. Linux, however, is still undergoing its makeover. The first improvement enables a user to open more than one window on-screen. To do so, the user needs special software known as *X Windows*. The next improvement involves jazzing up those windows with push buttons, drop-down lists, and all those things that Windows machines and Macs display. You need additional special software for this improvement. That software is known as *Motif*. So unless you intend to find out how to build your program so that you can use X Windows and Motif with it, you must live with a basic program that doesn't use the windowing features you see on Windows and Mac.

You can't write a pretty user interface for Linux like you see in Macs and PCs running Windows programs unless you know how to program X Windows and Motif (see Chapter 1). Linux is a plain-Jane operating system, like DOS. Expect your program only to wait patiently until someone presses the Enter key after typing each piece of information. In the meantime, your computer's collecting and storing all the keystrokes someplace inside it that's known as a *keyboard buffer*. After the user presses the Enter key, your program rushes to grab all those characters that the user entered at the keyboard and stuff them into the variables that you created for them.

Reading a string

Your computer isn't too bright whenever it must pick up data from the keyboard. (But, on the other hand, it would like to see *us* find the square root of 365 in less than a second.) Your computer doesn't know whether to treat a number as a character or a value to use in a calculation. It finds out only after *you* specify the kind of variable that you want to use to store the information.

After you tell the computer the correct variable to use, you must tell it to read the characters from the keyboard. The following code shows you how to tell the computer to read characters and then stuff them into a string variable:

```
#!/bin/bash
clear
echo " "
echo "Enter Your First Name: "
read FirstName
```

First, `#!/bin/bash` tells the computer to start the bash shell before clearing (`clear`) the screen.

Next, the computer skips a line on-screen (echo " ") and tells the user the kind of data to enter (echo "Enter Your First Name: ").

The reserved word read instructs your computer to take all the characters that the user enters at the keyboard and place them in the string variable FirstName. This command kicks in only after someone presses the Enter key, however.

Reading a number

If your program needs to read a number from the keyboard, you must take a slightly different approach. The instruction that you give your computer is the same that you give to read a string except that you use a numeric variable. The following code shows you how to tell your computer to read a numeric value from the keyboard:

```
#!/bin/bash
clear
echo " "
echo "Enter Your Age: "
read age
```

This code example is the same way that your computer reads a string from the keyboard.

The line #!/bin/bash tells the computer to start the bash shell before clearing (clear) the screen.

You don't need to declare the numeric variable at the top of your program.

The line echo " " then tells the computer to skip a line before it asks the user to enter some data (echo "Enter Your Age: ").

You use the reserved word read in front of the name of the variable (age). Doing so tells your computer to take all the data that the user enters at the keyboard and place it in the string variable age.

Mixing strings and numbers from the keyboard

You can mix the kind of information that your program collects from someone. Sometimes you can ask for a numeric value; other times you can ask for a string value. Your program doesn't care.

Keep in mind, however, that what you ask for *does* matter to the person using your program. You must ask for the information in a logical way. Someone using your program doesn't, for example, expect you to ask for a first name, age, and then a last name. That order just doesn't make sense. First name, last name, and age is an order that seems better.

Besides using common sense in requesting information, you also want to ask one question at a time. The following code illustrates how to read both string and numeric data in a logical order:

```
#!/bin/bash
clear
echo " "
echo "Enter Your First Name: "
read FirstName
echo "Enter Your Last Name: "
read LastName
echo "Enter Your Age: "
read age
```

This program does, of course, prompt the user for first name, last name, and then age.

Displaying Data That Someone Enters

After your program has the information that someone enters, it needs to do something with the information. The program can use the data in a calculation, store the information in a file on your disk, or do practically anything with it that you can imagine. (Well, almost anything.)

The most common thing to do with the information is to make it appear onscreen. Another thing to do is to compare the data with information that's already in your computer — but for now, you want to just try a simple display first.

Following are some things that you need to know about displaying information:

- ✔ Data appearing on-screen still remains in the variable. (You store data in a variable, and then the program copies the data from the variable to the screen. The data remains both on-screen and in the variable.)

- ✔ This process enables the program to do something else with the data while you're looking at it. Your program can store a salary in the MySalary variable, for example, and then display the salary on-screen. While the salary's on-screen, the program can still use it to calculate your new salary — assuming, of course, that you receive a raise in pay.

✔ Data always appears at the cursor on-screen. Say that your program displays the text `"Salary:"`. The cursor — that flashing little light that signals where you are on-screen — moves to the right of the colon (`:`). Next, your program displays the data that contains the salary.

✔ You can modify data appearing on-screen, but the changed data doesn't automatically appear on-screen. Your program displays the salary on-screen. It also stores the salary in the variable `MySalary`. Your program then proceeds to calculate the new salary and saves the result in the variable `MySalary`. The old salary, however, still remains on-screen until your program displays the variable `MySalary` again.

Nothing's special about the data that your computer collects from the keyboard and stores in a variable. This capability is the same as if your program itself told the computer to assign the value to the variable.

Displaying a string

A typical Linux program tells someone to enter a string of characters; the program then saves the characters in a variable before displaying them on-screen. You can choose to do either of the following:

✔ Display the characters on a single line.

✔ Display a combination of the characters with other characters on a single line.

You can have the computer show just the characters that someone enters into your program by using the `echo "$variable name"` on a line in your program. (Of course, replace *variable name* with the name of your variable.)

You can combine characters with other characters by placing them within quotation marks, as shown in the following code. Here, the program asks users their first names and then greets them with a big hello (but no kiss and hug).

```
#!/bin/bash
clear
echo " "
echo "Enter Your First Name: "
read FirstName
echo "Hello, $FirstName"
```

Although the program adds the text `Hello`, you could store this string in another string variable. (I do that in the following example.) By using the following code, you tell the computer to go to the $Greeting variable and display that string before going to the $FirstName variable and displaying those characters:

```
#!/bin/bash
clear
declare FirstName,Greeting
echo $Greeting = "Hello, "
echo " "
echo "Enter Your First Name: "
read FirstName
echo "$Greeting $FirstName"
```

Displaying a number

Telling your computer to show a number on-screen isn't different than telling it to display a string.

Take a look at the following code to see how to show numeric data on-screen. Remember that you don't need to declare the numeric variable at the top of a program.

```
#!/bin/bash
clear
echo " "
echo "Enter Your Age: "
read age
echo "$age"
```

Displaying strings and numbers

You collect numeric data and string data separately. Someone who uses your program, however, expects to see them appearing together on the same line. You don't want to disappoint anyone. So here's how you can show numeric data combining with string data on the same line:

```
#!/bin/bash
clear
echo " "
echo "Enter Your First Name: "
read FirstName
echo "Enter Your Age: "
read age
echo "$FirstName, $age really isn't that old."
```

The line echo "Enter Your First Name: " asks someone to enter a first name and then saves it to a variable (FirstName).

Next, echo "Enter Your Age: " asks the person to enter an age. It saves this information, too — but to a different variable (age).

Finally, the program shows the person's first name, age, and then a comforting comment (that no one believes): Jim, 82 really isn't that old.

Keeping Data in a File

Putting data that someone enters into your file on your hard disk is a common practice. A *file* is like a file drawer (but a lot better organized). Say that you want to keep your date book handy — but away from prying eyes. You can build a program that collects all those special phone numbers for you and then places them in an electronic hideaway on your computer's hard disk. Then, as Friday night rolls around, you can instruct your program to open the file, and you can choose the date of your dreams. (Of course, your dream date may already have plans. . . .)

Following are some reasons for saving data to a file:

- ✔ Data is always available to your programs.
- ✔ You don't lose information unless a disaster happens to your hard disk. And we all know that can *never* happen. (On the other hand, where's my tape backup?)
- ✔ You can use a Linux utility to search the file for particular information.

The way in which you organize the data that you save to a file is important; otherwise, your computer may have a difficult time finding it.

In Chapter 16, you explore how to create a simple database. A database is a special kind of file for holding information that you need to find fast. For now, however, I want to show you how to take the data that your program collects and stuff it into a simple file on your hard disk.

Saving data to a new file

Linus Torvalds decided that any time your program needs to display anything by using the echo reserved word, it uses the screen.

That's just fine for most of your programs, but you can easily change your program to display data someplace else — such as to a file. Such a process is known as *redirection*, which means changing the direction of the normal flow of data.

Test your programming knowledge

1. What does the following statement tell your computer to do?

```
read Telephone
```

a. Read the telephone number from the screen.

b. To take whatever someone enters at the keyboard and place it into the `Telephone` variable.

c. To find the money to pay your telephone bill.

d. To cut your phone bill in half.

2. What tells your computer to collect the information that someone enters into your program?

a. Your mother.

b. This little, tiny thing that lives inside your computer.

c. Someone pressing the Enter key.

d. The print command.

Answers: 1) b. See "Reading a string." *2) c. See* "Keyboard Input."

This redirection isn't hard to do at all. Take a look at the following example to see how. You see everything in this example elsewhere (Chapters 3 and 4), except for something in the last line in the program.

```
#!/bin/bash
clear
echo " "
echo "Enter Your First Name: "
read FirstName
echo "Enter Your Last Name: "
read LastName
echo "$FirstName $LastName" > employees.dat
```

The *greater-than sign* (>) tells your computer that, instead of showing the values of the variables on-screen, it's to store them in a file by the name `employees.dat` (and if I could get a peek, I could find out what's going on where you work).

Keep the following points in mind:

WARNING!

- Your computer creates a new file if you use the greater-than sign in your program to save something to a file.

- If a file with the same name already exists, your computer overwrites the old file with the new information. The old information is lost forever, which is a long time. So be careful.

Appending data to an existing file

Who wants to overwrite information in a file every time? No one does. That's why you need to use *two* greater-than signs (>>) instead of a single greater-than sign whenever you want to append information to the end of the file instead of than overwriting the data that's already there.

The *double greater-than sign* (>>) tells your computer to add the new data at the end of the file that you name rather than at the beginning of the file. Your computer never overwrites and loses existing data in the file.

The following code shows practically the same program as the code shows in the preceding example — except that it *appends* the new information to the file (assuming that the file already exists!). It automatically creates a new file if the file that you specify in the program doesn't already exist.

```
#!/bin/bash
clear
echo " "
echo "Enter Your First Name: "
read FirstName
echo "Enter Your Last Name: "
read LastName
echo "$FirstName $LastName" >> employees.dat
```

Data that you save to a file by using the echo reserved word appears on the same line in the file just as it appears on the same line on-screen.

Displaying data that you save to a file

You can show the information that your computer saves to a file on-screen by using the cat utility from within your program, as shown in the following example. You can tell your computer to run a utility program by entering the name of the utility in your program — just as you'd type the name of the utility on the command line. Programmers refer to this procedure as *calling a utility program*.

```
#!/bin/bash
clear
echo "Employee Data"
echo " "
cat employees.dat
```

Notice how the last line uses the cat command, following it with the filename.

The following example shows you what appears on-screen after this program runs with the cat utility.

The inside story of redirection

Your computer needs to know where to get information. The nerds call this standard *in* (short for input). Where does your computer get data? Linus Torvalds answered that question when he made Linux. His choice was the keyboard.

Your computer also needs to know where to show information. Computer folks call this standard *out* (short for output). And where does your computer display information? Linus Torvalds decided to show it on-screen.

Your computer needs to know one more thing: If something goes wrong, where do you want it to send the error message?

How about the screen? (Brilliant.) This standard is known as *error*.

You can change how information flows in your computer by using the redirection signs: the less-than (<) and greater-than (>) signs, as follows:

- ✔ The < sign tells the computer to get information from a file.

- ✔ The > sign tells the computer to send information to a file.

- ✔ The string 2> redirects all error messages to a file.

```
Employee Data

Bob Smith
Mary Jones
```

Of course, this example assumes that someone entered Bob Smith the first time that the program ran and Mary Jones the second time!

Chapter 6

Who Were Those Masked Operators?

● ●

In This Chapter

▶ Adding, subtracting, multiplying, and dividing numbers

▶ Using the *not*, *and*, and *or* operators

▶ Comparing values with comparison operators

▶ Establishing precedence for operators

● ●

*A*fter your computer receives information from someone who uses your program, the next step is to do something with the information. You can, for example, have your computer calculate a result.

Anytime that you want your computer to modify data, you must tell the computer to perform an *operation* by using one or more *operators* in your program. Linux recognizes the following three categories of operators (each with its own individual operators):

✔ Arithmetic

✔ Logical

✔ Comparison

In this chapter, I show you the operators that you can use in Linux and give you a tip or two on how to use them in your program.

Arithmetic Operators

Arithmetic operators transform your expensive computer into one of those pocket calculators that banks and other financial companies give away if you sign up for one of those high-interest credit cards.

These arithmetic operators enable your computer to add, subtract, multiply, and divide numbers or *variables* that contain numbers. (See Chapter 4 for the scoop on variables.) Table 6-1 shows these operators (as if you can't figure them out on your own).

Table 6-1	Arithmetic Operators
Operator	*What It Does*
+	Adds two numbers
–	Subtracts two numbers
*	Multiplies two numbers
/	Divides two numbers
%	Divides two numbers and returns only the remainder

Adding two numbers by using the + operator

To add two numbers together, use the + operator, as in the following example:

```
let a=30
let b=10
let sum="$a + $b"
```

Notice the lack of spaces around the = signs and the spaces around the + operator. Such spacing is true for all constructions of operators.

let a=30 tells the computer to create a variable by the name of a and to assign that variable the value 30.

let b=10 tells the computer to create a variable by the name of b and to assign that variable the value 10.

let sum="$a + $b" tells the computer to create a variable by the name of sum and to assign it the value of a plus the value of b. In this example, the value of sum equals 30 + 10 (which is 40!).

Subtracting two numbers by using the – operator

To subtract two numbers, use the - operator, as in the following example:

```
let Salary=3000
let Expenses=2500
let MyMoney="$Salary - $Expenses"
```

let Salary=3000 tells the computer to create a variable by the name of Salary and to assign that variable the value 3000.

let Expenses=2500 tells the computer to create a variable by the name of Expenses and to assign that variable the value 2500.

let MyMoney="$Salary - $Expenses" tells the computer to create a variable by the name of MyMoney and to assign it the value of Salary minus the value of Expenses. In this example, the value of MyMoney equals 3000 – 2500, or 500.

Multiplying two numbers by using the * operator

To multiply two numbers together, use the * operator, as in the following example:

```
let Computers=100
let Commission=5
let TotalCom="$Computers * $Commission"
```

let Computers=100 tells the computer to create a variable by the name of Computers and to assign that variable the value 100.

let Commission=5 tells the computer to create a variable by the name of Commission and to assign that variable the value 5. (This formula gives you a five-dollar commission on each computer!)

let TotalCom="Computers * Commission" tells the computer to create a variable by the name of TotalCom and to assign it the value of Computers times the value of Commission. In this example, the value of TotalCom equals 100 * 5, or 500.

Dividing two numbers by using the / operator

To divide two numbers, use the / (forward slash) operator, as in the following example:

```
let TotalCom=500
let Commission=5
let Computers="$TotalCom / $Commission"
```

`let TotalCom=500` tells the computer to create a variable by the name of `TotalCom` and to assign that variable the value 500.

`let Commisson=5` tells the computer to create a variable by the name of `Commission` and to assign that variable the value 5.

`let Computers="$TotalCom / $Commission"` tells the computer to create a variable by the name of `Computers` and to assign it the value of `TotalCom` divided by the value of `Computers`. In this example, the value of `Computers` equals 500 / 5, or 100.

Dividing by using the % operator

To divide two numbers and calculate the remainder, use the % (modulo) operator, as in the following example (and you probably get the idea by now, right?):

```
let a=10
let b=3
let c="a % b"
```

`let a=10` tells the computer to create a variable by the name of `a` and to assign that variable the value 10.

`let =3` tells the computer to create a variable by the name of `b` and to assign that variable the value 3.

Negating numbers by using the – operator

The – operator can transform a positive number into a negative number. This process is known as *negating a number* and you accomplish it by placing the – operator in front of any number or variable that contains a number, as in the following example:

```
let AfterTaxes=-3000
```

`let AfterTaxes=3000` tells the computer to create a variable by the name of `AfterTaxes` and to assign it the negative value of 3000. In this example, the value of `AfterTaxes` is **–3000**.

`let c= "a % b"` tells the computer to create a variable by the name of `c` and to assign it the value equal to the remainder of the value of `a` divided by the value of `b`. In this example, the value of `c` equals 10 % 3, or 1.

Logical Operators

You use *logical operators* to tell the computer to evaluate *true* and *false* values. A true value is any value that's not a zero, and a false value is a zero. Table 6-2 shows the common logical operators.

Table 6-2	Logical Operators
Operator	**What It Does**
!	Reverses the logic, as in saying, "I hope we're going to get a lot of rain today — *not*."
&&	Variable1 *and* Variable2, as in saying, "Bob *and* Mary are an item."
||	Variable1 *or* Variable2, as in asking, "Is Mary *or* Sue dating Bob?"

The ! (not) operator

Thanks to television, you have a new way of saying things today — for example: "I'm going to give you a 20 percent increase in pay — *not*!" Such a statement gets your hopes up and then slams reality in your face. The first part of the phrase leads you to believe that the statement is true. The speaker reverses this true meaning to a false meaning, however, by adding the simple word *not*.

You can change a true statement to false just as I did here by using the ! (*not*) operator.

You can also use the ! operator to change a false statement to true. Here's an example:

```
$Salary != 3000
```

By using $Salary != 3000, you're asking the computer to compare the value of the $Salary variable with the value 3000. (The != is a *comparison operator*, which I explain very soon.) If the variable has the same value, the statement is true. And in the following example, you can just assume that it's true:

```
!$Salary != 3000
```

By using !$Salary != 3000, you're asking the computer to perform the same analysis, which results in a true statement. But then you tell the computer to *reverse* the value of the statement. So instead of the computer saying that the statement is true (which it is), the computer says that the statement is false because of the ! operator.

The && (and) operator

The && (*and*) operator tells the computer to compare two variables. Each variable has either a true or a false value. Basing its conclusion on these values, the computer tells you that the statement is true or false. Here's how it works:

```
BuyCar = LowestPrice && LikeCar
```

The computer decides whether the value of the BuyCar variable is true or false by checking the values of the LowestPrice and LikeCar variables. The && operator tells the computer to return a true value only if the LowestPrice and LikeCar both have a true value. Following are all the possible outcomes:

BuyCar	LowestPrice	LikeCar
True	True	True
False	False	False
False	True	False
False	False	True

The || (or) operator

The || (*or*) operator tells the computer to compare two variables, each one having a true or false value. Basing its conclusion on these values, the computer returns either a true or false value, as in the following example:

```
BuyCar = LowestPrice || LikeCar
```

The computer decides whether the value of the BuyCar variable is true or false by checking the values of the LowestPrice and LikeCar variables. The

|| operator tells the computer to return a true value only if one or both LowestPrice and LikeCar have a true value. Following are all the possible outcomes:

```
BuyCar     LowestPrice     LikeCar
True       True            True
False      False           False
True       True            False
True       False           True
```

Comparison Operators

Comparison operators tell the computer to compare the values of two numbers or two strings to decide whether they're equal to, not equal to, greater than, or less than one another. Table 6-3 shows the common comparison operators.

Table 6-3	Comparison Operators
Operator	*What It Does*
-eq	Equal to
-ne	Not equal to
-gt	Greater than
-ge	Greater than or equal to
-lt	Less than
-le	Less than or equal to

The -eq (equal to) operator

To determine whether two values are the same, you use the -eq operator. Notice that no space falls between the hyphen (-) and the symbol eq. The following example shows you how to use this operator:

```
let Salary=3000
let NewSalary=2000
test $Salary -eq $NewSalary
echo "$?"
```

ANSI character codes

You understand more than your computer understands. Hard to believe, but computers know only two numbers — ones and zeros. These numbers are known as *binary numbers*.

Binary numbers are ideal for doing math. The computer can use these numbers to perform calculations just as you do with your calculator. If you need letters and punctuation marks, however, your computer falls flat on its face. But thanks to the American National Standards Institute (ANSI), your computer can compare our words against its binary numbers and figure them out. The institute devised the *ANSI*

character codes that assign each character a set of eight binary numbers. So if you type the letter *A*, the computer translates that *A* to the number *65* (the binary-number version, that is).

Now, how does your program know whether two words are the same? It subtracts the numeric representation of each letter of both words. If the result is zero, it's a match. If the first letter of both words is *A*, for example, the program subtracts the numeric equivalent of the letter *A* (65) in the second word from the numeric equivalent of the letter *A* (65) in the first word. The result is zero. They match.

`let Salary=3000` tells the computer to create a variable by the name of `Salary` and to assign that variable the value 3000.

`let NewSalary=2000` tells the computer to create a variable by the name of `NewSalary` and to assign it the value 2000.

`test $Salary -eq $NewSalary` tells the computer to test to determine whether the value of the `Salary` variable is equal to the value of the `NewSalary` variable. If so, `test` returns a true value; otherwise, `test` returns a false value. Finally, `echo "$?"` displays the value that test returns.

A true value is any value that's not a zero; a false value is a zero.

The -ne (not equal to) operator

To determine whether two values aren't the same, you use the `-ne` operator, as in the following example:

```
let Salary=3000
let NewSalary=2000
test $Salary -ne $NewSalary
echo "$?"
```

`let Salary=3000` tells the computer to create a variable by the name of Salary and to assign the value 3000.

`let NewSalary=2000` tells the computer to create a variable by the name of NewSalary and to assign that variable the value 2000.

`test $Salary -ne $NewSalary` tells the computer to test to determine whether the value of the Salary variable is *not* equal to the value of the NewSalary variable. If not, `test` returns a true value; otherwise `test` returns a false value. Finally, `echo "$?"` displays the value that test returns.

The -gt (greater than) operator

To determine whether the value of the first variable is greater than the value of the second variable, you use the `-gt` operator, as in the following example:

```
let Salary=3000
let NewSalary=2000
test $Salary -gt $NewSalary
echo "$?"
```

`let Salary=3000` tells the computer to create a variable by the name of Salary and to assign the value 3000.

`let NewSalary=2000` tells the computer to create a variable by the name of NewSalary and to assign that variable the value 2000.

`test $Salary -gt $NewSalary` tells the computer to test to determine whether the value of the Salary variable is greater than the value of the NewSalary variable. If so, `test` returns a true value; otherwise, `test` returns a false value. Finally, `echo "$?"` displays the value that `test` returns.

The -ge (greater than or equal to) operator

To determine whether the value of the first variable is greater than or equal to the value of the second variable, you use the `-ge` operator, as in the following example:

```
let Salary=3000
let NewSalary=2000
test $Salary -ge $NewSalary
echo "$?"
```

`let Salary=3000` tells the computer to create a variable by the name of `Salary` and to assign that variable the value 3000.

`let NewSalary=2000` tells the computer to create a variable by the name of `NewSalary` and to assign that variable the value 2000.

`test $Salary -ge $NewSalary` tells the computer to test to determine whether the value of the `Salary` variable is greater than or equal to the value of the `NewSalary` variable. If so, `test` returns a true value; otherwise, `test` returns a false value. Finally, `echo "$?"` displays the value that `test` returns.

The -lt (less than) operator

To determine whether the value of the first variable is less than the value of the second variable, you use the `-lt` operator, as in the following example:

```
let Salary=3000
let NewSalary=2000
test $Salary -lt $NewSalary
echo "$?"
```

`let Salary=3000` tells the computer to create a variable by the name of `Salary` and to assign that variable the value 3000.

`let NewSalary=2000` tells the computer to create a variable by the name of `NewSalary` and to assign that variable the value 2000.

Test your programming knowledge

1. Is the following statement true or false?

```
"I want a raise" --eq "Find another job."
```

a. False.

b. True.

c. Could be true or it could be false.

d. It all depends on how you look at it.

2. What does the following line tell the computer to do?

```
$BobSalary -le $MySalary
```

a. Determine whether `BobSalary` is less than or equal to `MySalary`.

b. Determine whether `BobSalary` is less than `MySalary`.

c. Tell me how much Bob is making.

d. Justify my request for a raise.

Answers: 1) a. See "The -eq (equal to) operator." 2) a. "The -le (less than or equal to) operator."

test $Salary -lt $NewSalary tells the computer to test to determine whether the value of the Salary variable is less than the value of the NewSalary variable. If so, test returns a true value; otherwise, test returns a false value. Finally, echo "$?" displays the value that test returns.

The -le (less than or equal to) operator

To determine whether the value of the first variable is less than or equal to the value of the second variable, you use the -le operator, as in the following example:

```
let Salary=3000
let NewSalary=2000
test $Salary -le $NewSalary
echo "$?"
```

let Salary=3000 tells the computer to create a variable by the name of Salary and to assign that variable the value 3000.

let NewSalary=2000 tells the computer to create a variable by the name of NewSalary and to assign that variable the value 2000.

test $Salary -le $NewSalary tells the computer to test to determine whether the value of the Salary variable is less than or equal to the value of the NewSalary variable. If so, test returns a true value; otherwise, test returns a false value. Finally, echo "$?" displays the value that test returns.

A true value is one; a false value is a zero.

Part III
Making Decisions

The 5th Wave — By Rich Tennant

"It's really made the job a lot less complicated. Oh jeez- now what?"

In this part . . .

Your program contains many instructions for the computer. Simply stated, programs contain a list of instructions that the computer follows one after the other.

But what if your computer needs to follow some of those instructions only if a particular condition exists? For this situation, you must tell the computer to make a decision.

Your computer's decision-making capability enables you to build complex programs that further enable your computer to perform mundane tasks that you'd otherwise get stuck doing.

In this part, you find out how to instruct your computer to make decisions.

Chapter 7

The if, if else, and if elif Statements

In This Chapter

▶ Specifying a condition

▶ Using the if statement

▶ Using the if else statement

▶ Using the if elif statement

Decisions, decisions, decisions. We're always asked to make decisions. Where, for example, do you want to go on vacation? To my mother's or to Hawaii?

Some decisions are obvious choices, but you base even those no-brainers on prevailing conditions: Do we have enough money for a trip to the islands? And if conditions aren't right, even the most desirable choice is just a memory. (It's Mom's again this year.)

Linux programming also can make decisions by checking conditions and then reaching a conclusion.

In this chapter, I show you how you can have your program make decisions for you based on information your program receives from the keyboard or from a file.

Conditions

A *condition* is a situation that must exist or must not exist. If the condition exists, the condition is true; otherwise the condition is false.

You either have enough money for the trip to Hawaii . . . or you don't. You have no room for an almost enough money condition. In Linux, a condition takes the form of the following:

▶ A single variable

▶ An expression

Say that you have all your money in your wallet. We can call the variable *wallet* and the value of the variable is thus the *amount of money* that you have in your wallet. So do you have enough money for the trip to Hawaii? Look in your wallet. You say that you don't have much money in it? You're broke! The value of the wallet variable, therefore, is zero — which means that you don't have enough money for the trip. The condition is false.

Say, however, that you have a good deal of money in the wallet. Is it enough money for the trip? You ask yourself whether the amount of money in the wallet is equal to or greater than $10,000 (the amount that you need for the trip). This question is an *expression* that results in either a true or false answer.

The condition as a single variable

The value of a single variable must be either *true* or *false*. You represent a *true* value as a *nonzero* value; a *false* value is a *zero* value. Following are two ways to determine whether the value of a variable is either true or false. The first method is to explicitly check the value of the variable, as in the following example:

```
if [ $HaveEnoughMoney -eq 1 ]
```

Your program checks whether the value of the variable is true or false by using the equal operator (-eq).

If you can have your program check whether a condition is true, you can also have your program check whether the value of the variable is false, as in the following example:

```
if [ $HaveEnoughMoney -ne 0 ]
```

The -ne (not equal) operator tells your program to reverse the logic. If you use the -eq operator, your program checks whether the variable is true. Place the -ne operator in the expression, and your program checks whether the variable is not true, which is false.

The condition as an expression

A condition can also be an *expression*. An expression tells your program to perform an operation on information. You can ask the program to check whether the value of a variable — your bank balance, for example — is more than a specific amount. In this case, the result of an expression is either true or false, as shown in the following example:

```
if [ $BankBalance -gt 3000 ]
```

Other operators useful for testing a condition

Whenever you need to tell your program to check whether a condition is true or false, you need to create an expression that uses an appropriate operator. Following is a list of the operators that you can use to test conditions in your program. These operators are for integers and for strings.

-gt	Greater than
-ge	Greater than or equal to
-lt	Less than
-le	Less than or equal to
-eq	Equals
-ne	Does not equal

Your program checks to see whether the value of BankBalance is greater than 3000. This expression results in one of two possible values: true or false. A bank balance greater than 3000 means that the expression is true (and the trip is on); otherwise, the expression is false.

An expression that contains a string can also be either true or false. In the following example, your program determines whether the variable GoingToHawaii contains the string Yes. If the string exists, the expression is true; otherwise, the expression is false.

```
if [ $GoingToHawaii -eq "Yes" ]
```

The if Statement

You use an if statement whenever you need your program to check whether a condition is true or false. An if statement simply tells your program that "If the condition is true, follow these instructions; otherwise, skip these instructions."

A true condition causes your program to follow a set of instructions. A false condition causes your program to ignore that set of instructions.

Cut to the chase and see how this all comes together in the following example:

```
if [ Condition ]
    then
    Instruction
fi
```

Basically, you're telling your program to follow the `Instruction` if a certain `Condition` exists — meaning that the `Condition` is true.

The `Condition` must always be true or false.

Following are some real-life examples. The first one tells your program to check whether the box is full. The box can hold only 100 cookies (something dear to my stomach).

```
if [ $Quantity -eq 100 ]
   then
   echo "The box is full."
fi
```

This statement tells your program to look at the variable `Quantity` and decide whether the value is 100 cookies. If that's true, your program displays the following message on-screen:

```
The box is full.
```

If the value isn't 100 cookies, however, your program skips this instruction and moves to the instruction that follows the `fi`. This `fi` is a reserved word that has a special meaning to your program (because it ends the `if` statement).

Try another example. In this case, your program must check to determine whether the box is full and check to see whether any sufficient boxes are available. Both conditions must be true for your program to report back that you can't package any more cookies.

```
if [ $Quantity -eq 100 ] && [ $AvailableBoxes -lt 1 ]
   then
   echo "The box is full and you have no more boxes."
fi
```

This statement tells your program to look at the variable `Quantity` and decide whether the value is 100 cookies. Your program also looks at the variable `AvailableBoxes` to see whether its value is less than 1. If both conditions are true, your program displays the message `The box is full and you have no more boxes.` on-screen.

If the value isn't 100 cookies, however, and boxes remain, your program skips this instruction and moves to the instruction that follows the `fi` reserved word.

You can place a bunch of instructions within the `if` statement; your program obeys these instructions only if the condition is true.

The if else Statement

The if statement enables your program to make a decision dependent on a condition and then to follow a specific set of rules if the condition is true.

A problem with using the if statement is that you may need to provide another set of instructions for the program to obey if the condition is false. You can use another if statement and tell your program to follow the other set of instructions if the condition is false. But another way is easier! Use something known as an if else statement. Following is the easiest if else statement:

```
if [ Condition ]
    then
        Instruction1
    else
        Instruction2
fi
```

This statement tells your program to obey the first group of instructions if the Condition is true . . . but to obey the second group of instructions if the Condition is false.

Here's a pop quiz to see whether you're paying attention: How do you modify the following instructions to tell your program to display the message The box is not full.?:

```
if  [ $Quantity -eq 100 ]
    then
      echo "The box is full."
fi
```

You can modify this statement in two ways. Each method depends on how you express the condition. If you leave the condition unchanged, you get the following:

```
if  [ $Quantity -eq 100 ]
    then
      echo "The box is full."
    else
      echo "The box is not full."
fi
```

You can, however, use the condition $Quantity -ne 100 to get the following:

```
if  [ $Quantity -ne 100 ]
    then
      echo "The box is not full."
    else
      echo "The box is full."
fi
```

Feel free to use either type of the `if else` statements. Both are acceptable, and the one you decide to use is up to your preference.

You can place a whole bunch of instructions between the expression and `else` reserved word and another whole bunch between the `else` and `fi` reserved words. The following example shows how the on-screen messages expand if you place more instructions between them:

```
if [ $Quantity -ne 100 ]
    then
        echo "The box is full."
        echo "Sorry, you need to stop."
    else
        echo "The box is not full."
        echo "Keep going!"
fi
```

The if elif Statement

Be careful! Your program blindly follows your instructions if the condition is false. Your program obeys the second bunch of instructions without asking a question. Sometimes you don't want this blind obedience to happen. Instead, you want your program to make another decision before following the second bunch of instructions.

You can have your computer make another decision by using the `if elif` statement. This statement looks confusing at first but is fairly easy to understand after you get used to it. Following's a simple `if elif` statement:

```
if [ Condition1 ]
    then
        Instruction1
    elif [ Condition2 ]
    then
        Instruction2
fi
```

In this statement, your program obeys the first group of instructions if `Condition1` is true. If `Condition1` is false, however, your program determines whether `Condition2` is true. If `Condition2` is true, your program obeys the second group of instructions. If `Condition2` is false, your program skips the second group of instructions.

Whenever you use the `if` statement, your program obeys at least one group of instructions. If you use the `if elif` statement, however, you always face a chance that your program may skip both groups of instructions. Following's an example:

```
if [ $Quantity -eq 100 ]
    then
        echo "The box is full."
    elif [ $Quantity -eq 95 ]
    then
        echo "You can add 5 cookies to the box."
fi
```

So what happens if the value of Quantity is 95 in the preceding example? Your program determines the value of the first condition and sees that the expression $Quantity -eq 100 is false.

Then your program determines the value of the second condition and sees that the expression $Quantity -eq 95 is true, so your program displays the message: You can add 5 cookies to the box.

Be careful as you answer this question: What happens if the value of Quantity is 94?

Your program checks the first condition $Quantity -eq 100 and determines that the expression is false. Your program ignores the first bunch of instructions. Your program then checks the second condition $Quantity -eq 95. This expression, too, is false. Your program ignores the second bunch of instructions.

Your program reaches the end of the if elif statement. None of the conditions are true, so your program doesn't obey any instructions!

Making multiple choices with if elif

You can have your program handle multiple possibilities by having more if elif conditions in your program to check the additional conditions. Following is the simplest way to use multiple if elif conditions:

```
if [ Condition1 ]
    then
        Instruction1
    elif [ Condition2 ]
    then
        Instruction2
    elif [ Condition3 ]
    then
        Instruction3
fi
```

In this statement, you're telling your program to obey the first group of instructions if Condition1 is true. If Condition1 is false, however, your program determines whether Condition2 is true. If Condition2 is true, your program obeys the second group of instructions. If `Condition2` is false, your program determines whether `Condition3` is true. If `Condition3` is true, your program obeys the third group of instructions — or, otherwise, skips the third group of instructions.

Watch out! All the conditions can be false, so your program may not obey any of the instructions within the `if elif` statement.

Caution! The more `if elif` lines that you use in your program, the more confusing it becomes to read the entire `if elif` statement. (It can prove worse than reading the instructions for filling out your taxes — unless, of course, you like jumping around the instruction booklet.)

Making sure that Linux follows at least one group of instructions

Imagine having a gigantic `if elif` statement only to find out that your program obeys no instructions. This sort of thing can happen in real life. You can avoid such a disaster by placing a `fi elif` statement at the end of the `if elif` statement. Following's a sample:

```
if [ Condition1 ]
    then
        Instruction1
    elif [ Condition2 ]
    then
        Instruction2
    elif [ Condition3 ]
    then
        Instruction3
    elif
        Instruction4
fi
```

In this statement, you're telling your program to obey the first group of instructions if `Condition1` is true. If `Condition1` is false, however, your program determines whether `Condition2` is true. If `Condition2` is true, your program obeys the second group of instructions. If `Condition2` is false, your program determines whether `Condition3` is true. If `Condition3` is true, your program obeys the third group of instructions — otherwise, your program obeys the fourth group of instructions.

Test your programming knowledge

1. How many instructions can you place within an if statement?

a. 24.

b. As many as you want.

c. 0.

d. As many as you can fit on-screen.

2. How can you make sure that your program follows at least one instruction in an if elif statement?

a. Write only if statement for your program.

b. Keep running the program until it follows an instruction.

c. Add a fi elif statement at the end of the if elif statement.

d. Complain to the system administrator.

Answers: 1) b. See "The if Statement." *2) c. See* "Making sure that Linux follows at least one group of instructions."

Chapter 8

The case Statement

In This Chapter

▶ Using the case statement

▶ Making the program follow at least one instruction

▶ Putting the case statement in the user interface

*Y*ou can run into a problem if you tell your computer to make a decision with many possibilities. Say, for example, that you want your computer to do something unique with each of five offices in your company. Your program requires a bunch of if elif statements, as in the following example:

```
if [ $region -eq "1" ]
    then
    echo "Hello, Bob"
elif [ $region -eq "2" ]
    then
    echo "Hello, Mary"
elif [ $region -eq "3" ]
    then
    echo "Hello, Joan"
elif [ $region -eq "4" ]
    then
    echo "Hello, Mike"
elif [ $region -eq "5" ]
    then
    echo "Hello, Tom"
fi
```

This program is probably a mess for you to read — although your computer can read it just fine. But just try to imagine tracking 20 if statements if you need to update 20 regional offices!

In this chapter, I show you how to make your program make decisions efficiently by using the case statement.

The case Statement

Suppose that you want your program to display a different message on-screen if someone in each office is using the program. You can set up the program so that, as it begins, it asks the user to enter the number of the office he's in and then matches the office number with the number of those offices for which you're creating a special message.

Chapter 7 shows you how to use a series of `if elif` statements to direct your program to determine whether a box is full of cookies. This code becomes difficult to read, however, especially if you have several boxes that you want your program to check. A better way to obtain the same result is to use the `case` statement.

The `case` statement tells your program to compare the value to the right of the `case` reserved word with the value that appears to the right of each of the close parentheses. The `case` statement looks as follows:

```
case VariableName in
  value1)
      Instruction
      ;;

  value2)
      Instruction
      ;;
esac
```

This statement — beginning with the `case` reserved word and ending with the `esac` reserved word — tells your program to look at the value of `VariableName`. If this value is equal to `value1`, the program follows the first set of instructions. If this value is equal to `value2`, the program follows the second set of instructions. The program follows all the instructions that appear between the `case` reserved word and the `esac` reserved word if it finds a match. You use double semicolons to tell Linux that it's at the end of the set of instructions.

In case you fail to notice it, a close parenthesis —) — follows each `value`.

In the following example, I replace the `if` statement that I use at the beginning of the chapter with the `case` statement:

```
case $region in
  1)
      echo "Hello, Bob."
      ;;
  2)
      echo "Hello, Mary."
      ;;
```

```
    3)
        echo "Hello, Joan."
        ;;
    4)
        echo "Hello, Mike."
        ;;
    5)
        echo "Hello, Tom."
        ;;
esac
```

This code is much easier to read (for humans) because it eliminates repetitive words such as elif. You can stuff as many values in this statement as you need. In effect, the case statement streamlines your program and enables you and your fellow humans to read it more easily.

You must keep a few things in mind, however, in using the case statement. (You knew it was too good to be true, right?) The following list clues you in:

- ✔ The value for the program to match must consist of one or more characters.

- ✔ You can use a variable or a value as a value for the program to match.

- ✔ A variable or a value can be a value that ends with a closed parenthesis.

Making the Program Do Something by Default

Your program can find itself unable to match the value if you don't supply it with the necessary matching value. (Whoops!) Sometimes this situation doesn't matter if you supply the value. A problem can arise, however, if someone else supplies the value that the program must match.

Say, for example, that another office opens and you don't have time to change your program to handle the new office. (Maybe you just misplaced that memo.) Your program's going to run fine. It simply ignores the new office because it doesn't match any value that you gave it.

You can have your computer act as your backstop by using the asterisk (*) reserved character. Following's an example of how you can use the asterisk reserved character:

```
case $office in
  1)
      echo "Hello, Bob."
      ;;
  2)
      echo "Hello, Mary."
      ;;
  3)
      echo "Hello, Joan."
      ;;
  4)
      echo "Hello, Mike."
      ;;
  5)
      echo "Hello, Tom."
      ;;
  *)
      echo "Sorry, your region is not on my list."
esac
```

This code tells your program to display the appropriate greeting if the value of $office is equal to an office number. If your program can't match the value of $office, however, it displays the last set of instructions: Sorry, your region is not on my list.

The case Statement in the User Interface

The most common use for the case statement is with your program's user interface. After your program displays your menu, it must wait for someone to type a key from the keyboard. The person using your program makes a selection, and then your program reads the selection and compares it to specific values by using the case statement.

Say that you want to create an electronic telephone book. I'm keeping it simple and saying that you want only two features: display a telephone number and add a telephone number to the electronic telephone book. First, these features appear on-screen as menu options; then the program reads the user's selection from the keyboard. You use the case statement to compare the user's selection with available features. In the following example, the program simply displays a message telling which selection the user makes. (Other instructions replace these messages in a more complex version of this program, of course.)

```
#!/bin/bash
clear
echo " "
echo "      The Telephone Book "
echo " "
echo "      1. Display A Telephone Number "
echo "      2. Add A New Telephone Number "
echo " "
```

```
echo "      Q Quit "
echo " "
echo "      Enter your selection: "
echo " "
read selection
case $selection in
  "1")
      echo "You want to display a telephone number."
      ;;
  "2")
      echo "You want to add a new telephone number."
      ;;
  "q")
      exit 0
      ;;
  "Q"):
      exit 0
      ;;
  *)
      echo "You made an invalid selection."
esac
```

Don't worry about the big space that you see between some quotation marks and the beginning of the on-screen display with the echo command (such as the fourth line of this preceding code) — that space (and the quotation marks) doesn't print anyway. I'm just indenting the text to make it easier to read.

To avoid any problem with the user trying to exit your program, you may want to indicate that either lowercase or uppercase letters are fine, as I do in the preceding example.

Test your programming knowledge

1. How can you make sure that your program follows at least one set of instructions in a case statement?

a. Use the asterisk (*) reserved character.

b. You have no way.

c. Kick it.

d. Don't forget to say "Please" in your code.

2. How do you end a case statement?

a. Use the reserved word end.

b. Use the secret word esac.

c. Yell "STOP!"

d. Politely say, "I'm done."

Answers: 1) a. See "Making the Program Do Something by Default." *2) b. See* "The case Statement."

Chapter 9

Nested Control Structures

*E*ver receive a gift in a big box? Quickly you open it only to find a slightly smaller box inside. Then you open that box, and another, smaller box is inside. This process continues until you finally find your present (and I hope it isn't a hunk of coal).

In programming, the concept of placing one box inside another is known as *nesting*. Nesting also occurs if you combine more than one `if` statement together or you combine more than one `case` statement together.

Nesting by Using if

Normally, an `if` statement contains one or more sets of instructions, such as in the following sample, which displays a personal greeting to the manager of the New York office:

```
if [ $office -eq "1" ]
then
    echo "Hello, Bob."
else
    echo "Sorry, your region is not on my list."
fi
```

Another way to write the preceding program is to replace the `if` statement with the `case` statement, as shown in the following example:

```
case $office in
 "1")
     echo "Hello, Bob."
     ;;
  *)
     echo "Sorry, your region is not on my list."
esac
```

Instead of placing a bunch of instructions in the if statement or the case statement, you can stuff an if statement and a case statement within other if statements and case statements. The following example shows how you do it by using the if statement:

```
if [ $office -eq "1" ]
    then
    if [ $RegionalMgr -eq "Bob" ]
        then
        echo "Hello, Bob."
fi
```

The program looks at the value of $office. If the value of $office is 1, the program then looks at the value of $RegionalMgr. If the value of $RegionalMrg is Bob, the program then displays a message greeting Bob.

Nesting by Using case

You can use the same nesting method with the case statement. Take a look at this use of nesting in action in the following example:

```
case $office in
 "1")
        case $RegionalMgr in
        "Bob")
                        echo "Hello, Bob."
            ;;
                esac
    ;;
  esac
```

The program looks at the value of $region. If the value of $office is 1, the program then looks at the value of $RegionalMgr. If the value of $RegionalMrg is Bob, the program then follows the instruction and greets Bob.

Don't forget that you must follow the value with a close parenthesis —).

Making Nested Statements Easy (for You) to Read

Your computer doesn't care how many if statements or case statements you place inside one another. *You*, however, are sure to care whenever you read your program. You can easily become lost reading a program containing multiple nested statements.

My advice is to indent each nested statement, as I do in the example in the preceding section. Indentation isn't a requirement of Linux, but it's a good style to use as you write a Linux program. Indenting makes reading your program a lot easier than jumbling all the nested statements together.

The following example shows what the code looks like without indenting:

```
case $office in
  "New York")
case $RegionalMgr in
  "Bob")
echo "Hello, Bob."
;;
esac
esac
```

Your computer doesn't have any difficulty reading this program. You're likely, however, to spend a few puzzling minutes matching the nested statements.

By the way, you don't even need a test for this chapter.

Part IV
Loops and Loops

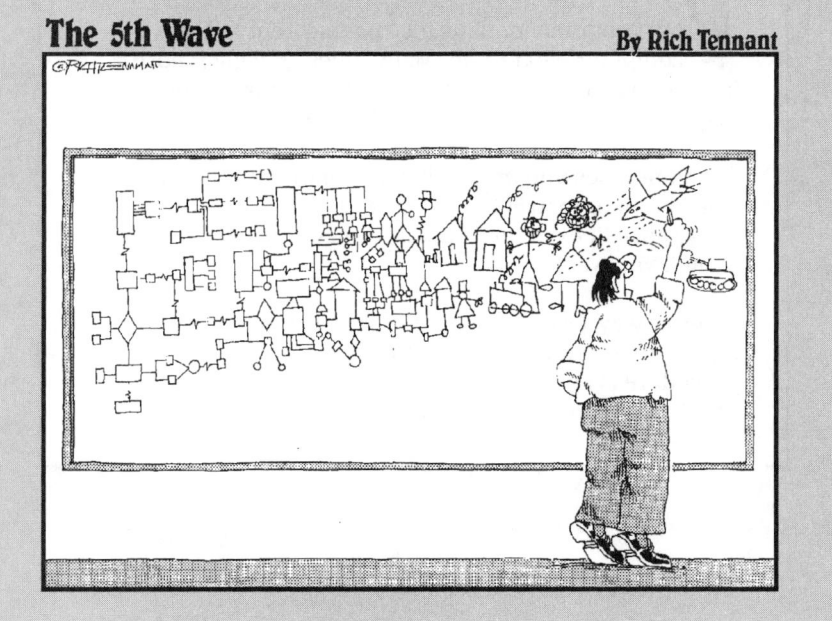

The 5th Wave   By Rich Tennant

In this part . . .

Your program contains instructions that tell the computer what to do. Many times, you give those instructions just once, such as whenever you need to display a welcome message for the user.

But sometimes you must tell your computer the same instruction or instructions over and over again. You *can* copy those lines of instructions to new lines in your program if you want.

A better way, however, is to simply tell your computer to repeat instructions that are already in your program. This procedure is known as *looping*. In this part, you find out how to make loops in your program.

Chapter 10

The while Loop

In This Chapter

▶ Using the while loop

▶ Determining how often the while loop repeats itself

▶ Using the while loop in a menu

*T*he while *loop* works like a group of people caught in the rain, standing under the awning of a store. Every so often, they check to see whether the rain's still coming down. While the rain continues, the people stay put. Otherwise, they begin walking toward their cars. Rain is a *condition* that determines whether the people can go for a walk.

You may write your program so that it continues to wait for the user to enter the correct response to a question before continuing with the program. Each time a response is given, the program checks it against the correct response. This checking for a correct response is similar to someone under the awning checking to see if it's still raining. If the program doesn't detect a match, it tells the user that he gave the wrong answer and returns to the top of the while loop to wait for the next response.

A while loop looks like what you see in the following example:

```
while [ Condition ]
    do
        Instruction
done
```

In this chapter, I show you how to use a while loop in your program so that your program executes your instruction only if a particular condition exists — such as someone entering the correct response at the keyboard.

You must include a variable or expression in the while loop that results in a true or false value. And you can place many instructions in a while loop.

Deciding Whether to Use a while Loop

As you write a program, you list all the instructions that you want the computer to follow, in order. At times, however, you want to repeat some of those instructions. Instead of writing those instructions over again, you can just place them within a while loop.

Use a while loop if you ever need to repeat a group of instructions — as long as a condition is true. If you need to prompt the user to enter a correct password, for example, and you put those instructions in a while loop, that group of instructions continues to execute until the user enters the correct password.

Don't, however, use a while loop if you don't want the group of instructions to repeat continuously. Say, for example, that you want to display the same message on-screen whenever someone makes an error using your program. Although the instructions that you need to display the message repeat in the program, instructions repeat only if an error occurs. Placing these instructions in a while loop causes the program to continually display the message. The best way to handle this problem is to place these instructions in a subprogram (see Chapter 14) and then call the subprogram whenever you need to display the message.

Using a while Loop in Your Linux Code

If your program sees a while loop, it checks the condition. It answers the following question: "Is this condition true or is it false?" Only if the condition is true does your program read the instructions that you put in the while loop.

The following code shows a while loop in action:

```
declare raining="1"
while [ "$raining" -eq "1" ]
    do
        echo "Still raining."
done
```

The following explanation describes what's happening in this while loop:

The declare tells your program to create a string variable by the name raining and assign it the value 1. This value indicates a true value.

The do tells your program to check whether the value of $raining is still 1. If true, this value means that the rain is still falling.

The echo tells your program to display the message on-screen only if the rain's still coming down.

The done tells your program that it's at the end of the while loop.

Of course, you need more instructions in this example to make it a working program. In the preceding block of code, for example, your program keeps displaying the message because the value of $raining never changes. This type of program is known as an *endless loop*. The condition in the statement is always true.

You need to add instructions that check to see whether the rain's still falling. You place these instructions within the while loop to change the value of $raining to 0 if the rain stops.

Using a while loop to create a menu

You commonly use a while loop to create a menu interface. In any program menu, the program user expects the following sequence:

1. See a menu.
2. Make a selection.
3. Have the program do something.
4. Return to the menu to make further selections.

The easiest way to program this menu stuff is to place all these instructions inside a while loop. Each time that the program finishes doing what the user requests, the program returns to the while loop and starts all over again. Take a look at the following example:

```
#!/bin/bash
declare flag="1"
while [ "$flag" -eq "1" ]
    do
            clear
            echo " "
            echo "The Telephone Book "
            echo " "
            echo "1. Display A Telephone Number "
            echo "2. Add A New Telephone Number "
            echo " "
            echo "Q Quit "
            echo " "
            echo "Enter your selection: "
            echo " "
            read selection
            case $selection  in
                "1")
                        #Run the subprogram to display a phone number
                        getnum
```

```
                        ;;
          "2")
                        #Run the subprogram to add a new phone number
                        addnum
                        ;;
          "q")
                        $flag="0"
                        ;;
          "Q")
                        $flag="0"
                        ;;
          *)
                        echo "You made an invalid selection. Try again."
          esac
done
```

The bash tells the computer that this program is a bash shell script. The declare creates a string variable by the name of $flag and assigns it the value 1.

Next, the program evaluates the expression in the statement to see whether the value of $flag is 1.

If so, the program displays the menu and waits for a user to enter a character at the keyboard; the program then stuffs this character into the variable. The program compares the value that $selection stores with all possible values by using the case statement.

If it finds a match, the program runs a subprogram — but only if the subprogram exists. In this example, an error occurs at that point because you didn't write those subprograms. Say, for example, that getnum is the name of a subprogram that runs after the user selects the first option on the menu. The subprogram returns to this part of the program after it finishes running, and the program continues with the instructions in the while loop.

Notice that the program looks for both upper- and lowercase Q. It does so because the user can enter Q — to quit the program — in either an upper- or lowercase character.

If the program doesn't find a match, however, it tells the user to try another selection. The program repeats this process until the user selects the Quit option. After this selection occurs, the value of $flag changes to 0 and the computer exits the while loop the next time that it checks the value of $flag.

Using a while loop to create a timing loop

You're likely to come across a problem if you want the program to pause before executing the next group of instructions. You may, for example, have a program that displays a series of messages on-screen automatically. Each message appears on-screen for a specific amount of time before the program changes to the next message — a kind of slide show without all the fancy type that you find in a Windows program.

The trick is to make the program pause long enough for someone to read the message. The way you can create such a pause is to use a timing loop. A *timing loop* is a simple while loop where the only instruction within the loop is an instruction to add 1 to a variable. Take a look at the timing loop in the following example:

```
declare counter=0
while [ "$counter" -lt 1000 ]
do
   let $counter="$counter + 1"
done
```

In this example, the program stores 0 in a variable known as counter and then the program enters the while loop. The single instruction within the loop adds 1 to the value of the counter and stores the new value back in the counter variable. The loop continues to count until the value of the counter variable is 999 — at which time the program leaves the while loop.

You can adjust the length of the pause by increasing or decreasing the value in the condition. In this example, the value of counter in the condition is 1000. Increase this value to lengthen the pause and decrease this value to speed up the pause.

Using a while loop to create a flashing message

Whenever you really want to catch the eye of the user and make sure that he reads your message, you can make your message flash on-screen by using a while loop. First, you instruct the program to display the message on-screen. Next, you start a timing loop (see the preceding section for information). This process causes your program to pause for a specific length of time. Finally, you clear the message from the screen and return to the beginning of the while loop. To see it in action, check out the following example:

```
clear
declare counter1=1
declare counter2

while [ "$counter1" -lt 6 ]
    do
             echo "Warning: There's a bug in your program."
        let counter2=1
             while [ "$counter2" -lt 200]
           do
              let $counter2="$counter2 + 1"
```

```
        done
    clear
        let $counter2=1
        while [ "$counter2" -lt 200 ]
            do
                let $counter2="$counter2 + 1"
            done
        let $counter1="$counter1 + 1"
done
```

Notice that I use three while loops in this program. The first while loop causes the message to flash five times. Each time the message flashes on-screen, the program adds 1 to the variable. After counter1 has a value of 6, the program exits the first while loop.

Each time the message appears on-screen, the program pauses by entering the second while loop. Simply put, the program counts to 200. You can change this value to any number. The higher the number, the slower the message flashes. And the lower the number, the faster the message flashes.

After this while loop counts to 200, the program removes the message from the screen; then the third while loop begins. The third while loop keeps the screen blank until that third while loop counts to 200; afterward, the first while loop adds 1 to its count and begins the process again.

Avoiding Endless while Loops

If the condition of the while loop is false, your program doesn't execute any of the instructions inside the loop. The instructions inside the while loop, therefore, never repeat. In fact, they never even execute. (And after all that work writing this code!) Following's an example:

```
declare raining = "0"
while [ "$raining" -eq "1" ]
    do
            echo "Still raining."
clear
```

Your program doesn't display the message in this example because the value of $raining is not 1. The program skips the instructions inside the while loop and continues on the line that follows the reserved word, clear, which in this case marks the end of the program.

If the condition of the while loop is true, the program executes all the instructions in the loop at least once.

If the condition of the while loop is always true, the program again executes all the instructions in the loop. Your program doesn't stop until you or the administrator who's responsible for your computer stops the program. Again, this situation is the infamous *endless loop*.

No cool programmer wants to put an endless loop in a program. You can avoid this situation by making sure that at least one instruction in the while loop changes the true or false value of the condition that the while loop uses. The following example shows how to do so:

```
#!/bin/bash
declare raining="1"
while [ "$raining" -eq "1" ]
    do
                clear
                echo " "
                echo "Is it raining? "
                echo " "
                echo "1. Yes "
                echo "2. No "
                echo " "
                echo "Enter your selection: "
                read raining
done
echo "It stopped raining."
```

The bash tells the program that this part is a bash shell script.

The declare tells the computer to create a string variable by the name of raining and assign it the value 1.

The while tells the program to check whether the value of $raining is 1. If so, the program executes the following instructions.

The clear tells the program to clear the screen.

The echo stuff displays a menu.

The read waits for the user to make a selection and then assigns the selection to the raining variable.

The program returns to the top of the while loop and checks to see whether the value of $raining is 1. If the value didn't change, the instructions execute again.

If the value isn't 1, the instructions don't execute again. The program jumps to the last instruction in the program and displays It stopped raining. on-screen.

Test your programming knowledge

1. How can the program break out of a `while` **loop?**

a. Use a file hidden in a birthday cake.

b. Make the condition false.

c. Make the condition true.

d. Use explosives.

2. How can a `while` **loop run endlessly?**

a. Your computer goes crazy.

b. Your program always changes the condition to false.

c. Your program never changes the condition to false.

d. The accelerator gets stuck.

Answers: 1) b. See "Avoiding Endless `while` Loops." *2) c. See* "Avoiding Endless `while` Loops."

Of course, the user can enter a character other than a 1 or 2. If that happens, the program treats the value as if the user is selecting 2. The value is no longer 1, so the program follows the same instructions as if the rain isn't falling.

Always indent instructions that you place in a `while` loop. If you don't, you usually must spend hours trying to understand what you told the program to do. (Although your program has no trouble reading your code whether you indent it or not.) Always indent lines of instructions so that you group similar instructions together.

Chapter 11

The for in Loop

In This Chapter
▶ Using the `for in` loop
▶ Using the `for in` loop in a program
▶ Using wordlists

Say that you want to print the same letter to each of your friends inviting them to the big bash you're throwing because you just won the lottery. You want to personalize these invitations. You could write a program to print the text, but each time the program runs, you find yourself entering the name of your next friend.

Of course, you avoid this problem by using the `for in` loop. The `for in` loop enables you to store all your friends' names in a list, and then your program uses each name in printing the invitation. It's like having a mail-merge feature built into your own program.

So, whenever you want your programming code to execute a series of instructions as long as a condition is true, use the `while` loop. Your computer keeps executing instructions that you place inside a `while` loop until one of the instructions in your code changes the condition to false.

If you know how many times that you want the instructions to execute, however, use the `for in` loop instead.

Just in case you can't wait, here's what a `for in` loop looks like:

```
for VariableName in wordlist
do
  Instruction
  done
```

The `wordlist` is a list of string values that you assign to the variable; I explain this wordlist stuff later in the chapter, so don't worry for now. (Remember that a string is any combination of letters and numbers.) The instruction inside the loop can use the variable.

You can stuff as many instructions as you need inside the loop. Your biggest challenge is your ability to keep track of the programming instructions that you enter. Use your common sense as a guide.

When to Use a for in Loop

No hard-and-fast rules exist to tell you when to use a for in loop. You just need to use your best judgment. (I guess you didn't need to go to MIT after all.)

The following list describes the times when you can use a for in loop:

- ✔ You need to do the same thing to more than one string value.
- ✔ You want to use a series of string values in a certain sequence.

Say, for example, that you want your program to give your five employees an increase in salary. Aren't you a nice person? The necessary steps are as follows:

1. Look up the employee's salary in the payroll file.
2. Calculate the new salary.
3. Save the new salary to the payroll file.

You place the name of each employee in the list that you associate with the for in loop. The program then uses the name of each employee in sequence to find the employee's record, perform the necessary math, and place the employee's record back into the file.

How the for in Loop Works

Here's something to do if you're ready to show off your new programming talents to your friends. Write a program that greets each one of them personally after you gather them around your computer. You can accomplish this task in either of a couple ways.

You can, for example, type the following code:

```
echo "Hello, Mary."
echo "Hello, Joe."
echo "Hello, Sue."
```

This program simply repeats the same instruction three times. Each time it changes the name to greet another one of your friends.

The following code also displays a Hello message to each of your three buddies:

```
let counter = 1
while [ "$counter" -lt 5 ]
do
   if [ "$counter" -eq 1]
      then
         echo "Hello, Mary."
   fi
   if [ "$counter" -eq 2 ]
      then
         echo "Hello, Joe."
   fi
   if [ "$counter" -eq 3 ]
      then
         echo "Hello, Sue."
fi
   let counter=$counter + 1
done
```

Here's what's happening:

Each time instructions within the while loop execute, the computer checks the value of counter.

Depending on the value of counter, a particular welcome message appears.

The last instruction in the while loop (let counter=$counter + 1) tells the computer to add 1 to the value of $counter and then assign this new value to counter. This instruction enables the computer to display all the messages.

After these instructions execute, the computer checks the value of counter to see whether the value is less than 5. If the value of counter is less than 5, the instructions execute another time. If the value of counter is greater than 5, the loop ends.

The preceding program took 16 lines of code to accomplish the same result as the following for in loop. I probably could have written in longhand in less time than it takes to simply read the code in the preceding example.

Use the following code to display a greeting to each of your three pals by using the for in loop:

```
for friend in Mary Joe Sue
do
     echo "Hello, $friend ."
done
```

In the first line of the preceding `for in` loop, you follow `for friend in` with the names of your friends, which you place after the word `in`. This creates a wordlist (see the following section) and designates the names as values, which you then assign to the variable.

Notice the space between `$friend` and the following period. If you don't include this space, the program looks for a variable by the name of `friend .` (with a period) and not `friend` (without a period).

Here's what happens as this program runs:

1. Your computer takes the first value and assigns it to `friend`.

2. Then the greeting appears on the computer screen.

3. Your computer goes back and assigns the next value to `friend`.

This sequence continues until your computer runs out of values, in which case it's greeted all your friends; then the `for in` loop ends.

So, you've cut down the amount of instructions that you need to type from the 16 lines using the `while` loop to three lines by using the `for in` loop. You've also made your program a lot easier to read by using the `for in` loop.

Using a Wordlist

The values that you assign to the variable are known as the *wordlist*. A wordlist is a list of string values (a mixture of characters and numbers) that you sequentially assign to a variable, one at a time.

By the way, you can use a wordlist with other statements besides the `for in` loop. (I think, however, that following a routine showing how you typically use a wordlist is a better way to demonstrate its use.)

Some points to remember about a wordlist:

✔ Values that you assign to a wordlist must be a string value.

✔ You must separate each value by a space.

✔ You need to place values within quotation marks if a space is part of the value.

Following's an example of how to use values that contain spaces:

```
for friend in "Mary Jones" "Joe Smith" "Sue Jones"
do
    echo "Hello, $friend ."
done
```

A for in loop is not a for next loop

Some computer languages, such as Visual Basic, use a `for next` loop, which enables you to determine the number of times the instructions inside the loop execute. The Linux `bash` shell language doesn't have a `for next` loop. A few inexperienced Linux programmers try to use the `for in` loop as a replacement for a `for next` loop. This attempt just doesn't work.

Here's a better way to control the number of times your computer executes instructions inside a loop: Use the `while` loop. (Refer to Chapter 10 for the lowdown on `while` loops.) Take a look at the following example:

```
let counter =1
while [ "$counter" -lt 4 ]
    do
        echo "This is my $counter
    time around."
        let counter=$counter + 1
done
```

This program tells your computer to follow the instructions inside the loop three times. The last line increases the `$counter` variable by 1. The loop continues to run as long as the value of `$counter` is less than 4; the loop ends as soon as the value of `$counter` reaches 4.

You can control the number of times that the computer executes instructions within the loop by changing the value of the condition of the `while` loop (`$counter -lt 4`).

Suppose that you want the program to execute the instructions ten times. Change the value 4 to the value 11. Changing the value to 11 means that the `while` loop continues as long as the value of `$counter` is less than 11.

Chapter 12

Nested Loops and Quick Exits

●●●

In This Chapter

▶ Using nested loops

▶ Indenting nested loops

▶ Avoiding pitfalls in nested loops

▶ Using the `break` statement for a quick exit

▶ Skipping over code by using the `continue` statement

●●●

*R*emember when Mom told you to clean up your toys? After complaining —
which never did any good — you picked up the first toy and dropped it in
the toy box. You repeated this action over and over again. Among those toys,
however, were dozens of blocks, and you needed to place each one in the canister that the blocks came in before you could put the canister into the toy box.

Picking up toys is the *outside loop,* and picking up blocks is the *inside loop* in
this example. You can jam loops inside other loops to form an endless series
of loops known as *nested loops.* Nested loops make your program better
organized — although they complicate things a bit more for you in reading
the program.

In this chapter, I show you how to make your program more efficient by creating nested loops. (See Chapters 10 and 11 for more information about loops.)

Using Nested Loops

A nested loop tells the program to do something a number of times (the
inside loop) for each time around the outside loop. The following block of
code contains a nested loop:

```
let flag=1
while [ "$flag" -lt 4 ]
    do
            for friend in Bob Mary Sue
```

```
                    echo "Hello $friend ."
            done
                    let flag="$flag + 1"
      done
```

In brief, the program greets Bob, Mary, and Sue with an on-screen message three times. Two loops are in the program: the `while` loop and the `for in` loop. The `while` loop goes around three times. The inner loop, which is the nested `for in` loop, displays the greeting to each friend every time that the `while` loop goes around.

The following paragraphs provide the line-by-line details.

The `let flag=1` says to create a numeric variable and assign the value 1 to it.

The `while [ "$flag" -lt 4 ]` says to check the value of the $ `flag` variable. If its value is 1, the program follows instructions that appear inside the `while` loop.

The `for friend in Bob Mary Sue` is the beginning of the nested loop. It says to assign each of the values in the wordlist (`Bob Mary Sue`) to the variable `friend`.

The `echo "Hello $friend ."` displays a greeting using the value of the `$friend` variable. (Notice the space between `$friend` and the period.)

The `done` says that the program is the end of the `for in` loop.

The `let flag="$flag + 1"` assigns a 1 to the $ `flag` variable.

The `done` indicates the end of the `while` loop.

The `for in` loop is the *inner loop*. The `while` loop is the *outer loop*. The inner loop must finish before the outer loop finishes.

Indenting Nested Loops

You can stuff as many loops as you need inside other loops. You don't confuse your computer by doing so. You may, however, confuse another programmer who may need to read your program if you use long blocks of code that contain lots of nested loops.

Avoid any confusion by indenting each inner loop in your code. Indenting your nested loops makes your code easier to read and makes finding where the loop begins and ends easier, too.

Test your programming knowledge

1. What's the limit to the number of loops that you can nest in a program?

a. 255

b. 256

c. You have no limit regarding the number of loops that you can nest in a program.

d. A number equal to the number of lines in your program.

2. How can you make nested loops easier to read?

a. Insert a blank line between lines in the program.

b. Use a separate piece of paper for each loop.

c. Indent each loop within the block of code.

d. Reduce the number of characters that you place on a line.

Answers: 1) c. See "Using Nested Loops." *2) c. See* "Indenting Nested Loops."

Take a look at the following code, for example, and notice how difficult picking out the nested loops is:

```
let flag=1
while [ "$flag" -eq 1]
do
for friend in Bob Mary Sue
echo "Hello $friend ."
let counter=1
while [ "$counter" -lt 4 ]
do
echo "$friend"
let counter="$counter + 1"
done
done
echo "Good-bye!"
let flag=0
done
```

Now, take a look at the same code where I indent the nested loops. Notice that identifying the nested loops is much easier in the following example:

```
let flag=1
while [ "$flag" -eq 1]
    do
        for friend in Bob Mary Sue
            do
                echo "Hello $friend ."
                let counter=1
                 while [ "$counter" -lt 4 ]
```

```
            do
               echo "$friend"
               let counter="$counter + 1"
         done
    done
    echo "Good-bye!"
    let flag=0
done
```

Indenting a nested loop doesn't affect how Linux processes the commands that the loop contains. Linux processes the commands in the same manner as it does those in the block of code that you don't indent — indenting a loop simply makes the code easier for you (and other programmers) to read and understand.

Avoiding Endless Loops

All right. You build your masterpiece of a program and fill it with loops inside other loops (nested loops), but it doesn't work correctly. The program keeps breaking out of an outer loop prematurely. It's a mess! This situation results from a common mistake that you want to avoid. Whenever code contains many nested loops, changes that you make within an inner loop are likely to inadvertently make the condition in an outer loop false — breaking your program out of the loop.

```
let flag=1
while [ "$flag" -eq 1 ]
    do
        for friend in Bob Mary Sue
            do
                echo "Hello $friend ."
                let counter=1
                while [ "$counter" -lt 4 ]
                    do
                        echo "$friend"
                        let counter="$counter + 1"
                done
        done
        echo "Good-bye!"
        let flag=1
done
```

Here's what's happening.

`let flag=1` creates a variable called flag and assigns the value 1 to the variable.

`while [ "$flag" -eq 1 ]` uses the value of flag as the condition for entering the loop. As long as the value of flag is 1, all the instructions inside the loop execute.

`let flag=1` near the last line in the program assigns the value 1 to the flag variable. This creates an endless loop because you never assign `flag` a value other than 1; the condition in the `while` loop is always true. The computer keeps running all the instructions inside the `while` loop . . . over and over again.

You can avoid breaking the loop by making sure that the condition for each loop is independent from other conditions and other variables that you use in the program. Programmers commonly use a variable known as `flag` as the condition for a loop — for example, `while [ "$flag" -eq 1 ]`. Inadvertently, you can use the same `flag` as the condition for all the nested loops. But what a mess results if you don't remember that you're using the variable as the condition for the loop and change the value of the `flag` variable in your program. It can potentially affect the condition of all the loops. You end up with an endless loop — and then you must untangle the mess.

Another common problem to avoid is ending the loop in the wrong place. This error trips many programs, especially if you nest loops. Each loop requires its own `done` reserved word. If you place `done` within the instructions of the loop instead of at the end of the instructions, the program probably produces unexpected results. This problem is a little different from other problems that you face as you write a program, because Linux doesn't tell you that a mistake is lurking in your program. Instead, the program executes as if nothing's wrong — except you recognize that the output of your program isn't correct. Only painstaking examination of your program reveals the problem.

The following code shows a potential problem that creating a nested loop introduces:

```
let flag=1
while [ "$ flag" -eq 1]
    do
        for friend in Bob Mary Sue
            do
                echo "Hello $friend ."
                let counter=1
                while [ "$counter" -lt 4 ]
                    do
                        echo "$friend"
                        let counter="$counter + 1"
                        echo "Good-bye!"
                        let flag=0
                done
        done
done
```

The `done` keywords are in the wrong places. Instead of displaying the `Good-bye!` message as part of the outer loop, the mix-up causes the `Good-bye!` message to appear as part of the inner loop.

Linux doesn't catch this mistake. You must hunt through your code to locate the problem.

Using break and continue in Any Loop that You Want

I know that the following stuff on `break` and `continue` closely connects to the `while` loop (which you can read about in Chapter 10), but I'm discussing them in this chapter because the topic usually comes up as you're finding out about nested loops and their potential problems. (So don't stop now. Read on.)

Using break for a quick exit

Did you ever try to run a mile on a treadmill just to stop halfway through? Practically the same thing can happen with your program as the program's executing a `while` loop. The treadmill has a safety button that you pull out to abort your run. The safety button in a `while` loop is the `break` reserved word.

A `while` loop runs continually until a condition proves true or false. Suppose that you want to exit the loop before the condition changes. How can you bow out of the loop before it finishes? You can use the `break` statement.

Take a look at the following code for an example of the `break` statement in action:

```
let n=1
while [ "$n" -eq 1 ]
    do
      echo "Enter your name or type stop to end: "
       read name
       case $name in
         "stop")
      break
       ;;
  esac
       echo "Good-bye!"
done
```

This program asks the user to enter his name or the word `stop` if he wants to end the program. Behind the scenes, the program displays a personal greeting on-screen as long as the user doesn't enter the word `stop`.

After the user enters `stop`, the program enters the `case` statement and skips to the next instruction, which causes the program to break out of the loop.

The break reserved word has practically the same effect as if you're changing the value of the flag variable to something other than go — which also causes the program to break out of the loop.

Finally, the program displays a farewell message on-screen.

Did you follow that sequence? If not, here's another explanation: You set up the program to ask the user to enter a name; after the user enters a name, the program then displays a personalized greeting on-screen. When the user wants to exit the program, he types the word stop instead of a name. Each time a user enters a name, the program checks whether the word the user enters is stop. If the user enters the word stop, the program moves to the next line and executes the break statement, which ends the loop.

After the user types the word stop, the case statement tells your program to break, it immediately leaves the loop and continues to follow the instruction that comes after the done reserved word. In this example, your program displays the Good-bye! message.

Using continue to reach the top of the loop

Your computer doesn't need to follow all the instructions that you place inside a loop. It can skip some instructions if you use the continue statement. The following code demonstrates the use of the continue statement:

```
declare n=1
while [ $n -eq 1 ]
    do
        echo "Enter your name or type stop to end: "
        read name
        echo "Enter your employee number:"
        read num
        case $name in
            "stop")
                    if [ "$num" -eq 1 ]
                        then
                            continue
                    else
                            break
                    fi
                ;;
            *)
                    echo "Hello, $name"
        esac
done
```

Here's what's happening in this sequence:

You're telling your computer to ask the user to enter a name and also to enter the number 1 — or to enter the word `stop` and a number other than the number 1 to end the program. After the person enters his name, the program greets the person. If the user enters the word `stop` and a number other than 1, however, the program doesn't actually end. Instead, it uses the `break` reserve word to break out of the loop and jump to the last instruction in the program: `Good-bye!`

The `continue` statement tells your program to skip the rest of the instructions within the loop and go directly to the top of the loop without displaying the greeting on-screen. After it gets there, the program checks the condition and decides whether to follow the instruction inside the loop again.

Part V

Writing Subprograms

The 5th Wave   By Rich Tennant

Before installing Linux,
Dwayne prepares to partition
the hard drive.

In this part . . .

One of the tricks to writing large, complex programs is to divide the program into smaller programs known as *subprograms* and, within each subprogram, to group together repeating code into a *function*. Functions and subprograms perform one particular task of your program. Your job is to make your main program call the function and subprogram whenever you need them. You discover how to use this trick with your own programs in this part.

Chapter 13

Waxing Efficient with Functions (So You Don't Have to Retype Code!)

As you begin to write Linux programs, you find yourself repeating the same commands over and over again. You may want to personalize and print an invitation to your next bash (pardon the pun), for example, and then send the invitation to your friends. You can write the message inside a `for in` loop and place your friends' names in a *wordlist,* which you can read about in Chapter 11. You can also rewrite the invitation many times in your program for each of your friends. Or you can use a function.

A *function* is part of your Linux program that you set aside from the rest of the program. Think of a function as a compartment inside your program. You identify a function with a unique name (known as, logically enough, a *function name*), and then you store one or more commands that you frequently use inside the function.

You can enter the name of the function in your program whenever you want Linux to use the commands that you store in the function. You can, thereby, use the same commands over and over simply by using the name of the function instead of rewriting all those commands again. I'd place the invitation to my bash inside a function.

You can pass information to the function each time that you call the function. You refer to this procedure as *passing a parameter to the function*. So if you create a function to print an invitation, you're passing the function a name. The function automatically assigns your friend's name to a variable inside the function. You then use a variable instead of the friend's name whenever you refer to that friend in the invitation.

You commonly use functions to do something with information that you pass to the function. The results of whatever the function is doing then return to the part of the program that called the function. The result of the function is known as the function's *return value*, which you can use within your program.

You want to use functions whenever you find yourself rewriting the same code in your program. In this chapter, I show you how to create and use functions in your program.

Creating a Function

You must define a function before you use that function in a program. The best place to create a function, therefore, is at the beginning of your program. Creating a function is also known as *defining* a function, the results of which you refer to as a function definition.

You can create as many functions as you want, but limit your enthusiasm to a few. Otherwise, you're almost certain to lose track of all the functions that you create. Start with one function if you're rewriting code and then add others as they become necessary. Keep in mind that your program doesn't require a function if the program doesn't contain any repeating code.

Follow these steps to define a function:

1. **Begin your program by typing the word** function **into your program.**

   This action tells Linux that you're creating a function.

2. **Give your function a name that you don't use anywhere else in your program.**

   Make sure that the name reflects the purpose of the function. Don't, for example, call a function that displays text on-screen *bob* if the name *display* is more informative.

3. **Type an open French brace ({) between the function name and the first command.**

   The brace tells Linux that commands follow.

4. **Type any commands that you want to execute after the function calls.**

   You can use any commands that I discuss in this book within a function.

5. **Type a semicolon (;) after each command and before you type the next command.**

   Don't place a space before the command and the semicolon. The semicolon tells Linux that the specific command is ending.

6. **Type a close French brace (}) after the semicolon of the last command.**

   Don't place a space between the last semicolon and the brace. This final action tells Linux that the function definition is complete.

Following are the components of a function definition:

```
function name
{
    command;
    command;
}
```

Following is a typical function definition that displays a welcome message on-screen. (I refer to this function later in the chapter, so keep it handy!)

```
function display
{
    echo "Welcome to the world"
    echo "of functions"
}
```

Calling a Function

Calling a function is pretty easy after you define the function. All you need to do is use the name of the function in your program wherever you want to use the commands that the function contains. By *calling a function*, you order Linux to find the definition of that function and execute each command that it finds. After reaching the close French brace, Linux returns to the line following the function line in your program. Linux continues to execute your program as if the function never existed.

Following is a typical command that calls a function:

```
#! /bin/bash
clear
function display
{
    echo "Welcome to the world"
    echo "of functions."
}
display
```

The following steps walk you through each line of this program:

1. The first line (#! /bin/bash) tells Linux to run the bash shell.

2. Clear wipes the screen clean.

3. The program uses the function keyword display to define a function.

4. Between the French braces, you tell Linux to display two lines of text on-screen.

5. Following the closing French brace, you call the function by using the name of the function (display), and Linux then displays the text on-screen.

Passing Arguments to a Function

Passing arguments sounds like avoiding a heated discussion with the guy who cut you off on the highway. But the term *passing arguments* really refers to a way to give changing information to a function.

Suppose, for example, that you write a function that validates an ID and password. The function contains the commands and information necessary to perform the validation — all except for two pieces. The missing pieces are the ID and the password, which are different each time that the program calls the function.

The ID and password can pass as arguments to the function if you call the function in your program. Linux assigns the ID and password to variables whenever you call the function. These variables are $1 and $2. Each number refers to the next argument passing to the program. You can't substitute the number in these variables with another name such as var1 because Linux expects to see numbers.

So you can use the variable in place of the information in the function definition. Say that the ID is the first argument passing to the function and the pass-word is the second argument. You can, therefore, use $1 in the function definition whenever you want to refer to the ID and use $2 to refer to the password.

The program looks as follows:

```
#! /bin/bash
clear
function verify
{
    if [ $1 -eq "Bob" ] && [ $2 -eq "555" ]
```

```
        then
            echo "Verified"
        else
            echo "Rejected"
}
verify Bob 555
```

The following steps describe what's happening in this program:

1. The bash shell starts.

2. The screen clears of unnecessary information.

3. The program calls the verify function.

4. Following the open French brace, the program compares the value of variable $1 with "Bob" and the value of variable $2 with "555". $1 is the ID passing to the function. $2 is the password passing to the function. "Bob" is the valid ID, and "555" is the valid password.

5. The function displays Verified or Rejected on-screen, depending on whether the correct ID and password pass to the function.

6. Following the close French brace that ends the function definition, the program calls the function and passes "Bob" as the ID and "555" as the password. The function, of course, displays Verified.

Verifying the number of arguments passing to a function

A function may get into deep trouble if the program fails to pass the function all the information that the function needs. A function may, for example, perform a calculation that it bases on information that the program provides. Or, in a truly horrifying situation, it may pass your spouse's name but not the birth date (because you can't remember it). Not only do you run into trouble with Linux in such a situation, but with your spouse, too! A mistake may also occur, however, if the program passes no information at all to the function.

Never assume that information passes correctly to a function. Instead, build commands into your function to verify the correct number of arguments that it receives before the function processes the information. Say that your function needs two pieces of information to pass to it as arguments, such as a first and last name. Only the first name, however, passes to it. Unless you verify that the correct number of arguments pass, your function assumes that the last name also passed and tries to use the second argument. This situation can cause an error in your program.

The $# variable contains the number of arguments that pass to the function. You stop the function from processing information by comparing the value of the $# variable to the number of arguments that the function expects to receive from the program. The following example shows you how to do so:

```
#! /bin/bash
clear
function verify
{
      if [ $# -ne 2 ]
         then
              echo "Wrong number of arguments!"
         else
            if [ $1 -eq "Bob" ] && [ $2 -eq "555" ]
               then
                  echo "Verified"
            else
                echo "Rejected"
            fi
      fi
}
verify Bob 555
```

The following steps describe what's happening in this program:

1. The bash shell starts.

2. The screen clears.

3. The program calls the function verify.

4. Following the open French brace, the program compares the value of the $# variable with the value 2 and displays an error message if they differ. If so, Linux skips the rest of the commands in the function.

5. If it receives the correct number of arguments, the program compares the value of variable $1 with "Bob" and the value of variable $2 with "555". $1 is the ID passing to the function. $2 is the password passing to the function. "Bob" is the valid ID, and "555" is the valid password.

6. The function displays Verified or Rejected on-screen, providing that the correct ID and password pass to the function.

7. Following the closed French brace (ending the function definition), the program calls the function and passes "Bob" as the ID and "555" as the password. The function, of course, displays Verified.

Sharing a Function with Subprograms

You can use a function that you create in a program in subprograms as well. Think of a *subprogram* as a program within your program. Chapter 14 tells you everything thing that you need to know about subprograms.

Say that you create a program that uses the function that verifies an ID and password, as I describe in the preceding section. But you also want to use the same function in another program that doesn't contain the function. Instead of copying the function into the second program, you can make the function in your first program available to the second program.

You can share functions between subprograms by using the `export` command to export the function. You then call the subprogram from within your second program. The following example shows you how to do so:

```
#! /bin/bash
clear
function verify
{
        if [ $# -ne 2 ]
           then
                echo "Wrong number of arguments!"
           else
                if [ $1 -eq "Bob" ] && [ $2 -eq "555" ]
                   then
                        echo "Verified"
                else
                        echo "Rejected"
                fi
        fi
}
export verify
subprogram1
```

Following is a description of what you add to the last lines of the function definition to share the function:

1. Following the close French brace that ends the function definition, you use the `export` command to make the `verify` function available to the subprogram that I call `subprogram1`.

2. The last line of the program calls `subprogram1`, which the following example shows. Notice that `subprogram1` doesn't contain the function definition for `verify`, but the subprogram calls the `verify` function, because the *export command* exports the `verify` function before calling the subprogram.

```
#! /bin/bash
clear
verify "Bob" "555"
```

Returning Information from a Function

A function is like a two-way street because you can send information to the function and the function can send information back to your program. Say that, instead of the `verify` function displaying a message stating whether the

ID and password are valid, the `verify` function sends the results to your program. Your program can then decide the appropriate action to undertake.

Your program assigns the information that a function returns to the $? variable. The value of that information must be an integer from 0 to 256. You can't, therefore, send a string as a return value of a function.

Your program sends a value back from a function by using the `return` keyword, following it with the value that it's returning. Because the `return` value is an integer, you must assign meaning to each integer that's returning. You typically use a zero, for example, to indicate that the function is operating correctly. Any other integer indicates that something's wrong.

You can place a `return` anywhere in your function, but the `return` usually falls somewhere in the program *after* the place where function tests the values — such as where the program compares the ID and password. After Linux executes `return`, the function stops executing and Linux returns to the line in the program that calls the function.

The following example shows you how to return a value from a function:

```
#! /bin/bash
clear
function verify
{
      if [ $# -ne 2 ]
         then
             return 1
      else
            if [ $1 -eq "Bob" ] && [ $2 -eq "555" ]
               then
                   return 0
               else
                   return 2
               echo "Rejected"
            fi
      fi
}
verify Bob 555
                          case $? In
    do
       0)
          echo "Verified"
          ;;
       1)
          echo "Wrong number of arguments!"
          ;;
       2)
          echo "Rejected"
          ;;
    done
```

The following steps describe what's happening in this program:

1. The bash shell starts.

2. The screen clears of unnecessary information.

3. The programs defines the function verify.

4. Following the open French brace, the program compares the value of the $# variable with the value 2 and returns a value of 1. If the values are the same, Linux skips the rest of the commands in the function.

5. If it receives the correct number of arguments, the program compares the value of variable $1 with "Bob" and the value of variable $2 with "555". $1 is the ID passing to the function. $2 is the password passing to the function. "Bob" is the valid ID, and "555" is the valid password.

6. The function returns a 0 or a 2 depending on whether the correct ID and password pass to the function.

7. Following the close French brace that ends the function definition, the program calls the function and passes "Bob" as the ID and "555" as the password.

8. The program uses the case statement to compare the $? variable that contains the return value and values in the case statement.

Test your programming knowledge

1. When do you use a function?

a. Whenever you find yourself repeating code in your program.

b. Whenever you want to give yourself a raise.

c. Whenever you get tired of typing.

d. Whenever you want to copy instructions.

2. What information can a function return?

a. Any characters or numbers.

b. Characters only.

c. An integer between 0 and 256.

d. The winning lottery number.

Answers 1) a. See "Creating a Function." *2) c. See* "Returning Information from a Function."

Chapter 14

Getting Down with Subprograms

● ●

In This Chapter

▶ Creating a program plan

▶ Creating subprograms

▶ Naming subprograms

▶ Using subprograms

▶ Sharing subprograms

● ●

*A*lthough you design each program to perform a specific task, every program that you write shares some basic functions in common with other programs. Every program, for example, displays text on a screen, reads information that a user enters on the keyboard, saves the user's input to a variable, and then works with the information.

You piece each of these tasks together to build large, complex programs that tell the computer to perform some useful tasks. At times, you want your program to perform a specific group of related tasks, such as displaying an error message on-screen if the user does something wrong with your program. Pretty soon, you're writing Linux programs that enable your computer to do all sorts of fancy things.

Because errors can occur practically anywhere in your program, duplicating the necessary instructions to display an error message throughout your program doesn't make sense. Such duplication takes up too much space and is a nightmare to maintain. Every time that you want to change a part of the error message, you must remember all the places in your program where you duplicate those instructions.

You can avoid the problems that result from duplicate instructions in your program simply by placing those instructions in a small program known as a *subprogram*. A subprogram is identical to a regular program in that you create a subprogram by using an editor and the `chmod` command to transform the file into an *executable program* (a file that your computer can run).

The only thing special about a subprogram is that the instructions you place in a subprogram are those that you design to perform a *specific* task, such as displaying an error message or checking for the correct user's password. Those same subprograms can then execute from within your program whenever you need it to perform a special task.

You often find yourself building large, complex programs from many subprograms. To make sure that your program works smoothly and is also easy to read, however, you need to *map out* the tasks that you want your program to perform and then decide how each task relates to the other tasks in the program. In this chapter, I take you through the steps for creating an overall program plan and describe how subprograms contribute to a well-designed and efficient program.

Why Use a Subprogram?

Subprograms are the building blocks of your program. First, you create each building block, and then you assemble them to develop the whole program.

Suppose that you need the computer to display an opening menu and respond to whatever the user selects. You call both of these activities one task, because whenever a menu appears, the program always waits for a response from the user. You can place all the code that's necessary to perform this task into the same subprogram. Your program then calls this subprogram whenever you want to perform the task.

The following list describes some reasons for using subprograms:

- ✔ Subprograms isolate all code performing a specific task. If you're having a problem with your menu display, for example, you don't need to hunt through your entire program for the piece of code that's causing the problem. You just need to look in the display-menu subprogram.

- ✔ Building your program from subprograms saves you from repeating the code in your program. You simply execute the subprogram whenever you need the program to perform that task.

- ✔ You make changes or updates to code in just one place in your program. (What a timesaver!)

- ✔ Subprograms are reusable, and you can use them to build other Linux programs — and share them with other programmers who want their programs to perform some of the same tasks that your program performs.

You need to use a little common sense in deciding the number of subprograms to create for your program. If you find that you're losing track of the subprograms that you create, you're probably making too many of them (although no particular rule tells you how many subprograms are too many). If you feel that tracking subprograms is getting out of control, you probably need to consolidate some of them or devise a better planning tool to help you organize your subprograms. Probably the best planning tool is the *flowchart,* which graphically organizes your program plan.

Creating a Program Plan by Using a Flowchart

Just the mention of creating a Linux program plan can send most new programmers off to get a bottle of aspirin. Why must computers be so complicated? I thought that I'd never figure out Microsoft Project (a tool that many programming gurus love to use in building a plan), but with a little patience, I overcame this perceived obstacle. You, too, may find creating a Linux program plan daunting at first, but it's really pretty easy.

First, you want to figure out what you need Linux to do and then break down the overall plan into individual functions. The flowchart helps you organize your program and place the subprograms to maximize efficiency.

Divide and conquer

How do you eat an elephant? One bite at a time, of course. How then do you plan a large, complex Linux program? You break the program down into its individual functions and create a list of what you want Linux to do. (You can also chomp on the program, but you quickly find that it's rather stringy and in need of garlic.) By dividing your Linux program into logical chunks, with each performing a unique and important task, you make your overall programming task much easier.

Suppose, for example, that you want to create a Linux program with the overall objective of maintaining your telephone directory. You can further divide this overall program objective into the individual tasks that you want the program to perform, which may include some of the following:

- Logging into the program.
- Displaying a main menu that enables the user to make a selection.

- Finding a listing in the telephone directory.
- Adding a listing to the telephone directory.
- Modifying a listing in the telephone directory.
- Printing the telephone directory.

Your Linux program may have more or fewer tasks than appear in the preceding list. Most programs that work with data, however, incorporate subprograms that find data, add data, modify existing data, and print data.

Plugging a task list into a flowchart

You need to take pencil in hand and organize your thoughts about how your program is going to work. The simplest approach is to draw a flowchart where each box in the flowchart represents a task that your program must accomplish. You must arrange each box on the flowchart in the order that you want your program to accomplish the task, and then you can draw lines connecting the boxes.

Take an example close to my heart (actually close to my stomach). I call this creation the Get a Snack program. The examples in this section describe how I organize this nightly trip. (Now if I could only get my computer to do the fetching, I'd have it made.)

A flowchart for the Get-a-Snack program, for example, may look something like the chart shown in Figure 14-1.

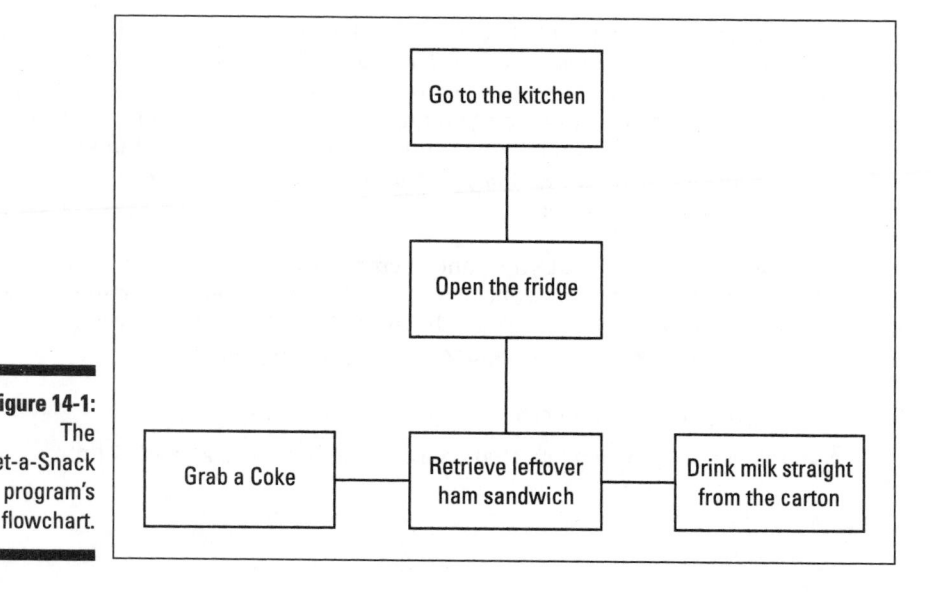

Figure 14-1:
The
Get-a-Snack
program's
flowchart.

To start your program flowchart, then, you first need to assemble the long list of tasks that you want your Linux program to perform. The next step is to draw a picture of your program. All you need to draw is a box for each task; then you place the name of the task inside the box, similar to what you see in Figure 14-2 — just as I'm doing with the Get-a-Snack program. (And this time, I'm starting from the very beginning.)

Figure 14-2:
The beginnings of a fine flowchart.

Find Listing

This little task doesn't add much to your plan, but you're just on the first step. The next step in creating a flowchart is to map out how each task relates to the other tasks. Now the process is getting a little more complicated, isn't it?

The flowchart in Figure 14-3 shows how the Linux user progresses through your program. The user first logs in (`Login Task`), and the main menu appears (`Display Menu`). From the main menu, the user can then choose one of the four options that you provide in the program: `Find Listing`, `Add Listing`, `Modify Listing`, or `Print Listing`.

Adding detail to a flowchart

You can further divide each task on your flowchart into more specific tasks. The task Find Listing, for example, requires that your program perform the following more-detailed tasks:

✔ Prompt the user to enter a name to find.

✔ Search the database for the name the user enters.

✔ If the search is successful, display the listing.

✔ If the search is unsuccessful, tell the user that it can't find the listing.

✔ Return to the main menu.

Draw another flowchart that shows each of these more detailed tasks and how each task logically follows from the preceding one. Figure 14-4 shows how the Find Listing flowchart looks.

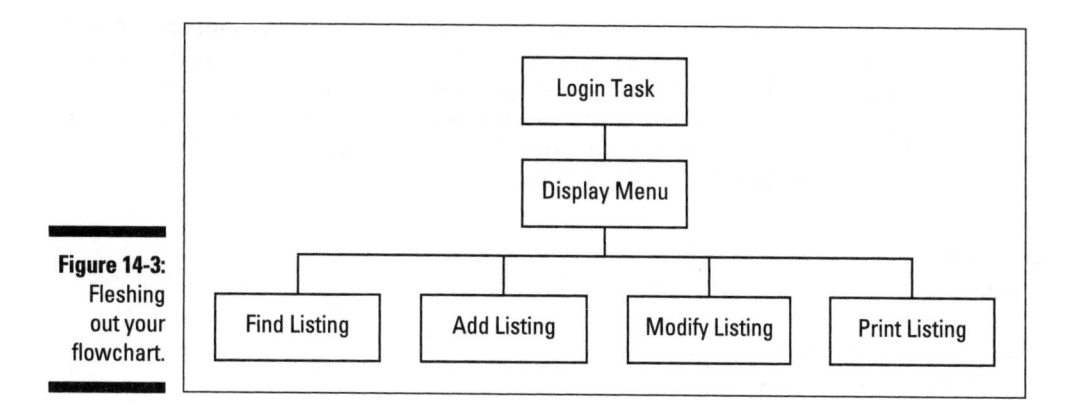

Figure 14-3:
Fleshing
out your
flowchart.

The shape of the flowchart in Figure 14-4 is a little different than that of Figure 14-3 because the relationships among the tasks are now different.

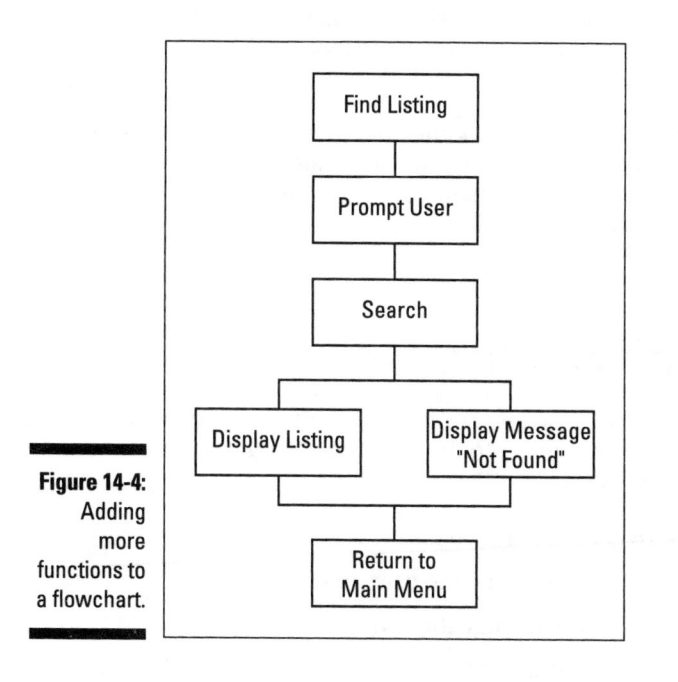

Figure 14-4:
Adding
more
functions to
a flowchart.

As you become more specific about what each task (subprogram) does in your Linux program, the flowchart that depicts that task also becomes more detailed — kind of like branches sprouting from the trunk of a healthy tree.

Arrow your flowcharts

You can dress up your drawings by placing arrows on the lines that connect tasks. The arrows show the direction of the next task. Using these arrows isn't a requirement, but they do add clarity to your drawing.

Each box in the flowchart is a task that associates with other boxes (tasks) on your flowchart by a connecting line. The line does more than just join boxes. The line shows how each box relates to another box by using an arrow at the end of the line. The task of displaying the menu, for example, comes before the user enters one of the selections from the menu. So you draw a line connecting the first box (displaying the menu) to the second box (selecting from the menu) with an arrow pointing to the second box because this task comes after the first task.

Linking subprograms in a flowchart

As you map out more and more tasks on your Linux program flowchart, keeping track of all those subprograms may become tough. By numbering a subprogram, as shown in Figure 14-5, you can refer to another flowchart that contains more details about that subprogram.

Suppose that you're building a program that requires a user to enter a name and password into the program before using the program. So you label the first box on the flow chart Login Task. This label tells you generally what takes place at this portion of your program.

But what exactly does the Login Task involve? You need to know this information as you build the subprogram that handles the login task. You don't, however, have enough room in the Login Task box on your flowchart to place all these details.

Here's the solution: Number each box on your flow chart. The first box is 1; the second is 2; and you get the idea from there. If a box needs more detail, you can create a separate flowchart for that box. You have plenty of room on the second flowchart to identify all the tasks relating to that box on the previous flowchart.

Suppose that you assign a number 1 to the Login Task on the first flowchart. You then create an entirely new flowchart just for the Login Task box. The first box on the Login Task flowchart you number as *1.0*, and this box contains the same text that you use on the corresponding box on the first flowchart — Login Task.

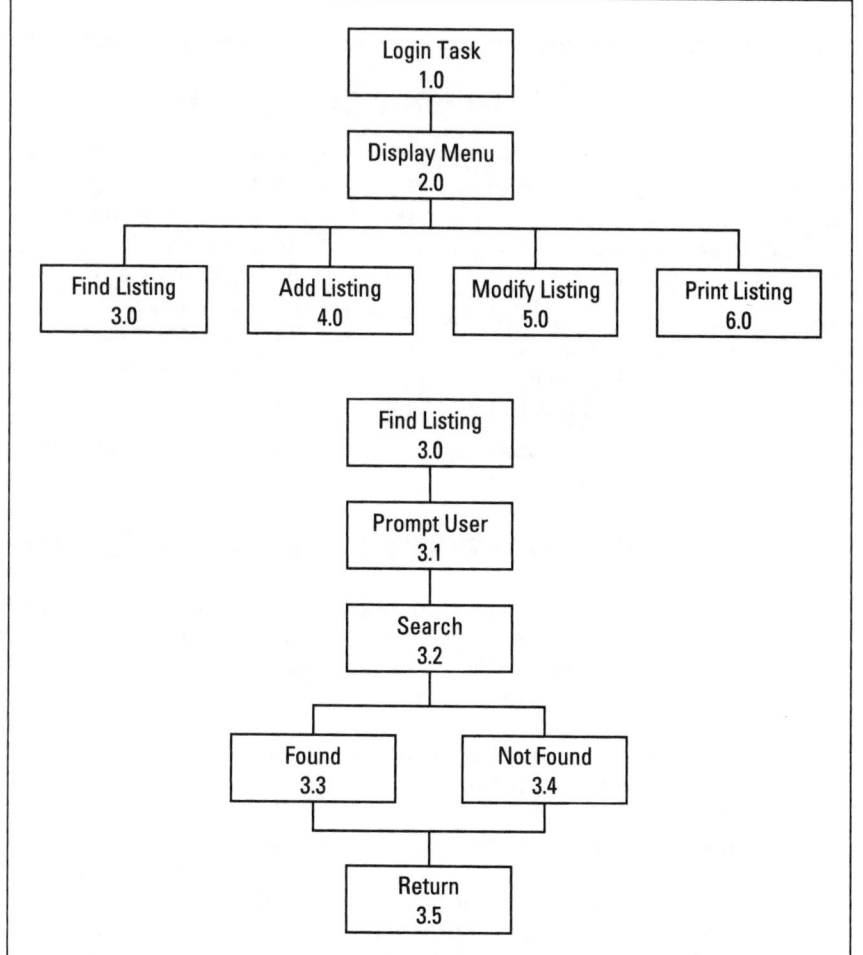

Figure 14-5:
The bottom
flowchart
contains the
details of
the Find
Listing task
shown on
the top
flowchart.

Create boxes on the Login Task flowchart, using the procedures that I describe in the preceding section, to represent all the tasks that are necessary for the user to log into the program. You must also number each box on the Login Task flowchart. Instead of numbering the boxes as 1, 2, 3, and so on, however, you number them as 1.1, 1.2, 1.3, and so on. This numbering method enables you to quickly know that the box you're looking at associates with a particular box on the first flowchart. The first number (1) is the number of the related box on the first flowchart. The second number (.1) is the number of the box on the second flowchart.

The technical name for associating boxes on one flowchart with those on another flowchart is a *leveling diagram*. The first flowchart is level one, and the second flowchart is level two. And you can have a level three, level four, and so on, as necessary.

Using a Flowchart to Create Linux Subprograms

After you map out your Linux program on a flowchart and number each box appropriately, the next step is to write the programming code for each task. Each module or box on the flowchart represents a distinct function or task for which you write code.

You must decide whether to include the code for a task directly in your program or in a subprogram. The criterion to use in making this decision is that any task that requires little or no help from the program or from a subprogram and that the program uses repeatedly is a good candidate to become a subprogram.

How to create a subprogram

You create a subprogram the same way that you create a program. The flowchart that you create shows all the steps that you must include in the subprogram. Your job is to translate these steps into Linux programming instructions. (See Chapter 2 for more information on Linux programming instructions.)

After you determine the instructions that you need to make the program carry out the task, you type those instructions into a text file by using a text editor such as vi. (I introduce vi in Chapter 3; refer also to Appendix B for vi details.) Then you need to save the file to your hard disk. Make the file an executable file by using the chmod command (refer to Chapter 1) and execute your new subprogram from the command prompt. This process enables you to test your subprogram before you use it in your program.

Some rules for writing subprograms are as follows:

- ✔ Instructions must appear in the subprogram in the order in which you want the program to perform those instructions.
- ✔ You must save each subprogram in its own file.
- ✔ You must convert each subprogram file into an executable file by using the chmod command.
- ✔ You want to run each subprogram at the command line to make sure that it runs smoothly. If not, you must debug the subprogram until you resolve all the problems. (See Chapter 19 for information on debugging.)

Say that you want to create a program that manages your personal telephone directory. The program incorporates the following tasks:

- Display a menu.
- Read the user's selection.
- Determine the selection that the user makes.
- Find a telephone listing.
- Add a new telephone listing to the file.
- Modify an existing telephone list in the file.
- Quit the program.
- Print a telephone listing.

Placing the first three tasks in the program itself makes sense because these tasks are the central functions of the program. You make the task of quitting the program a part of the program. The other tasks you build into subprograms, because these tasks are relatively self-contained pieces of the program. You don't really need the menu, for example, to find a telephone listing. You can simply run a subprogram that takes care of this task.

You give each subprogram a name that identifies the task that the subprogram performs. The `findlisting` subprogram, for example, finds a telephone listing in the file. After you build this subprogram, you can run it from the command line — independent from the program. The instructions to ask the user for the name of the person that the user wants to call and the instructions to locate and display the telephone number on-screen are all part of the `findlisting` subprogram.

After you determine that each of these subprograms runs smoothly, you can make the names of the subprograms part of your program. As your program sees the name of a subprogram, the program executes the subprogram just as you do at the command line in testing it. This process is also known as *calling the subprogram* from your program. The following example shows you how the instructions look:

```
clear
echo "Telephone Directory"
echo " "
echo "1. Find Listing"
echo "2. Add Listing"
echo "3. Modify Listing"
echo "4. Print Listing"
echo "Q. Quit"
echo " "
read selection
case $selection in
```

```
"1")
    findlisting
    ;;
"2")
    addlisting
    ;;
"3")
    modifylisting
    ;;
"4")
    printlisting
    ;;
"Q")
  exit
esac
```

After the user makes a selection, the program determines whether it needs to run a particular subprogram to complete the task that the user requests. If so, the program calls the name of the subprogram and the instructions in the subprogram take over. After the task is complete, the subprogram ends and the program retakes control by executing the next instruction in the program.

Choosing a name for a subprogram

A subprogram's name is important to a programmer. The subprogram's name helps the programmer recognize the subprogram, and you can also use it to identify the purpose of the subprogram. You can, for example, name a subprogram something short and easy, such as sub1. But then try to remember what the sub1 subprogram does as you're rushing about writing your code. (Hmmmm — is sub1 the Login Task subprogram or is it the subprogram to print a name list?)

I call the sample subprogram in the preceding section displaymenu. This subprogram name briefly describes what the subprogram does — it *displays the menu*. The name displaymenu is also an easy one to remember.

Keep the following points in mind as you name your subprograms:

✔ You want to make the subprogram name informative. Although the name displaymenu appears to meet this requirement, for example, displaymenu doesn't actually mention *which* menu the subprogram's displaying.

✔ Use abbreviations in the subprogram name. You can rename the displaymenu subprogram to something such as dispopenmu, which implies *dis*play *open*ing *menu*. Make sure that the meaning of the abbreviations are easily recognizable.

✔ Try to reflect the name of the main program in the name of the subprogram. The name `dispopenmu`, for example, states that this subprogram *disp*lays the *open*ing *m*enu — but the opening menu for which program? To make this subprogram name more informative, you can rename this subprogram to add the name of the main program — `tddispopenmu` to imply *t*elephone *d*irectory *disp*lay *open*ing *m*enu.

✔ You need to make the subprogram name easy to read — you can play around with the capitalization to help its readability. The name `tddispopenmu`, for example, identifies the subprogram, but it's hard to read. The name is better if you make it `TdDispOpenMu`.

Keep in mind that no hard and fast rule shows you how to correctly name a subprogram. You can stay out of trouble, however, by using your common sense.

How to use a subprogram

You first want to create and test your subprograms and then create your program itself. Some programmers call this latter creation the *main program* because it contains the instructions for your program. As you create your program, place the name of the appropriate subprogram into it wherever you want your program to perform the subprogram's task.

Test your programming knowledge

1. What's the first step in writing a complex Linux program?

a. Begin to write instructions.

b. Hit your head against the wall repeatedly (which always feels better after you stop).

c. Draw a flowchart of the program before writing your code.

d. Read this book.

2. Why are subprograms helpful?

a. They have a few instructions.

b. Subprograms fit better inside your computer.

c. Little guys are easier to control.

d. Subprograms reduce a large, complex Linux program into smaller, manageable modules.

Answers 1) c. See "Creating a Program Plan by Using a Flowchart." *2) d. See* "Why Use a Subprogram?"

You insert the name of the subprogram as an instruction into your program the same way that you place the other instructions into your program. In fact, you can write a program that contains only one instruction — the name of a subprogram. The following example shows how such a program looks:

```
#!/bin/bash
displaymenu
```

Not much to this program. It simply starts the bash shell and then calls the displaymenu subprogram. The subprogram does all the work in this case. The displaymenu subprogram displays a menu on-screen.

You can build large, complex programs from many subprograms. And sometimes you can reuse subprograms in other programs without even modifying the subprogram. Suppose, for example, that you create a subprogram that prompts the user to enter a name and password and then validates the password. You can use this same subprogram with other programs that also need this task.

Sharing Subprograms

Don't throw away the subprograms that you build! Programmers treat their collection of subprograms almost as collector's items. A subprogram that's working smoothly is worth its weight in gold. Okay, maybe it's not *that* valuable yet. But a programmer who can choose between building a subprogram from scratch or getting one from a friend always opts for the latter.

But don't go looking for a formal trading post where you can exchange subprograms. You really aren't going to find any. You can, however, post your request for subprograms on the appropriate newsgroups on the Internet (see Chapter 21 for details). You can also ask other programmers that you meet whether they have any good subprograms that you can take a peek at.

Chapter 15

Understanding Arguments ... Not the Ones with Your Mother-in-Law

*H*ere's a good excuse to use the next time that you want to argue with your significant other: Just say, "I'm not arguing; I'm simply passing you information." Feel free to use this expression (but don't attribute it to me).

Most of us think of an argument as words of disagreement that can heat up and sometimes lead to blows. But to your computer, an *argument* is information that goes to a program (or subprogram) from the command line after the program (or subprogram) executes.

Using Arguments — Why?

The capability to pass arguments enables you to build flexible programs and subprograms. Remember that a program can really consist of a group of subprograms. Each subprogram performs one task very well. After you build a subprogram and get it running smoothly, you don't need to modify the instructions within the subprogram. (If it ain't broke, don't fix it.)

The best way to use information between the program and subprogram is to pass the specific data to the subprogram as an argument on the command line. Although you don't fool with the "innards" of a subprogram, you enable the subprogram to share the information that pertains to your current program.

Say that you build a subprogram to fetch you snacks from the kitchen (just dreaming). The subprogram is all ready to do the legwork for you. But the subprogram needs to know what snacks you want. How can you give it this information? Well, as you call the subprogram, you use the command line to pass to it the name of the snack. If you write the subprogram to receive the snack information, you can just sit back in your recliner and keep surfing the tube.

Although I say that you pass arguments from the command line to the program (or subprogram), you can also pass arguments to the programs (or subprograms) from within your program by typing the name of the program (or subprogram) and following it with the argument.

Passing an argument to a program (or subprogram) is different from the way that I show you to write programs in earlier chapters. In all the programs that you create in the preceding chapters of this book, you always provide to your program the information that it needs in the form of *values* that you assign to *variables*. With some programs, however, you place information inside your program as part of the code, as in the following example:

```
declare FirstName="Bob"
```

In the preceding line of code, you assign the name Bob to the string variable FirstName. This type of assignment is known as *hard coding* the information into the program. *Hard coding* is a term that programmers use to say that you type the information directly into the program. Every time that you want to change the data — if, for example, you need to change "Bob" to "Robert" — you must change the program.

In Chapter 5, you see another way that a program gathers information: It can ask the user to enter the information while the program's running, as in the following example:

```
declare FirstName
echo "Enter your first name: "
read FirstName
```

Here, the program asks the user to enter his first name. The program then assigns the name to the string variable FirstName. The information that the user enters changes every time that the program runs, without the programmer needing to change anything inside the program.

Hard coding information is not always the best way to get information into your program, because the programmer needs to change that program each time that the information changes.

Asking the user to enter the information each time that the program runs is generally better than hard coding the information into the program. At times, however, the user can't provide the necessary information. Say, for example, that you write a program to send out an invitation to your big promotion bash to everyone whose name appears in your personal telephone directory — but you don't want to enter each name individually. So you sit down to write a Linux program to do the work for you.

You follow all the tips that I give you in this chapter and create a subprogram that prints the invitation. Each time this subprogram prints, however, it needs one name from your telephone directory. Of course, you don't expect the subprogram to prompt you to enter each name. Instead, your program recalls each name from your telephone directory and passes the name as an argument whenever the program calls the subprogram and requests the name variable.

Passing Arguments

The transfer of the information from the command line to the program (or subprogram) is commonly known as *passing arguments*. (The information that passes to the program resides *outside* the program or subprogram that's using the information.)

Say that you want to run the subprogram that finds a listing in your personal telephone directory. You call this subprogram findlisting and assume that the subprogram doesn't prompt you to enter the person's name that you're trying to locate. Instead, you pass the name of the person as an argument to the program. The following example shows how you enter the information at the command line:

```
findlisting Jones
```

The Linux operating system automatically passes the name *Jones* to the findlisting subprogram. The findlisting subprogram then uses the name to search for Jones' telephone number. After it finds the number, the findlisting subprogram displays the number on-screen — if the programmer provides the subprogram the necessary instructions to do so.

You start your program by entering its name on the command line, as follows:

```
$ displaymenu
```

The $ sign is the command prompt for the bash shell. This prompt already appears on-screen. The name of the program that Linux is calling is displaymenu. You can send data to the program by placing the data to the right of the name of the program, as follows:

```
$ displaymenu yes
```

The word yes is the information that you're sending to the program displaymenu.

You can also pass information to a subprogram. You call a subprogram from within a program or from another subprogram by using the following command (`displaymenu` being the name of the subprogram):

```
displaymenu
```

REMEMBER

Notice that the $ sign is missing. It doesn't appear because you're calling the subprogram from within another program. The $ sign appears only if you start the program from the command line.

You can send data to a subprogram the same way that you send data to a program from the command line, as the following example shows:

```
displaymenu yes
```

TIP

Following are some rules to go by in sending data to a program from the command line:

✔ Place a space between the name of the program and the data.

✔ Place a space between each data item if you're sending multiple data to the program. See the section "Passing Multiple Arguments," later in this chapter, for more of the lowdown on multiple data.

Accepting Arguments

Well, if you can pass information to your program (or subprogram), you must write instructions in your program (or subprogram) to do something with the information after it receives it. This activity that the program performs is commonly known as *accepting arguments*.

Linux stores the information that it passes to your program in a variable by the name of $1. The number 1 tells your program that you want to refer to the first piece of information that passes to the program. (As you see in the section "Passing Multiple Arguments," later in this chapter, you can pass more than one piece of information to the program.) To refer to this information, for example, you type the following code at the command line:

```
$1
```

If your program is the one that's getting you a snack from the kitchen, giving it this information is like telling it what kind of snack you want. You write something such as the following line:

```
getsnack chips
```

The program sees `chips` as the value that you assign to the $1 variable. The program just goes about its business, using $1 whenever it needs to refer to the snack that you want from the kitchen.

Now, you need to get real and take a look at a practical way of using this information. In the following example, I do something sneaky. I create a `displaymenu` program that displays a menu, receives a response from the user, and then executes the appropriate subprogram. This program, however, displays the menu and does all the other stuff only if you pass the magic word — yes — to the program. Otherwise the program skips directly to the end of the program without showing anything on-screen.

Your program can do more than just display the data item it receives. Sometimes your computer uses the data as the criteria to make a decision.

The following example shows you how I set up the `displaymenu` program that I mention a couple paragraphs earlier:

```
#!/bin/bash
if [ "$1" -eq "yes" ]
   then
   clear
   echo "Telephone Directory"
   echo " "
   echo "1. Find Listing"
   echo "2. Add Listing"
   echo "3. Modify Listing"
   echo "4. Print Listing"
   echo "Q. Quit"
   echo " "
   read selection
   case $selection in
"1")
               findlisting
               ;;
"2")
            addlisting
            ;;
"3")
            modifylisting
            ;;
"4")
            printlisting
            ;;
"Q")
            exit
      esac
fi
```

This example is an involved version of the `displaymenu` program, because the program is receiving information from the command line. The menu appears only if the user sends the program a magic word. (The magic word is yes.) The following steps describe what happens in a nutshell:

1. The computer starts the bash shell.

2. The program compares the data the user sends it to the word yes.

3. If the data and the magic word match, the menu appears and the computer does something after the user makes a selection.

4. If the data and the magic word don't match, the program ends.

Passing Multiple Arguments

A program can pass your program (or subprogram) more than one argument from the command line. This capability becomes very useful whenever your program requires more than one piece of information to perform a task.

Say that you write a program that displays names on-screen — names of your friends. If you write the program to accept these names from the command line, you can place each name on the command line, making sure that you separate each one with a space. The space character enables your program to recognize where one piece of information begins and the other ends. Take a glance at the following example:

```
$ displayfriends Bob Mary Joe Sue
```

Each piece of information must appear to the right of the program name. A space must separate each data item.

Your program can use this information by using the $1 variable (which I explain in the preceding section) with the corresponding number of the data item, as in the following example:

```
#!/bin/bash
echo "My friend $1"
echo "My friend $2"
echo "My friend $3"
echo "My friend $4"
```

This program shows the names of your friends on-screen, as follows:

```
My friend Bob
My friend Mary
My friend Joe
My friend Sue
```

Knowing how to pass multiple arguments to your program and subprograms provides flexibility to your programming. You no longer must write into the code all the information that your program requires. Nor do you need to constantly prompt the user for information. Instead, you can simply enter the information on the command line or as your program calls a subprogram, and the information passes to the program or subprogram.

Problems with Sending Arguments

Two common problems can occur whenever anyone sends your program or subprogram arguments: Someone can send you the wrong number of arguments or the wrong kind of arguments.

The wrong number of arguments

You can plan to receive a fixed number of arguments, but nothing forces someone to send you the correct number. Suppose that your program expects the following two arguments:

```
#!/bin/bash
echo "First Name: $1"
echo "Last Name: $2"
```

Now suppose that someone supplies only one of those arguments, as follows:

```
$ displayname Bob
```

Your program is still telling your computer to use the second data item that it expects to pass to the program — in this case, the phantom data.

The wrong kind of argument

Your program depends on someone else to pass it the correct information. If this person isn't dependable, your program experiences problems. Say that someone calls your program and sends the following information:

```
$ namegame car truck
```

Your program assumes that the information is just what it's looking for in the following example:

```
#!/bin/bash
echo "First Name: $1"
echo "Last Name: $2"
```

But that information isn't what your program expects and your program is using incorrect information. So who's going to get the blame for the problem? The person using your program or the programmer? (Who, you? Why, it's not your fault . . . is it?) You have no easy way to avoid this situation or the blame (except by not answering the phone if the user calls to complain). As long as you note in the documentation of your program that the user needs to enter specific kinds of information at the command prompt as the program runs, your job is done. You can't force the user to read the documentation before running your program. But you still hear such excuses as "*Of course I . . . didn't . . . read the instructions.*"

Does Your Argument Exist?

Your program sometimes needs for someone to send data to it; otherwise, your program can't perform the task. So the first thing that your program needs to do is to determine whether anyone's sending any data to it.

You can use the $#$ variable to determine the number of data items that your program receives. The $#$ variable contains the number of arguments that pass to your program. Notice the difference between $1, which you use to reference an argument, and $#$, which just contains the number of arguments that your program receives.

The following example shows you how you use the $#$ variable:

```
#!/bin/bash
echo "$#"
```

This program displays the number of data items it's receiving. As you run this program, you don't see the data itself; instead, you see a number on-screen, which represents the number of data items your program's receiving.

You can compare the value of $#$ with the number of data items that your program requires by using the following example:

```
#!/bin/bash
if [ "$#" -eq 2 ]
    then
       echo "You entered the correct number of arguments."
    else
       echo "You didn't enter the correct number of arguments."
fi
```

In the preceding code, the program starts the bash shell and then determines whether the correct number of arguments pass to the program. In this case, I decide that two arguments are necessary, basing my decision on the specifications for the program.

So the program uses the if statement to compare the value in $#$ with the value 2. If it finds a match, the program displays a message and continues (although I don't show the rest of the program in this example). If it doesn't find a match, the program ends.

Test your programming knowledge

1. How can your program access the first argument it receives from the command line?

a. By calling my mother-in-law. She has access to everything.

b. A heavy-duty tire iron does the trick.

c. By referencing the $1 variable.

d. By referencing the $argx[1].

2. How can you make sure that your program receives the correct number of arguments?

a. Ask the person who uses your program for the number of arguments she typed.

b. Check the value of the $# variable.

c. Get your program a subscription to *Argument Digest*.

d. Check the whatchamacallit chip in your computer.

Answers:1) c. See "Accepting Arguments." *2) b. See* "Problems with Sending Arguments."

You can also determine whether a user enters any arguments at all by writing something such as the following example in your program:

```
#!/bin/bash
if [ "$#" -lt 1 ]
    then
        echo "You didn't enter the correct number of arguments."
fi
```

This program checks to determine whether the value of $# is less than 1 — meaning that no one entered any arguments on the command line. If so, the following message appears: You didn't enter the correct number of arguments. And although I don't show the instructions to do so, you're likely to end the program if no information passes from the command line.

Part VI
Database Programs and Printing

The 5th Wave   By Rich Tennant

"YEAH, I USED TO WORK ON REFRIGERATORS, WASHING MACHINES, STUFF LIKE THAT—HOW'D YOU GUESS?"

In this part . . .

*I*nformation that your program gathers you usually save in a file for later use or print on paper. In this part, you find out how to save information to a file as a *database*. You also discover how to find a particular piece of information that you store in a file. Finally, you get the scoop on how to print information on paper. What more can you ask?

Chapter 16

Working with Database Files

May I have the file on Jones? Sure can. And with a few strokes of the keyboard, up comes the information about Jones on-screen. It's a miracle. Those mystical computers get the data you need in seconds and without ever making a mistake (ha!).

Exactly how a computer locates all the information that you think is confidential involves very little magic. You, too, can perform this trick by following a few simple steps:

✔ Decide what information you want to store and retrieve.

✔ Plan how you want your computer to store the information.

✔ Know the correct words to use to ask your computer to find the information that you want.

What Is Data?

Information is a bunch of words that contain some meaning for people. You recognize the letter *B,* for example, as a letter of the alphabet that represents the phonetic sound *ba.* If you combine the letter *B* with two more letters, *ob,* you come up with a different meaning for the letter *B.* Now it's part of the word *Bob.*

Combine the word *Bob* with the numbers *555-55-5555* (which looks a lot like a Social Security number). This data then identifies a specific individual whose first name is Bob. By combining letters into words and words into meaningful data, you form information that you can use to manage your affairs.

Keep in mind, however, that this data is meaningful only to us. To the computer, it looks very confusing — that is, until you translate the letters into something that your computer understands: a series of zeros and ones.

What Is a File?

Words that you type at the prompt by using your computer's keyboard appear on-screen. You can read this data, but you can't do much else with it.

To make the information useful, you need to save it to a file. A *file* is a place on the computer's hard drive (or floppy disk) where you store data; the data stays there after you turn off your computer. Think of a file as a folder that you place in a file drawer. The drawer, in this case, is the computer's hard drive.

Saving information to a file

The easiest way to save information to a file in Linux is to use the `echo` reserved word. The following example shows you how to do so:

```
echo "Bobbie" > friends
```

This command tells the computer to take the word `Bobbie` and, instead of displaying it on-screen, put it into a file by the name of `friends`.

Notice that you use the greater-than operator (>) in this command. This particular operator is known as the *redirection* operator. It tells the computer to change the place where it normally shows data, which is the screen. (Nerds call this process redirecting the *output* from standard *out* to the disk.)

Be careful if you save information to a file by using the redirection operator. If the file already exists, you replace the information currently in the file with new information.

Appending information to a file

You don't want to overwrite information each time that you save new information to a file. A better way is to place the new information at the end of the existing information. This process is known as *appending* information to a file, as in the following example:

```
echo "Bobbie" >> friends
```

You use two greater-than signs (>>) to tell the computer to put the information at the end of the file. If the file doesn't exist, the computer creates a new file and places the information into the file.

Displaying information that you store in a file

After you save the information to a file, you can turn off your computer and go do something exciting. After you come back, you find that the information still resides on the hard drive. You can show the information that you save to a file by using the cat utility, as follows:

```
cat friends
```

This command tells the computer to copy each character in the file friends and display these characters on-screen. (The whiz kids call this process *concatenating* the information that you store in the file to standard out, which is the screen.)

Information that appears on-screen is a copy of the information that you're storing in the file. The original information remains in the file until you overwrite or append the file.

A File and a Database

Some programmers confuse a file with a database — an understandable mistake, because a database *is* a kind of file. Information that you store in a database you also store in a file on a disk. But not all information that you store in a file goes into a database. (You knew I was going to say that, right?)

A file displays the following characteristics:

- ✔ Contains information in no particular order.
- ✔ No organization to enable you to find the information quickly.
- ✔ Can contain mixed kinds of information.

A database, however, displays the following traits:

- ✔ Contains information in a particular order.
- ✔ Its organization enables you to find the information quickly.
- ✔ Contains a unique kind of information.

Think of a database as way to organize information that resides in your file folder. Placing information in a file folder is similar to storing information in a file. Organizing that information in the file folder so that you can quickly find what you're looking for is similar to storing information in a database.

Databases and Database-Management Systems

Whenever most programmers talk about a database, they're really talking about a database-management system. A *database-management system* is a group of programs that works together to create and maintain a database file.

You can purchase many popular database-management systems for your computer. They're expensive, however, and you often find them only on large commercial computer systems. But with a bit of effort, you can create your own database-management system.

A word of caution: Don't expect your system to manage any important data. You need a commercial database-management system for any serious database jobs. If you use your homemade system, you can't find important data fast enough to keep up with your database needs. Your homemade system, however, is perfect for working with small amounts of data and finding out how a database system works.

Creating a Database

The first step in creating a database is to decide how you're going to organize your information. You must ask yourself what information you want to store in the database. Consider storing, for example, the information that a telephone directory contains (the data in the electronic version of your black book). Make a list of the things that you normally find in such a directory, as I do in the following list:

- ✔ First name
- ✔ Last name
- ✔ Telephone number

Columns and rows

A *row* is a horizontal line that contains a set of data (known as a *record*). All the information about `Bob Smith`, for example, appears on the same line. Each person gets a separate line in the database.

A *column* is a vertical grouping of the same kinds of data (known as a *field*). All the first names, for example, appear in the same column, as do all the last names.

This data appears similar to that in the following example:

```
Bob Smith   555-1212
Mary Jones  555-5555
Tom Adams   555-7777
```

Notice that each line contains the same kind of information in the same order (first name, last name, telephone number). Organizing data this way forms a database.

The following example displays the same information but not in a database format:

```
555-1212 Bob Smith
Mary Jones 555-5555
Adams, Tom, 555-7777
```

Information about each person appears on its own line, which is fine for a database. The columns, however, don't contain similar information. The data is simply unorganized.

Saving information to a database

Although a file isn't always a database, a database *is* a file. (Am I confusing you?) You save information to a database the same way that you save information to a file. The following example shows you how to do it:

```
echo "Bob Smith 555-1212" >> friends
echo "Mary Jones 555-5555" >> friends
echo "Tom Adams 555-7777" >> friends
```

The first line tells the computer to save information about `Bob` to the file `friends`. If the file doesn't exist, the computer creates this file.

The second line tells the computer to save information about Mary to the end of the file friends.

The last line tells the computer to save the information about Tom to the end of the same file.

Finding Information in a Database by Using vi

The kind of file that you use as the database file is known as a *text file*. This file is almost like the file that you create by using your word processor — except that all the instructions for those fancy features (for example, font size) are missing. If you want to find information in the file, your computer must search each line in the database file.

Start vi

You can use a number of methods to locate data in your database file. The easiest and yet most time-consuming method is to use a text editor, such as vi. (See Appendix B for all the details that you want to know about vi.) Try entering the following line at the command prompt:

```
vi friends
```

Press Enter, and a page of the database file appears on-screen (assuming, of course, that you have a file by the name of friends).

Search methods in vi

You can then use either of the following two methods to find information in your database by using vi:

✔ The hunt-and-peck method. You hunt through each page on the screen and then peck at the PgDn key to access another page.

✔ The find feature of vi. Ask the program to locate the data for you.

These methods, of course, aren't the best ways to search for information in a database file. A much better method is to use a Linux utility, which is a program that's designed to search your database.

Finding Information in a Database by Using gawk

The gawk utility is one of the most popular tools that programmers use to search a database file. It consists of the following two parts:

- ✔ A search pattern.
- ✔ Data that you want to display.

The following example shows you how to use this command:

```
gawk '/Smith/ {print $1, $2, $3}' friends
```

This command tells your computer to look for the character Smith in the database file friends. Then the computer displays the first, second, and third column of all rows that match Smith. Notice the use of the curly brackets ({ }) and the single quote marks with the gawk command.

Create the search expression

The information that you're looking for in the database file is known as the search expression. The *search expression* tells the computer how to identify the rows in your database that you want to see.

The search expression has the following characteristics:

- ✔ It must appear at the beginning of the gawk command line.
- ✔ You must place the information that you're looking for within the forward slash character (/).

Building a search expression for the gawk utility can become complex because it's a very powerful utility. If you really want to dig into building complex search expressions, use the man pages to see the online documentation. The man command displays the manual pages relating to a particular Linux utility or command. The following example shows you how to issue the command at the Linux prompt:

```
man gawk
```

Match characters

The simplest search expression tells the computer to find an exact match for a pattern. The *pattern* contains the characters that appear somewhere in the database file.

Perhaps you want to see all the rows from the `friends` database file that have `555` as the first three digits of the telephone number. The pattern that you want to match is `555-`.

Notice that you place the hyphen (-) at the end of the pattern for which you're searching. You do so because the first three digits of the telephone number end with a hyphen, at least in your database file. If you omit the hyphen from the search expression, the computer selects any occurrence of `555` in a row.

The following example shows how the search expression looks:

```
gawk '/555-/ {print $1, $2, $3}' friends
```

This command results in the computer displaying all the rows in the `friends` database file, because each telephone number begins with `555-`.

Watch out for spaces

Whenever you tell the computer to find an exact match in a database file, you must consider that spaces separating columns can be a required part of the search expression because the spaces are actually part of the data.

Consider, for example, adding the name `John Smith` to the `friends` database file. The following example shows what the file looks like after you finish:

```
Bob Smith   555-1212
Mary Jones  555-5555
Tom Adams   555-7777
John Smith  555-4444
```

Now you can ask the computer to show you Bob Smith's telephone number. Because two lines contain `Smith`, you make it clear in the search expression that you want to see `Bob Smith` and not `John Smith`.

The following example shows how the search expression looks:

```
gawk '/Bob Smith/ {print $1, $2, $3}' friends
```

The search expression includes the space between the first and last names of `Bob Smith`.

Match only the beginning of the line

You can be clever and tell the computer to match characters from the beginning of the line. You accomplish this feat by including a *caret* (^) as the first character in the search expression. Why do you need to do so? Good question. Look at the following database file:

```
123786 Bin 123987
123987 Bin 134444
134444 Bin 123986
133333 Bin 123986
```

It doesn't look like much, but perhaps the first column contains part numbers and the second and third columns contain location numbers in a warehouse. Now you want the computer to show you the location of all the parts that have a part number beginning with 123.

At first glance, you may think of just matching the characters, as I show you in the preceding section. The command for such a search looks as follows:

```
gawk '/123/ {print $2, $3}' inventory
```

This command, however, causes your computer to return all the rows because each row contains the pattern 123 in it. What you really want is to match just the first column. The following example shows what you actually need to type:

```
gawk '/^123/ {print $2, $3}' inventory
```

Now only the first two rows meet the search expression.

Choose the column to match

You can specify the column that contains the data to match as part of the search expression. Say that you want the computer to find all the rows that contain the pattern 123 at the beginning of column 3. In addition, you know that the column can contain other characters after the pattern 123. Use the following expression:

```
gawk '$3 ~ /^123*/ {print $1}' inventory
```

The $3 represents the column that you want to search.

The tilde character (~) tells the computer that you're looking for a match. It's like an -eq operator that you use in the if statement (see Chapter 6).

The caret (^) tells the computer to start matching at the beginning of the column.

The asterisk (*) tells the computer that other characters in the column in addition to the ones that you're seeking are okay.

Do not match

You can also tell the computer to show rows that don't match the search expression. To display the part numbers that *aren't* in locations that begin with 123, use the following expression:

```
gawk '$3 !~ /^123*/ {print $1}' inventory
```

The only difference between this example and the preceding search expression is the *not* operator (!) that you place before the tilde (~). This operator tells the computer to find lines that are "not equal to" those in the search expression.

Extract information to a file

You can copy all or part of the data in a database file to another file simply by using the redirection operator (>). The following example shows you how to do so:

```
gawk '/^123/ {print $2, $3}' inventory > locations
```

In this expression, you're telling the computer to copy to the locations file only columns 2 and 3 of rows from the inventory database file where 123 are the first three characters on the line. You can view the locations file by using a text editor such as vi, or you can use your word processor.

Delete information from a file

Your computer can also quickly remove information from a database file. Just give it the correct command, and your computer takes out an eraser and wipes away the row. In reality, the computer rewrites the database file, omitting the unwanted row.

The friends database file, for example, contains a row with information about Tom Adams, as follows:

```
Bob Smith   555-1212
Mary Jones  555-5555
Tom Adams   555-7777
John Smith  555-4444
```

Perhaps Tom Adams is no longer your friend. To delete that row from the database file, use the following expressions:

```
gawk '$2 !~ /^Adams/ {print $1, $2, $3}' friends > newfriends
rm friends
cp newfriends friends
rm newfriends
```

The following steps provide a blow-by-blow account of what's happening:

1. The line gawk '$2 !~ /^Adams/ {print $1, $2, $3}' friends > tells your computer to find rows that don't contain the name Adams in the second column. After the computer finds a column that fits the search criteria, it copies all the columns to the new database file newfriends.

2. It doesn't copy the row that contains Adams to the newfriends database file.

3. The line rm friends deletes the friends database file.

4. The line cp newfriends friends copies the newfriends database file to a new file by the name of friends. Now both database files contain the same information.

5. The line rm newfriends deletes the newfriends database file, leaving you with the revised friends database file.

Displaying information on-screen

You can pick which columns appear from the database file in your search by using the print statement and the column number. Your search must include the following criteria:

✔ You must precede each column that you want to appear on-screen with a dollar sign ($).

✔ A comma must separate each column reference.

The following example shows how this search expression looks:

```
gawk '/123/ {print $2, $3}' inventory
```

Test your programming knowledge

1. What's the difference between a file and a database?

a. A file stores data organized into fields.

b. A file is something that you use to break out of jail.

c. A database must store information in an organized format, but a file doesn't.

d. You use a file to hold data, while a database is what Data calls home in *Star Trek: The Next Generation*.

2. How can you copy only some data in a database file to another file?

a. Use the indirection operator.

b. Use a No. 2 pencil to copy the data from the screen.

c. No one would ever want to copy data from the database file.

d. Use the redirection operator.

Answers: 1) c. See "A File and a Database." *2) d. See* "Extract information to a file."

Chapter 17

Making Your Program Print Stuff Out

· ·

In This Chapter

▶ Printing a line of text

▶ Printing a file

▶ Printing a database

· ·

Showing information on-screen is fine if you're looking for a quick answer to a question. But taking the information away with you is a bit difficult. (You grab the monitor, and I can take the computer.)

You don't need to break your back lugging the computer around with you. Nor do you need to get writer's cramp jotting down the information on scrap paper. A better way is to tell your computer to send the information to the printer.

Give Me Some lp Service

A printer is similar to your computer screen in that it takes characters from your computer and displays them. Instead of displaying information on a monitor, however, the printer prints out the information on paper.

You don't need to concern yourself with the kind of printer that attaches to your computer as you write information to your printer. You do need to know how to tell your computer to send the information to the printer. You do so by calling the lp utility. This utility takes the information that you supply and makes sure that it goes to the printer correctly.

Essentially, you worry only about the text that you want to print, and the lp utility worries about how to get it to the printer. And, of course, the printer worries about how to get the information on the paper.

Printing a Line of Text

The simplest program that you can write is one to display a line of text on-screen by using the echo command.

The following example shows you how to do so:

```
echo "Hello world."
```

Your screen thus shows the following text:

```
Hello World.
```

You can send the same line of text directly to the printer by using the pipe operator (|), following it with the call to the lp utility, as in the following example:

```
echo "Hello world." | lp
```

You're telling your computer to use the echo command to display the phrase Hello world. You then tell the computer to take those characters and send them to the lp utility. This process is known as *piping*. (Nerds call this process taking the output of the echo command and piping it into the input of the lp utility.) The lp utility then takes these characters and sends them to your printer.

Printing a File

Sending a single line of text directly to the printer isn't very smart programming. A better sign of programming is not to repeat any code.

In the following example, the program is calling the lp utility a couple of times:

```
echo "Hello world." | lp
echo "How are you doing?" | lp
```

A better way of printing is to write all the text to a file. After you safely store the information on your hard disk, you can send the entire file to the lp utility. The following example shows you how to put all the text into a file by the name of myfile:

```
echo "Hello world." > myfile
echo "How are you doing?" >> myfile
```

TECHNICAL STUFF

Pipes and redirection (and other Linux 101 things)

If you're a little confused about pipes, redirection, and all the other nerdy stuff, don't let it concern you.

Think of it this way: You're a traffic cop trying to keep cars (information) flowing in the right direction. You can give one of three signals to control the flow: none, redirection (>), or piping (|).

Consider that you want traffic to flow normally. The best signal to give is none. Nerds call this sending information to *standard out*, which is usually the screen. After the cars get there, they stop. The trip is over.

Now you want to change flow away from the normal destination (the screen) and send it to another destination (a file). Just give the computer the redirection signal (>). After the cars get there, they also stop. The trip is over.

Finally, you may want to send the traffic to another highway (utility). Give your computer the pipe signal (|). After the cars get there, they don't stop. Instead, another program takes control, and the cars keep moving.

Next, you can use the cat utility to read the information from the file and send it to the lp utility for printing. The cat utility requires only the name of your file. You issue the following command:

```
cat myfile | lp
```

You're telling your computer to call the cat utility. The cat utility opens the file myfile and reads each character. Normally, as it reads each character, the cat utility displays the character on-screen. The pipe character (|), however, tells the computer to send the characters to the lp utility rather than to the screen. The lp utility then passes the characters to the printer.

Printing a Database

You print information in a database (see Chapter 16) in the same way that you print a file. First, you create a database, as follows:

```
echo "Bob Smith 555-1212" >> friends
echo "Mary Jones 555-5555" >> friends
echo "Tom Adams 555-7777" >> friends
```

Each line of this program appends the information to the `friends` database. After the program finishes, the database contains the names and telephone numbers of three persons.

You use the following command to print all the information from the database:

```
cat friends | lp
```

You print database information the same way that you print the contents of a file.

Printing the entire database is sometimes useful, but frequently you want to print only a portion of the information. To do so, you need to call the `gawk` utility (which I discuss in Chapter 16).

Use the following command to print all the information in the database that refers to our friend `Smith`:

```
gawk '/Smith/ {print $1, $2, $3}' friends | lp
```

This command tells your computer to take the following steps:

1. Look for the character `Smith` in the database file `friends`.

2. Send the first, second, and third columns of all rows that match `Smith` to the `lp` utility.

3. Tell the `lp` utility to send the rows that it receives from the `gawk` utility to the printer.

Avoid searching again

One major drawback to sending the results of your search directly to the printer is telling the computer to search the database each time that you want to reprint the information. This process is time consuming, because your computer must perform the same task repeatedly.

A better way is to tell the computer to put the results of the search into a file and then send the file to the printer. You issue the following commands to do so:

```
gawk '/Smith/ {print $1, $2, $3}' friends > myfriends
cat myfriends | lp
```

The following steps describe what's happening:

1. You tell the computer to use the gawk utility to find rows in the friends database that contain the word Smith.

2. It copies columns 1, 2, and 3 of each of those rows to the myfriends file.

3. The program calls the cat utility to read the myfriends file into the lp utility.

4. The lp utility then sends the contents of the myfriends file to the printer.

Printing comments before the data

Sometimes you need to print comments before the information from the database prints. This procedure isn't so difficult, as the following example shows:

```
echo "Here are some of my best friends" > myfriends
gawk '/Smith/ {print $1, $2, $3}' friends >> myfriends
cat myfriends | lp
```

The following steps describe how this procedure works:

1. The first line tells the computer to copy a comment to the file called myfriends.

2. The second line tells the computer to find rows that contain Smith and to append the entire row to the file myfriends (which means that the data appears below the comments in the file).

3. The last line tells the computer to use the cat utility to send the contents of the file myfriends to the lp utility for printing.

Printing comments after the data

You can also print comments after the data. Issue the following commands to do so:

```
gawk '/Smith/ {print $1, $2, $3}' friends > myfriends
echo "I have more friends than this." >> myfriends
cat myfriends | lp
```

This technique is the same one that you use in the preceding example except that the comment statement appears below the call to the gawk utility.

Test your programming knowledge

1. What is 1p?

a. The L programming language.

b. It's a utility that sends characters to the printer.

c. A very long program (long program = 1p).

d. The last program command.

2. Why do you want to store the results of your search in a file instead of printing it directly?

a. This process gives the computer time to remember how to print.

b. You can always reprint the data without needing to conduct another search of the database.

c. So that you don't lose the information.

d. To justify buying a bigger disk.

Answers: 1) b. See "Give Me Some 1p Service." *2) b. See* "Avoid searching again."

Part VII
Debugging Your Program

The 5th Wave   By Rich Tennant

SURE, HE'S A LITTLE DIFFERENT, BUT HE WORKS HARD, AND KEEPS THE SYSTEM FREE OF BUGS.

In this part . . .

After building your first program, you're likely to discover that the program doesn't work just the way that you had in mind. Geez, your program may contain a bug! What next? Time to *debug* your program. Don't fret. You discover the best ways to debug your programs in this part.

Chapter 18

Getting Chatty with Comments

● ●

● ●

*Y*our Linux program may be clear to you, but ask your friends to take a look at it, and they may spend several hours trying to figure out what's happening.

After they write a program, some programmers put it aside, work on a different project, and then come back to the program. If you do so, you're likely to need to study your own code to recall what you wanted your program to tell the computer to do.

How can you keep from forgetting what you want your Linux program to do? You have only one solution: Place comments throughout your program. A *comment* is a line in your program that tells you what's happening in your code. Your computer ignores any comments it encounters, as though it's saying, "Keep your remarks to yourself — you already gave me instructions."

How to Create Comments

You create a comment in a program by typing # (the number sign) anywhere on the line. Your program ignores characters between the number sign and the end of the line. Following are examples of comments:

```
#This is the beginning of my program
clear #This clears the screen
```

The first line in this example doesn't tell the computer to do anything. This comment line does, however, tell those reading the program that the program begins here. The second line instructs the computer to clear the screen and adds a comment for anyone who reads the program (just in case they need help!).

You can use as many comment lines as you want. Just make sure that each line begins with a # sign.

Make Your Comments Worthwhile

The main reason for placing comments in a program is to enable you to easily remember what you want the computer to do with your instructions. Most programmers use comments at the beginning of important sections of their programs.

To introduce the purpose of your program to whoever may read it, you always want to place comments at the beginning of your programs. (You never know when you may want to share your programming secrets with a friend.) Although you can create any kind of introductory comments you want for your program, you want to include at least some of the following information in this list:

✔ Program name

✔ Programmer's name

✔ Purpose of the program

✔ Name of the intended user of the program

✔ Date on which the programmer wrote the program (and sometimes the time)

✔ Date of the last change that anyone made to the program

✔ Name of the programmer who made the last change

Now that you know what to include at the top of your program, you want to see how your program looks with this information in place. The following example of commented code incorporates all the information in the preceding list:

```
#Title: Regional Reporting Program
#Programmer: Mary Jones
#Purpose: Provide business tracking for each regional office.
#Primary user: All regional office managers and their staff.
#Originally written: 12/26/95
#Last changed: 2/4/96
#Changed by: Roger Smith
```

Use comments throughout your program to identify key actions that the computer takes. In the following example, you're instructing the computer to call a subprogram by the name of menu1, and the comment reminds you of this action:

```
#Display the opening screen
menu1
```

The name of the subprogram menu1 doesn't provide much information. You can guess that it somehow involves a menu, but which one? And anyone reading your code has even less of an idea. The comment in front of the instruction, however, answers that question.

If you're trying to decide whether to use a comment in your program, follow this rule: If in doubt, add the comment.

Make Your Comments Easy to Read

Keep in mind that you and your friends are probably reading your Linux programs (so you better watch what you say). You can make your program much easier to read if you use blank lines to separate chunks of your program.

In addition to making your comments understandable to anyone who reads them, you must also present them in a clear way. Look at the following example to see how difficult identifying the different sections in the program is:

```
#Title: Regional Reporting Program
#Programmer: Mary Jones
#Purpose: Provide business tracking for each regional office.
#Primary User: All regional office managers and their staff.
#Originally Written: 12/26/95
#Last Changed: 2/4/96
#Changed By: Roger Smith
#Change these values for each region
declare REGIONAL_OFFICE="Boston"
declare REGIONAL_MGR="Mary Smith"
let REGIONAL_SALES=1000000
#Display the opening screen
menu1
```

Can you quickly see where comments end and the code begins? Probably not. Now compare the preceding example with the following one:

```
#Title: Regional Reporting Program
#Programmer: Mary Jones
#Purpose: Provide business tracking for each regional office.
#Primary User: All regional office managers and their staff.
#Originally Written: 12/26/98
#Last Changed: 2/4/99
#Changed By: Roger Smith
```

```
#Change these values for each region
declare REGIONAL_OFFICE="Boston"
declare REGIONAL_MGR="Mary Smith"
let REGIONAL_SALES=1000000

#Display the opening screen
menu1
```

This example is much easier to read because it uses blank lines to break up the code into sections. You add blank lines to your program by inserting a carriage return (also known as a *hard return*) on a line that doesn't contain any text. The easiest way to insert a hard return is to move the cursor to the end of a line of text and press the Enter key. Rather than type text on the line, press the Enter key again. Voilà — a blank line!

How to Disable a Pesky Instruction

Beware! Bugs can work their way into your program. A *bug* is an error in your program, and sometimes it's hard to uncover. Suppose that you write a program to tell your computer to do something, but the computer doesn't do it. You have a bug in your program! What do you do? The following list provides your choices:

✔ Scream, "I hate computers!" This technique doesn't do anything to get your program to work, of course, but it certainly can relieve some of your frustrations.

✔ Test your program to determine which instruction isn't working. Keep in mind that the computer does what you tell it to do. You've probably simply given it an incorrect instruction.

You can use comments to disable instructions in your program. Although programmers use a number of techniques to locate bugs in their programs (and I discuss these techniques in depth in Chapter 19), most methods consist of the following basic steps:

1. **Disable an instruction.**

2. **Test the program.**

3. **Review the results.**

You can disable a part of your program by placing the number sign (#) at the beginning of the line that contains the instruction.

Suppose that you run a program (a snippet of which appears in the following example), and for some reason, it displays an incorrect regional sales value. As you inspect your code, you see — and suspect — an instruction that creates a REGIONAL_SALES environment variable that displays a value of 1000000. Can this item be causing the problem? You can erase this instruction and rerun the program to see what happens. If this particular instruction isn't causing the problem, however, you must remember which instruction you deleted so that you can add it to your program again. Check out the following example:

```
#Change these values for each region
declare REGIONAL_OFFICE"Boston"
declare REGIONAL_MGR="Mary Smith"
let REGIONAL_SALES=1000000

#Display the opening screen
menu1
```

You can now delete the suspect line and try again. A better method, however, is simply to place a comment sign (#) as the first character of the instruction, as follows:

```
#Change these values for each region
declare REGIONAL_OFFICE="Boston"
declare REGIONAL_MGR="Mary Smith"
#let REGIONAL_SALES=1000000

#Display the opening screen
menu1
```

The computer then ignores the instruction let REGIONAL_SALES=1000000 just as though you erased it. To restore the instruction, all you need to do is remove the comment sign.

Test your programming knowledge

1. What do you use the number sign (#) for in your program?

a. To send the line of code to the printer.

b. To tell the computer to ignore all the characters that follow the number sign on the line.

c. To create a tic-tac-toe board on-screen.

d. To draw a border around the screen.

2. Why do you want to use comments in your program?

a. To tell a private joke to your friend who's reading your program.

b. To summarize how your program works.

c. To reduce the amount of code.

d. To prove that your program works.

Answers: 1) b. See "How to Create Comments."
2) b. See "How to Create Comments."

Chapter 19

Stamping Out Bugs in Your Program

*Y*ou create your dream Linux program. It tracks all those significant others in your life, so you don't face two of them showing up on your doorstep at the same time. Well, what's that saying about mice and men? Your program just missed the mark. It lost track of one. Now you're in hot water.

You can't do anything about what happened, but in this chapter, I describe the steps that you can take to correct your program so that the mistake doesn't happen again.

What's a Bug?

Your program doesn't work because a bug's lurking in the program. Now don't go looking for your bug spray. That can only damage your computer. You can call any problem with a program a *bug*. You need to blame something for the problem, after all (but not the programmer, of course). So why not blame this tiny little critter that scares everyone as it quietly crawls across the floor?

The bug in your program may not be real, but the problem that causes your program to work incorrectly is very real. Following are some common reasons why programs don't work:

- ✔ **An instruction is out of place.** This situation's like putting the cart before the horse.

- ✔ **You give the wrong instruction to your computer.** This situation, on the other hand, is like telling your computer to move on a red light. It's the right time in your program to make a decision, but it's the wrong decision.

✔ **You use the wrong word.** Instead of using a word that your computer understands, you use sort of a different word (which kind of looks like the right word to you).

✔ **You put the right word in the wrong place.** Nerds call this problem using the wrong *syntax*. It's like saying, "I'm Hawaii to going," but you mean to say, "I'm going to Hawaii."

How a bug gets into your program

Bugs fly in the open window and land on your computer's hard drive just in the spot where you store your program. (Don't believe anyone who tells you that story.)

Bugs get into your program in very predictable ways, as the following list describes:

✔ Because you rush to write code without first planning what you want to write.

✔ Because of typographical errors (whoops).

✔ Because of poor computer-language grammar. (Grammar checkers don't catch the misuse of words that make up computer languages.)

You may, for example, use an if statement to have your program make a decision (see Chapter 7). The if statement ends with endif. A spelling and grammar checker may indicate a problem with endif. You realize, however, that endif is correct. But you may have typed endf in the program, leaving out the i. This error, too, confuses the spelling and grammar checker. You, on the other hand, can recognize that endf is not part of the computer lanaguage because the i is missing.

✔ You put some code in the wrong place.

✔ You guess at the correct word to use. (You don't want to get up to check. The book's on the shelf downstairs.)

Don't feel too concerned if you find a bug in your program. Bugs lurk in every program, even those that Bill Gates' people write. But just because you find something in common with the pros doesn't mean that you can ignore stamping out the bug.

Don't lose the war

Trying to get your program to work correctly is a test of persistence between you and the bug. This task can become very frustrating — almost to the point where you want to give up.

You want to remember the following items in debugging your program:

- ✓ **Computers do what you tell them to do.** If the computer is doing something other than what you intend, you're giving it the wrong instruction.

- ✓ **Don't work around the bug.** Trying this approach is like getting caught at the office without an umbrella in the middle of a downpour. You can work around the problem by waiting until the rain stops. You face the same situation, however, the next time that a downpour occurs. The smart solution is to leave an inexpensive umbrella in the office.

- ✓ **Remember that most bugs are simple and obvious.** Your debugging gets more difficult, however, as the complexity of your program increases.

Here's a hidden reward for being persistent about debugging your program: Your knowledge of Linux programming grows tremendously. After you find the answer to the problem, you most likely never forget it.

Retracing Your Steps

You begin to discover why your program isn't working by reviewing each line of your program. This process can become a time-consuming task depending on which technique you use.

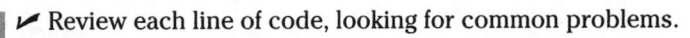

Following are a few common ways that programmers tackle this job:

- ✓ Review each line of code, looking for common problems.
- ✓ Watch each line of code as your computer reads the instructions.
- ✓ Have the computer check your code for syntax errors.

You must trace your entire program, no matter how insurmountable the review process seems. Doing so is the only way to get your program to run correctly.

Proofread your code

Pretend that you're your computer; then begin reading your program just as the computer reads it. Follow each direction carefully.

This suggestion may sound absurd. How can you stuff things into your computer's memory? How can you display characters on-screen? You can't, but you can take a pencil and a piece of paper and draw computer memory and a screen. One sheet of paper can serve as the memory and another as the screen. It's that simple.

Consider that the following program isn't working. It says "Hello" to all your friends and then "Good-bye" — but keeps repeating these messages endlessly. Look through the following example to see whether you can determine the problem:

```
#!/bin/bash
let flag=1
while [ "$flag" -eq 1 ]
do
for friend in Bob Mary Sue
do
echo "Hello $friend."
done
echo "Good-bye!"
let flag=1
done
```

The first thing that you need to do is to indent your code to make it readable, as in the following example:

```
#!/bin/bash
let flag=1
while [ "$flag" -eq 1 ]
    do
        for friend in Bob Mary Sue
            do
            echo "Hello $friend."
        done
    echo "Good-bye!"
    let flag=1
done
```

Next, on the piece of paper that represents your computer's memory, write the line let flag=1. That's what your computer is doing.

The next instruction tells your computer to check whether the value of $flag is 1. So look at the piece of paper, and you can see that, yes, it's equal to 1 (and for this discovery you went to college?). You must, therefore, follow the instructions inside the loop.

The first of these instructions tells the computer to place the string Bob into the string variable friend. Write this information on the paper. Your paper version of your computer memory should now appear as follows:

```
let flag=1
declare friend="Bob"
```

The next line tells the computer to display Hello Bob. on-screen. Write this greeting on the paper that you're using as your screen.

Continue this process until all the names appear on-screen. Your paper should now look as follows:

```
Hello Bob.
Hello Mary.
Hello Sue.
```

You don't find any more values in the for in loop, so the loop ends and the next line executes. This line tells your computer to display Good-bye! on-screen.

Now write that same line on your paper so that what appears on your paper is as follows:

```
Hello Bob.
Hello Mary.
Hello Sue.
Good-bye!
```

The next line tells your computer to place the value 1 in the $flag variable. Go to the piece of paper that contains the variables, find the $flag variable, and erase whatever value appears there. Place a 1 next to the $flag variable.

Why erase the value? You're doing exactly what your computer does as it reads your program. It always overwrites whatever value you already assigned to a variable (picky, picky).

Return to the top of the loop, check the value of the $flag variable, and repeat the process.

Wait! Do you see the bug? The computer keeps displaying the same messages because the value of the $flag variable is now always 1.

The following example shows how you fix the bug:

```
#!/bin/bash
let flag=1
while [ "$flag" -eq 1 ]
    do
        for friend in Bob Mary Sue
            do
                echo "Hello $friend."
        done
    echo "Good-bye!"
    let flag=0
done
```

The value of let flag now changes to 0 at the end of the loop.

Look at your code while the program's running

Reviewing each line of your code is fine for short programs, but it's a nightmare if you're using this method to debug a much larger and more complex program.

Debugging a program (that's nerd talk for finding the problem with your program) is tedious work. Regardless of what method you use to locate the problem, you still need to review the lines of your code as the final step in this process.

Your inability to see your instructions while your program is running is a drawback in debugging your program. You simply can't see what's happening in that black box.

The following list describes two ways that you can solve this problem (assuming that the name of your program is myprogram and you're using the bash shell):

✔ Use the -v option, also known as the *verbose option,* to tell your computer to display each line of code before it executes it. You use the following expression:

```
$ bash -v myprogram
```

You call the bash shell explicitly with the -v option and the name of your program by using this expression.

✔ Use the -x option, also known as the *echo option,* to make your computer display each line after it executes it. Use the following expression to do so:

```
$ bash -x myprogram
```

The major difference between these two methods is that -v shows you the instruction before the computer executes it, and -x shows it to you after it executes the instruction.

Laying a Trap for the Bug

Sometimes you can look at your code until you can't see straight, and you still can't determine why your program isn't working. This situation can become very frustrating, but don't give up. Instead, try another tactic.

Following are some good fallback plans that you can try:

- **Set flags for yourself throughout the program.** A *flag* is a message that appears on-screen to tell you what part of your program your computer is currently reading (see Chapter 4).

- **Display the value of all the variables in your program on-screen.** This procedure gives you a glimpse of what's happening behind the scenes (see Chapter 4).

- **Turn parts of your program off and on by making the expression true or false.** This process helps you to isolate the part of your program that's causing the trouble (see Chapter 3).

Just use a little common sense in using any of these methods. You must decide where to place the flags and which parts of your program you turn off and on.

Setting flags

A *flag* is simply a message that appears on-screen. The message of a flag can be as simple as "I got this far."

The following example shows you how to use flags in your program (and notice that the `let` command designates the flag):

```
#!/bin/bash
let flag=1
echo "Outside of while loop"
while [ "$flag" -eq 1 ]
    do
        echo "inside of while loop"
        for friend in Bob Mary Sue
            do
                echo "inside of for in loop"
                echo "Hello $friend."
        done
    echo "outside of for in loop"
    echo "Good-bye!"
    let flag=1
    echo "last line in while loop"
done
echo "last line in the program"
```

You see the following messages on-screen as you run this program:

```
Outside of while loop
inside of while loop
inside of for in loop
Hello Bob.
inside of for in loop
```

```
Hello Mary.
inside of for in loop
Hello Sue.
outside of for in loop
Good-bye!
last line in while loop
inside of while loop
inside of for in loop
Hello Bob.
inside of for in loop
Hello Mary.
inside of for in loop
Hello Sue.
outside of for in loop
Good-bye!
last line in while loop
```

Take a close look at these flags. Do you see anything strange? Following are some clues:

- ✔ All the flags inside the `while` loop repeat. They repeat endlessly if you run this program.
- ✔ The flag `last line in the program` doesn't appear on-screen.

Where's the problem? The computer *enters* the `while` loop but doesn't *leave* the `while` loop; the value of flag is always equal to 1. The condition in the `while` loop, therefore, is always true, and the loop never ends.

Display hidden values

You can ask the computer to show you values of variables while the program's running. You can combine this method with the flag method to give you more clues to the puzzle. Normally, the value of the flag variable doesn't appear on-screen because you use the flag variable only to control active instructions. You can, however, use the `echo` command to display the value of the flag variable on-screen.

The following example shows you how to use this method:

```
#!/bin/bash
let flag=1
echo "Outside of while loop flag = $flag"
while [ "$flag" -eq 1 ]
    do
        echo "inside of while loop flag = $flag "
        for friend in Bob Mary Sue
            do
                echo "inside of for in loop flag = $flag "
                echo "Hello $friend."
```

```
        done
    echo "outside of for in loop flag = $flag "
      echo "Good-bye!"
  let flag=1
    echo "last line in while loop flag = $flag "
done
echo "last line in the program flag = $flag "
```

Following is what you see on-screen as a result of running this program:

```
Outside of while loop flag = 1
inside of while loop flag = 1
inside of for in loop flag = 1
Hello Bob.
inside of for in loop flag = 1
Hello Mary.
inside of for in loop flag = 1
Hello Sue.
outside of for in loop flag = 1
Good-bye!
last line in while loop flag = 1
inside of while loop flag = 1
inside of for in loop flag = 1
Hello Bob.
inside of for in loop flag = 1
Hello Mary.
inside of for in loop flag = 1
Hello Sue.
outside of for in loop flag = 1
Good-bye!
last line in while loop flag = 1
```

Now you realize that your program never assigns the let flag variable the
value of 0. You know the cause of the problem because it creates an endless
loop (see Chapter 10).

Using a file to help find the problem

Displaying flags and the value of variables on-screen is helpful in finding a
problem in your program. With some programs, however, this method isn't
practical. You have just too much information to keep on-screen.

A better approach is to make the computer save the stuff that appears on-
screen to a file. You use the following command to do so:

```
myprogram > flagfile
```

In this example, you tell the computer to run myprogram and to redirect to
the file flagfile anything that goes to the screen. You can review the flagfile by using a text editor such as vi.

You use the following command to get vi to review a file:

```
vi flagfile
```

If you really want to get down and dirty trying to locate the trouble inside your program, you can print a copy of the file. You can use this printout as a guide as you review lines in your program.

Use the following command to print a copy of the file:

```
cat flagfile | lp
```

Turning off parts of your program

Another beneficial method that programmers use to find trouble spots in their program is to turn parts of the program off and on.

The first step in this process is to place the comment character (#) as the first character of each line of the program — at the very beginning because there it's easier to remove and doesn't affect the indentation of the other instructions — as in the following example:

```
#!/bin/bash
#let flag=1
#while [ "$flag" -eq 1 ]
#   do
#       for friend in Bob Mary Sue
#           do
#               echo "inside of for in loop flag = $flag "
#               echo "Hello $friend."
#           done
#       echo "Good-bye!"
#       let flag=1
#done
```

The computer ignores lines that begin with a comment character, except where the first line of the program contains only the comment character. This initial line tells the computer to start the bash shell.

Next, remove the comment character from lines that are necessary to perform the same task. The for in loop, for example, and the lines within the for in loop display a greeting to your friend. These lines all perform one task.

The following example shows what the program now looks like:

```
#!/bin/bash
#let flag=1
#while [ "$flag" -eq 1 ]
#   do
        for friend in Bob Mary Sue
            do
```

```
            echo "inside of for in loop flag = $flag "
            echo "Hello $friend."
      done
#     echo "Good-bye!"
#     let flag=1
#done
```

The computer starts the bash shell. It ignores the next two lines because they're comments. The for in loop and the code inside this loop execute, and the program ends.

This process tells you that the problem isn't with the for in loop. It must lie somewhere else.

Move to the next line, which displays a farewell message, and remove the comment character. The following example shows how it looks now:

```
#!/bin/bash
#let flag=1
#while [ "$flag" -eq 1 ]
#    do
        for friend in Bob Mary Sue
            do
                echo "inside of for in loop flag = $flag "
                echo "Hello $friend."
        done
      echo "Good-bye!"
#     let flag=1
#done
```

You then see that the program works fine.

The only part of the program that isn't on is the while loop and related instructions. By the process of elimination, you know that the problem with the program lies in the while loop.

You can make sure that the problem lies there by removing the rest of the comments from the program; then run the program again. The following example shows how it now looks:

```
#!/bin/bash
let flag=1
while [ "$flag" -eq 1 ]
    do
        for friend in Bob Mary Sue
            do
                echo "inside of for loop flag = $flag "
                echo "Hello $friend."
        done
      echo "Good-bye!"
      let flag=1
done
```

You're correct. Now the program no longer works, and you can concentrate your troubleshooting on the while loop.

Running parts of your program by hand

You build many Linux programs from subprograms. Some of these subprograms are `bash` shell scripts that you or your friends build. Others are Linux utilities that have been around for years. You can run all subprograms from the command prompt as well as from inside your program.

Instead of running your large program many times to find the problem, you can run each subprogram from outside your program to see whether the subprogram is causing the problem.

This technique is especially useful if your program uses the `gawk` utility. This utility searches a database file for a particular pattern of characters (see Chapter 16).

A common place for trouble to occur is with the expression that you use in the `gawk` utility. You simply don't ask the `gawk` utility the right question; therefore, it comes up with the wrong answer.

You can modify the expression and execute the `gawk` utility from the command line rather than from within your program. This strategy speeds the debugging process.

Use the following command to execute `gawk` from the command line:

```
gawk '/123/ {print $2, $3}' inventory
```

This command executes the `gawk` utility on the command line and asks it to display the second and third columns from the inventory file for each row that contains the characters 123.

Test your programming knowledge

1. What's a bug?

a. A tiny, crawly thing that sometimes irritates you as you're sleeping.

b. Part of a program that works all the time.

c. Part of a program that doesn't work.

d. An insect inside your computer.

2. How can you turn off parts of your program?

a. Run your program in half-time.

b. Take off your shoes while writing code.

c. Use the X switch.

d. Use the comment character (#) as the first character of each line that makes up the part of the program that you want to turn off.

Answers: 1) c. See "What's a Bug?" 2) d. See "Turning off parts of your program."

Part VIII
Automating E-Mail

In this part . . .

This part shows you how to use your newfound Linux programming skills to make your programs automatically send e-mail to your friends, relatives, or to anyone with an e-mail address. Here you can find valuable tips on how to create programs that take full advantage of all the features available in e-mail.

Chapter 20

Getting Goofy with E-Mail

. . . .

In This Chapter

▶ Understanding e-mail

▶ Creating a new user

▶ Using the `mail` utility

▶ Enhancing e-mail

. . . .

*T*o send the same e-mail to many friends at the same time, you can write your e-mail by using a text editor such as `vi` (which I show you how to use in Chapter 3). You can then use `vi` to write your program that sends the e-mail, too. Run your program, and the e-mail leaves your computer and goes to its recipients faster than a speeding bullet.

Your program uses the Linux `mail` utility, which handles the nitty-gritty work of combining the e-mail addresses with the message and makes all the necessary connections to help your e-mail follow the right path to your friends.

Your job is to give the `mail` utility all the information it needs to process your electronic letter. I like to think of the `mail` utility as the postal carrier who picks up your mail from the mailbox and needs to place the mail into the correct postal bag at the post office so that the mail can arrive at your friends' mailboxes.

The `mail` utility is like a postal carrier who's very particular about the mail I give him to take to the post office for processing. It inspects the envelope, and if any critical piece of information is missing, such as the stamp or the mailing address, it refuses to accept the letter.

Understanding E-Mail

The `mail` utility in Linux inspects the e-mail before processing my electronic envelope. The `mail` utility requires the first two pieces of information in the following list, and common courtesy requires the third piece of information:

- ✔ The destination address.
- ✔ The name of the file that contains the letter.
- ✔ The subject, although this information is optional.

The destination address consists of the person's name and the computer that contains that person's electronic mailbox. The filename tells the `mail` utility the name of the file that you create in `vi` that contains the letter you want to send. The subject consists of the word or two that describes the topic of the e-mail.

The pathway to the outside world

The computer running Linux must connect either directly or indirectly to your friend's electronic mailbox; otherwise, it can't deliver your e-mails. Don't expect your e-mails to go across the Internet if your computer running Linux doesn't connect to the Internet correctly. You can send an e-mail to `bgates@microsoft.com` by using the `mail` utility on your computer, but your message can't get to him if your computer doesn't connect to the Internet.

The pathway to the inside world

Linux is a *multiuser operating system,* which is the fancy way of saying that more than one person, each known as a *user,* can access your computer at the same time. You can use complex wires and gizmos to connect each of your friends' computers to your computer that runs Linux and create your own intranet. But you don't need to do so to discover how to send e-mail automatically. Nor do you need to hook your computer to the Internet.

You can create any number of users on your own computer and then have each of them log in to your computer by using your computer's keyboard. This approach, however, means that your friends must come over to your house to read their e-mails that you send them by using Linux. Not very practical — unless, of course, they bring refreshments over with each visit. But this method does offer a very practical way to find out how to write programs that send mass e-mails.

Creating a New User

Before you send your first e-mail, you want to create several users on your own computer. A *user* is a person who can log in to your computer and access the disk, modem, and other resources that attach to the computer. Pick up a copy of *Linux For Dummies*, 2nd Edition, by Jon Hall (published by IDG Books Worldwide, Inc.) to find out more about user logins.

Two pieces of information are necessary to create a user: the *user ID* and *password*. The *user ID* is a set of letters and characters that uniquely identifies the user on your computer.

You can use `bgates` as a user ID, for example, as long as no one else on your computer already claims `bgates` as a user ID. Bob Gates and Barbara Gates may both want `bgates` as a user ID, but only one of them can have it.

The *password* is a series of letters and numbers that associate with a specific user ID. You create the initial password for each user ID. Each user then can change his password to something unknown to you. Unlike with user IDs, people *can* duplicate passwords, which means that Bob Gates and Barbara Gates both can use the same password.

You create new users and assign user IDs and passwords in this chapter only so that you can practice sending and receiving e-mail. You don't, therefore, need to take precautions to use letters and words for the password that are difficult to guess. You do, however, need to devise a procedure to inhibit a hacker from guessing your passwords if you connect your computer to the outside world through the Internet.

The root user

The *root user* is the user ID with the right to do anything in Linux, such as configuring hard disks, shutting down the computer, and creating new users. As you first install Linux, it prompts you to enter a password for the root user ID. This password, along with the root user ID, enables you to log in to Linux as the root user and gives you full access to Linux.

Follow these steps to log in as the root user:

1. **Type** login root **at the command line.**

2. **Press the Enter key.**

3. **Type the root password (whatever you want it to be) at the command line after Linux prompts you for it.**

4. **Press the Enter key.**

You must log in as the root user before you can create a new user. Linux prompts you if you enter the wrong password and gives you a chance to enter the correct password. You must reinstall Linux, however, if you ever can't recall the root ID password.

User IDs and passwords

After you log in by using the root ID, you're all set to create your first user. Think of a user ID that you want to give the new user before you begin. Because this computer is mine and I don't have any friends who share the same first name, I like to use their first names as their user IDs. You can, of course, use any name you that you want as long as the names are unique — and you can remember them.

Whenever they need to assign user IDs to many users, many Linux administrators create a program to automatically create user IDs by combining information about the person to form the user ID. Following are some of those techniques that such a program uses:

- ✔ Using the initials of the person's first and last name, following them by the last five digits of the person's Social Security Number.

- ✔ Using the initials of the person's first and last name, following them by the person's employee number.

- ✔ Using the initial of the first name, following it by the first four characters of the last name. The program then assigns each person whose name includes the same five characters a number in sequence, such as `jkeog1`, `jkeog2`, and so on.

You can create a program that automatically generates passwords, too. Because passwords don't need to be unique, the program typically assigns the same password to each user ID and then requires the person to change the password the first time that he logs in to the computer.

Sometimes Linux administrators use the day of the week that they create the user ID as the password. That way the Linux administrator can easily remember the password, because his records indicate when he created the user ID.

Adding a new user

You create a new user on your computer by using the `useradd` utility. The `useradd` utility requires that you enter the user ID of the new user as you call the `useradd` utility. The following example shows how I create a user ID for my friend Bob:

```
useradd bob
```

I use Bob's first name as the user ID and I enter it in lowercase letters. I can use any letters or numbers for the user ID and also can use a mixture of upper- and lowercase or all uppercase letters. Bob's user ID, therefore, can also appear as any of the following variations (whichever one I may choose to make it):

```
Bob
BOB
BOb
BOB
```

I prefer to keep user IDs simple, however, because Linux user IDs are *case sensitive,* which means that Linux treats each of the preceding four examples as unique user IDs — in addition to the original version, `bob`. All the user IDs that I create, therefore, are in lowercase, which enables users and me to remember them more easily.

After I press the Enter key, Linux prompts me to enter a password for the new user ID. Again, I like to keep things simple, especially because I'm creating this user ID to practice my e-mail programming. So I use the user ID as the password, too, as follows:

```
passwd bob
```

Don't get confused if you see `passwd`. Instead of using `password` as the prompt, Linux just uses `passwd`. (You notice that Linux likes to abbreviate.) Simply enter the password after the prompt and press the Enter key.

Don't get surprised if Linux becomes a little temperamental and yells at you, saying that it doesn't like the password you select. Linux doesn't like most of the passwords that you come up with because those passwords appear in the Linux dictionary. You can almost always expect to see the following message after you enter the password.

```
New Unix password: bob
BAD PASSWORD: it is based on dictionary word.
Retype new Unix password:
```

Of course, Linux substitutes your own password for the word `bob` in this example. This message is merely a warning, which you can ignore. Linux is simply telling you that a hacker can create a program that uses each word in the dictionary as the password. If your password is in the dictionary, the likelihood that a hacker can figure out your password is high.

I don't worry about hackers because the hacker needs to gain physical access to my computer, as my computer doesn't currently link to the Internet. Besides, even if a break-in occurs, all the hacker gets are example Linux programs, which are available to him already simply by buying this book.

Linux prompts you to retype the new Unix password. Don't get upset, by the way, that Linux uses Unix instead of Linux in its error message. Remember that Linux is the child of Unix and inherits Unix utilities, including the adduser utility.

Enter the same password again. This action assures both you and Linux that you didn't mistype the password the first time you entered it. You receive an error message if you enter a different password the second time. In this case, Linux permits you to re-enter the password again. The following example shows what you see on-screen before retyping the password:

```
New Unix password: bob
BAD PASSWORD: it is based on dictionary word.
Retype new Unix password:
```

Notice that you don't see the password as you retype it. That's because Linux doesn't display the password as you type it to prevent any Peeping Toms from seeing the new password. After pressing Enter, Linux returns you to the shell prompt as if nothing's happened.

Testing the new user ID

Try logging in to your computer as the new user after you create the user ID. You do so the same way that you log in as the root, although you use the new user ID instead of the root ID and use the new password instead of the root password.

Type login at the prompt, following it with the user ID, as shown in the following example:

```
login bob
```

After you press the Enter key, Linux prompts you to type the password.

After you press the Enter key, Linux validates your user ID and password, and if you pass, the user ID appears as part of the command prompt. I enter bob as the user ID and bob@mycomputer appears as part of the new command prompt, as in the following example:

```
bob@mycomputer%
```

Test your programming knowledge

1. What does the following Linux command do?

```
useradd tom
```

a. Orders the user tom to perform addition.

b. Declares a variable by the name of tom.

c. Tells the computer to create a new user with the user ID tom.

d. Tells the computer to add the word user to tom.

2. What is the purpose of Linux telling you that your password is in the dictionary?

a. So that you can keep your password secret from hackers.

b. So that you can use the dictionary whenever you forget your password.

c. So that you can check the spelling of the password by looking it up in the dictionary.

d. Linux is showing off that it can automatically look up words in a dictionary.

Answers: 1) c. See "Adding a new user." *2) a. See* "Adding a new user."

The user's e-mail address

An e-mail address and a mailbox for each user ID resides on the computer on which the user logs in to Linux. The e-mail address consists of the user ID, the *at* symbol (@), and the name of the computer that saves the user ID.

Linux gives your computer the name mycomputer as you install Linux. As I create the user ID bob, therefore, I create bob as a user on mycomputer. The e-mail address for bob then becomes bob@mycomputer.

This designation is like saying *bob at mycomputer* or *bob at New York City.* Thousands of bobs live in New York City, of course, but I can't have more than one bob on mycomputer. Remember that bob is a user ID that must be unique to mycomputer. So e-mail that you send to bob on mycomputer doesn't misroute anywhere else.

Logging out

After you're sure that your test of the new user login is successful, you must log out so that you can log back in as the root. This action enables you to do anything that you want in Linux, including shutting down Linux — something that you can't do as the new user.

Type the logout command and then press the Enter key to log out of the user ID, as follows:

```
Logout
```

After you log out, you again find yourself at the command prompt.

You can log in as root by typing the following and then pressing the Enter key:

```
login root
```

Linux prompts you to enter the root password. Do so and press the Enter key. Linux changes the prompt to the following:

```
root@mycomputer
```

Using the Mail Utility

The mail utility is a tool available in Linux to automatically process outgoing and incoming e-mails. All you need to do is provide the mail utility with specific information and sit back, knowing that the electronic postal carrier is handling your message.

The mail utility performs the following tasks:

- ✔ Receives e-mail someone sends to a user's e-mail address.
- ✔ Displays incoming e-mail on-screen.
- ✔ Creates e-mails.
- ✔ Sends e-mails.

You have two mailboxes: an *incoming box,* where you receive e-mail for a user ID, and an *outgoing mailbox,* where the utility keeps e-mails that the user ID sends out for transmission. The mail utility uses the user IDs to identify the user mailboxes.

Creating e-mail

Although you can use the mail utility to create an e-mail, I find that using a text editor such as vi to create my e-mail is more efficient.

To use vi to create an e-mail, type the following at the command line and press the Enter key:

```
vi memo1
```

This command starts vi and opens an empty document by the name of memo1. You can, of course, replace memo1 with the name of your e-mail. You can call the e-mail any name that you want. vi uses the name that you assign to the e-mail as the file name for the document.

Create your e-mail message in vi. (If you need more help with vi, see Chapter 3.) After you finish, follow these steps:

1. **Press the Esc key.**
2. **Press and hold the Shift key as you type** ZZ.

Linux saves your file, you exit vi, and you return to the command prompt.

Remember the name of the document, because you need the name to send the e-mail.

Sending e-mail

You can use the mail utility from the command prompt without first needing to write a program to send e-mail. Doing so is a good way to become familiar with using the mail utility before incorporating the mail utility into your program.

The mail utility requires the following two pieces of information:

- ✔ The destination address.
- ✔ The filename containing the e-mail message.

The *destination address* is the e-mail address of the person to whom you're sending the e-mail. In our first example, I'm sending the e-mail to my closest friend — me! Yes, you can send e-mails to yourself whenever you get lonely or, in this case, whenever you want to practice sending e-mails.

Composing and editing e-mails by using the Linux mail utility

The mail utility uses its own commands for composing and editing text of an e-mail message. These commands can prove confusing, especially if you already know vi commands. The vi text editor does the job quite well, so you don't really need to pick up unnecessary mail-utility commands — unless you're really looking for a challenge. If so, you can use the online manual pages available in Linux by typing the following command and pressing the Enter key:

```
man mail
```

My e-mail address is the same as your e-mail address, because both of us use the root user ID. My e-mail address, therefore, is `root@mycomputer`. I first create an e-mail and save the e-mail in a file with the name `memo1`. You can call the file anything you like.

At the command prompt, I type the name of the `mail` utility, following it by the destination address and the name of the file that contains the e-mail message, as shown in the following example:

```
mail root@mycomputer < memo1
```

The name of the `mail` utility is `mail`. (Not very creative is it?) A space separates `mail` from the destination address, which is `root@mycomputer` in this example. I use the less-than symbol (<) to tell the `mail` utility the name of the file that contains the e-mail message.

The geeks call the less-than symbol *redirection of input*. This term sounds confusing, but as is the case with many terms that you use in programming, this one is very easy to understand. *Input* refers to where the `mail` utility receives the e-mail.

If we leave out the less-than sign and `memo1`, the `mail` utility assumes that you're going to enter the e-mail message directly into the `mail` utility from the keyboard. You can do so, but you need to know the `mail` utility's text-editing commands. (For more about mail text-editing commands, see the sidebar "Composing and editing e-mails by using the Linux `mail` utility," in this chapter.)

The less-than sign, however, tells the `mail` utility to get the e-mail message from the file `memo1` instead of from the keyboard. In essence you're *redirecting* words that you normally type from the keyboard to the file `memo1`.

After you press the Enter key, the `mail` utility sends the file `memo1` to the e-mail address `root@mycomputer`.

Reading e-mail

You can use the `mail` utility to read your e-mail. First, type `mail` at the command prompt. (After you press the Enter key, the `mail` utility goes to your incoming mailbox and displays a list of all e-mails.) Just use the following command to summon the list:

```
mail
```

All incoming e-mails appear in a list, along with their subjects, if any, and a unique number so that the `mail` utility doesn't confuse e-mails with similar addresses and subjects. At the end of the list, you see an ampersand (&) command prompt. Enter the number of the e-mail that you want to read at the prompt and press the Enter key, as follows:

```
& 1
```

In this example, I'm asking the `mail` utility to display the first e-mail in my incoming mailbox. The full text of the e-mail appears on-screen. This text consists of the same information that memo1 contains. Type **q** at the prompt and press the Enter key to quit the `mail` utility after you finish reading the message, as follows:

```
&q
```

Sending e-mail to a friend

You can send an e-mail to someone other than yourself by replacing your e-mail address with your friend's e-mail address and then repeating the same process that I describe in the section "Sending e-mail," earlier in this chapter, to send the e-mail. The following example shows how I send an e-mail to bob, the user ID that I create in the section "Adding a new user," earlier in this chapter:

```
mail bob@mycomputer < memo1
```

After I press the Enter key, the `mail` utility sends bob my e-mail message that memo1 contains. I can't read this message; however; only bob can read this message after he logs in to the computer.

Because I know bob's user ID and password, however, I can log in and pretend to be bob. First, I log in by using bob's user ID, press the Enter key, and then enter the password, pressing the Enter key again, as the following example shows:

```
login bob
password bob
```

Remember that you must use a user ID and password that you create on your computer to complete this exercise. (The ID and password that you must use may be different from what I'm showing here if you don't first create a user ID for bob that uses bob as its password, too.)

You notice that Linux displays one of two messages after you log in as bob. Following is the message that appears if Linux successfully delivers your mail to bob:

```
You have new mail
```

Otherwise, Linux displays the following message if no e-mails are in the incoming mailbox:

```
No mail for bob
```

In this message, of course, bob is the user ID and, therefore, you see a different user ID in your message if you don't log in as bob. After you log in, you can use the mail utility as I describe in the preceding section, "Reading e-mail," to read your incoming mail.

Enhancing E-Mail

If you call the mail utility, e-mail can include a subject, and you can copy it to another person by providing the mail utility with this information. This process is similar to how you provide the destination e-mail address, but it uses a special symbol to identify the subject and any additional e-mail address.

The geeks call the special symbol (a hyphen that you follow with a character) a *switch* that you use to turn on a feature of the mail utility. The switch is more like a railroad switch that moves a train from one set of tracks to another rather than a light switch.

If you turn the switch in one direction, for example, the mail utility reads and processes the subject from the command line. If you turn the switch in the opposite direction, the mail utility knows to process the e-mail without the subject.

The same logic is true if you use switches to include or exclude sending a copy of the e-mail to another destination address. If you turn on the switch for the copy, the mail utility copies e-mail to the other e-mail address; otherwise, it sends no copies.

A *switch* is a symbol that you proceed with a hyphen (-) and follow with the additional information that the mail utility requires to process the e-mail. If the switch is missing from the command line in the examples that I use throughout in this chapter, Linux assumes that the switch is off.

You use switches to tell the `mail` utility to perform the following tasks:

- Include a subject in the e-mail.
- Copy the e-mail to one or more addresses.
- Blindly copy the e-mail to one or more addresses (blocking names of people to whom you sent the e-mail so that each person receiving the message can't see who else is receiving the same message).

You don't need to include a subject in your e-mail or copy the e-mail to another address, although sometimes you find both beneficial if, for example, you want to get the attention of the purchasing clerk who lost your computer order. The subject alerts the clerk to your problem before he reads the e-mail. The copy also tells the clerk that you're informing your boss about the problem.

Inserting a subject

Including the subject of your e-mail on the subject line is always a good practice. The subject line appears whenever the list of e-mail appears if you're using the `mail` utility — and the person to whom you send the e-mail often uses the subject line to determine which e-mail to read first (which may be the case if he receives many e-mails).

You want to write the subject line to attract the person's attention and ensure that he reads your e-mail before other e-mails. Furthermore, you want the subject to describe the content of the e-mail. The word `URGENT` as the subject, for example, screams for the person's attention but doesn't give him a clue as to the content of the message.

On the other hand, the subject `customer problem` tells the general topic of the e-mail but doesn't provide any information on the urgency of the problem. Using `URGENT Customer Problem`, as the subject, however, clearly implies that the recipient needs to read the e-mail immediately because the customer problem is serious.

Be careful not to overuse attention-grabbing words such as `URGENT`, because such overuse waters down their meaning after a while. If half the messages with the subject `URGENT` aren't really urgent, using `URGENT` as the subject no longer attracts the same amount of attention.

Some words don't require any indication of urgency because they normally attract the person and are read first. An e-mail that refers to promotions, for example, is one that people are likely to read immediately, because everyone wants to find out who's receiving promotions.

You can include a subject line to your e-mail by using the `-s` switch, following it with the text of the subject. Insert the switch and the subject between the mail and the destination address at the command prompt, as shown in the following example:

```
mail -s "Promotions" bob@mycomputer < memo1
```

The `-s` switch tells the `mail` utility to use `Promotions` as the subject of the e-mail. Always include the subject within double quotation marks.

Inserting multiple addresses

The `mail` utility can send the same e-mail to many destination addresses and copy the e-mail to many other addresses. You can achieve this task by inserting the additional addresses next to each other, separating each address with a space.

Say, for example, that I want to send the e-mail to my co-workers Sandy, Joanne, and Anne, in addition to good old Bob. The following example shows how I do it:

```
mail bob@mycomputer sandy@mycomputer joanne@mycomputer anne@mycomputer < memo1
```

The `mail` utility treats each address as a destination address, which means that these addresses all appear in the `TO` portion of the e-mail. You can also insert multiple addresses to send copies of the e-mail by placing the addresses after the `-c` switch. You must separate each address with a space.

Say that I want to send one e-mail to Bob and copy the e-mail to Sandy, Joanne, and Anne. The following example shows how I do it:

```
mail bob@mycomputer -c sandy@mycomputer joanne@mycomputer
        anne@mycomputer < memo1
```

Inserting a copy address

A *copy address* is another e-mail address that receives a copy of the e-mail, along with the destination address of the e-mail. Everyone who receives the e-mail also sees the copy addresses.

Say, for example, that I send the promotion memo to Bob and his boss, Mary, and Mary's boss, Mark. Bob sees Mary's and Mark's e-mail addresses as `"cc"` on the e-mail. Mary also sees that her boss is receiving the e-mail, too, just as Mark knows that Mary's receiving the same e-mail.

Be careful in copying anyone on an e-mail, because you may not want everyone who receives the e-mail to know about all the other people who receive the same e-mail. You may not want Mary, for example, to know that her boss is also receiving the e-mail. Yet, you have no problem with Mark knowing everyone who's receiving the e-mail.

You can use the *blind-copy* feature of mail to restrict the people who see who else receives the e-mail. I discuss this feature in the following section, "Inserting a blind-copy address." In the previous example, Mary doesn't know that her boss is receiving a copy of the e-mail if you send her boss a blind copy of the e-mail.

You use the `-c` switch to include a copy e-mail address, as shown in the following example:

```
mail bob@mycomputer -c mary@mycomputer < memo1
```

In this example, `mary` and `bob` both receive a copy of the `memo1` e-mail message.

Inserting a blind-copy address

The *blind copy* is a feature of the `mail` utility that enables you to send a copy of the e-mail to someone without the other recipients knowing who else is receiving the e-mail.

Blind copies often come in handy if the e-mail involves an internal political struggle, where covering your . . . well, you know . . . is important. You can send the e-mail without tipping your hand to your adversary by using the blind-copy feature.

The switch `-b` is the switch that you use to create a blind copy, as shown in the following example:

```
mail bob@mycomputer -b boss@mycomputer -c mary@mycomputer < memo1
```

In this example, the `mail` utility sends the `memo1` to `bob` and a copy to `mary`. Bob can see Mary's e-mail address in the e-mail, so he knows that Mary's receiving a copy of `memo1`. The boss also receives a copy, but neither Bob nor Mary sees the boss' e-mail address in the e-mail. On the other hand, the boss sees all the e-mail addresses of everyone who's receiving the `memo1`.

You accomplish the task of sending blind copies to many addresses in a similar fashion. Say that, instead of sending Sandy, Joanne, and Anne a standard copy, I want to send them a blind copy. The following command shows how I do it:

```
mail bob@mycomputer -b sandy@mycomputer joanne@mycomputer
          anne@mycomputer < memo1
```

I can, of course, include multiple destination addresses, multiple copy addresses, and multiple blind-copy addresses, plus a subject line by placing them on the same line.

Inserting all features in an e-mail

You can include a subject, a copy address, and a blind copy in an e-mail by using all the switches that I mention in the preceding sections of this chapter. Simply insert the switches after the destination address as you call the mail utility.

The following example shows you how to do so:

```
mail bob@mycomputer -s "Promotions" -b boss@mycomputer -c
          mary@mycomputer < memo1
```

The mail utility sends Bob, Mary, and the boss memo1 and identifies the subject as Promotions.

Test your programming knowledge

1. How can you turn off an enhanced feature of the mail utility?

a. Use the W switch.

b. By using switches with the mail utility.

c. Don't use switches with the mail utility.

d. Stand on a ladder and stretch to reach the switch.

2. What's a blind copy?

a. A copy of the e-mail where you hide the text.

b. The address of the person receiving a blind copy is hidden from everyone else who receives the e-mail.

c. An e-mail where the mail utility guesses the destination address.

d. An e-mail where you close your eyes while writing the text of the e-mail.

Answers: 1) c. See "Enhancing E-mail." 2) b. See "Inserting a blind-copy address."

Chapter 21

Automatic E-Mailing

• •

In This Chapter

▶ Sending e-mail from a program

▶ Passing an argument to an e-mail program

▶ Passing multiple arguments to an e-mail program

▶ Overriding default e-mail values

• •

*I*f you want to send the same e-mail to many friends, you use the Linux `mail` utility and insert the different addresses at the `mail` command line. (If you need more information on the basics of e-mail, refer to Chapter 20.) This process can become cumbersome if you frequently e-mail a long list of friends, because each time that you want to send an e-mail, you must retype all the addresses and the name of the message file. After you modify your program, you can send an e-mail without directly using the `mail` utility. Cool, eh?

Linux automates the e-mail process by creating a program that does all this work for you. You enter the list of addresses only once by entering those addresses into the program and not directly into the `mail` utility.

You can also write a program that changes the e-mail message without needing to rewrite the program. You can then send e-mails to all your friends by running the program and giving the program the filename that contains the e-mail message. The program takes care of sending the e-mail to your friends.

Sending E-Mail from a Program

Say that you want to send an e-mail message that you keep in a file to a friend by using a program. To do so, you simply write your program in a text editor, save the program, close the text editor, and then make the program file executable so that Linux knows that the file contains a program. The following instructions take you step by step through this procedure:

1. **Open your text editor.**

   In this example, I use the vi text editor and call my program mailprogram, but you can call your program anything that you want. To start vi, for example, you need to type the following:

   ```
   vi mailprogram
   ```

2. **Next, type the following code into vi (and if you need to brush up on your vi commands, review Chapter 3):**

   ```
   #!/bin/bash
   mail -s "Good News" bob@mycomputer < memo1
   ```

   Here's what this program does: The first line, #!/bin/bash, tells Linux that this program is a bash program and that Linux must first run the bash shell before running this program. Remember that, if your copy of Linux complains about this line (such as saying that #!/bin/bash is an unknown command), you can also run the program by typing the following line at the command prompt:

   ```
   /bin/bash mailprogram
   ```

   The last line of the program calls the mail utility and tells it to send the message Good News in the memo1 file to bob@mycomputer.

3. **Before you can run this program, you must save the program file by pressing Esc, Shift+ZZ.**

   This command automatically saves the file as mailprogram and closes vi.

4. **At the command prompt, type the following:**

   ```
   chmod 711 mailprogram
   ```

   This last step is to make the program file executable, which simply means that you do something to tell Linux that the mailprogram file contains a program.

   This command calls the chmod utility, which you use to change the status of a file. The 711 isn't a telephone number; it's the code that makes the mailprogram an executable file. You can read more about the chmod utility in *Linux For Dummies*, 3rd Edition, by Dee-Ann LeBlanc, Melanie Hoag, and Evan Blomquist (published by IDG Books Worldwide, Inc.). After you press Enter, Linux runs the chmod utility.

To execute the mail program, type the following at the command prompt and then press the Enter key:

```
mailprogram
```

The mailprogram program sends the e-mail to Bob. You can verify that the program works and that Bob receives your e-mail by logging in to your

computer as bob. (See Chapter 20 for further information on reading e-mail.).
You see the message You have new mail after you enter Bob's user ID and
password. You can then use the mail utility to read the mail.

Passing an Argument to an E-Mail Program

You can modify how the mail utility works after you call the mail utility from
a program by *passing changes*. The geeks call this *passing an argument from
the command line*.

Say that you want to send a message that you keep in a file you call mysecret
to your friend Bob, whose e-mail address is bob@xyz.com. You pass the mail
utility mysecret and bob@xyz.com as an argument as you call the mail utility
from the command line.

You can write a program that asks the user of your program to enter an e-mail
address as the name of the file that contains the message to be sent to that
e-mail address. Your program can then call the mail utility and pass the
e-mail address and document name to the mail utility so that it can send the
document.

Following is information that you can change if you call the mail utility from
the command line or from within your program:

✔ The e-mail message.

✔ The destination address.

✔ The copy address.

✔ The blind-copy address.

✔ The subject.

To review how you use these features of the mail utility, see Chapter 20.

Passing the e-mail message

You probably send many e-mails to your friends, so writing a program that
contains the filename of the hard-coded message doesn't make too much
sense, because you want to send many different messages to your friends.
(*Hard coding*, by the way, is a geek's way of saying that you type the name of
the file that contains the message as part of the program, as I do in the section "Sending E-Mail from a Program," earlier in this chapter.)

By using a variable, however, you can easily change the message without changing the program. (Chapter 4 contains lots of juicy material on variables). Say that I create a program to send e-mail messages to my friends. Each time that I run the program, I want to send a different message. I pass the name of the file that contains the message to the program each time that I run the program. I include information and the name of the program by using the $1 special variable at the command prompt.

Inside your program, you can use the argument variable $1 to represent the name of the file that contains the message that you want to e-mail to your friends. Say that I want to send my friends a message that I keep in the file mysecret and I call my program myfriends. I type myfriends mysecret at the command line. As you run your program, you place the filename beside the program name on the command line. Every time that Linux sees $1 in your program, Linux replaces the $1 with the file's name. In my example, mysecret replaces $1 in my program. Just follow these steps:

1. **Display the mailprogram in vi by typing the following and pressing the Enter key:**

   ```
   vi mailprogram
   ```

2. **Make your program look as follows by typing these commands into your program.**

   These instructions start the bash shell and then calls the mail utility to send an e-mail to Bob. Good News is the subject line of your message:

   ```
   #!/bin/bash
   mail -s "Good News" bob@mycomputer < $1
   ```

3. **Save your changes by pressing the Esc key and then pressing and holding the Shift key as you type ZZ.**

4. **At the command prompt, type the following to make the program an executable program:**

   ```
   chmod 711 mailprogram
   ```

5. **Whenever you're ready to run the mailprogram, type the following at the command prompt and press Enter:**

   ```
   mailprogram memo1
   ```

Here's what the program's going to do: By typing mailprogram memo1, you're telling Linux two things. First, you want to run the program mailprogram. Next, you want to pass the mailprogram a value you call memo1. The geeks call this procedure *passing the program an argument*. (I don't know why, because Linux rarely complains about the value that you pass to the program.)

Linux then follows all the instructions that you place inside your program. The first instruction tells Linux to run the bash shell. Next, you tell Linux to run the mail utility to send bob@mycomputer the e-mail message that variable $1 refers to. The mail utility also includes the subject Good News.

Whenever Linux sees $1, Linux immediately knows that $1 is a placeholder for the value that you type beside the program name at the command prompt.

Before Linux calls the mail utility, Linux replaces the $1 with memo1; then it starts the mail utility and passes all the information necessary to send the e-mail to the mail utility.

Passing the destination address

On several occasions, I've written a program to send an e-mail. Each time that I ran the program, I wanted to change the destination address. Originally, I wrote the address as part of the program, which made sense at the time but became cumbersome. Each time that I wanted to change the destination address, I needed to load the program in vi and make the changes.

I discovered, however, that I can avoid the hassle of changing the program by passing the destination address as an argument to the program. To do so, follow these steps:

1. **First load the program that you use in the section "Passing the e-mail message," earlier in this chapter, into vi and change the program to look as follows:**

   ```
   #!/bin/bash
   mail -s "Good News" $1 < memo1
   ```

2. **Next, save your program by pressing Enter and using the Shift+ZZ key combination.**

   See the preceding section, "Passing the e-mail message," for further information on using this shortcut. Because you can use the same program that you use in that section, you don't need to use the chmod utility to make the program an executable program. The program is already executable from the last time that you saved it.

3. **As you call your program, include the destination address on the command line, as shown in the following example:**

   ```
   mailprogram bob@mycomputer
   ```

The following steps describe what happens as I run this program:

1. Linux sees the first line #!/bin/bash and knows to run the bash shell.

2. Then Linux substitutes the $1 with the command-line argument bob@mycomputer. This argument is, of course, the destination address.

3. Finally, Linux runs the mail utility that sends the message that the memo1 file contains to bob@mycomputer with the subject of Good News.

Passing the copy address

You pass the copy address to the e-mail program by using basically the same method that you use to pass the destination address to the program. The copy address is the e-mail address of the person who's going to receive a copy of the e-mail that you send to the destination address.

Follow these steps to modify the e-mail program:

1. **Start vi and load the program, as I show you in the section "Passing the destination address," earlier in this chapter.**

2. **Next, change the program to look like the following example:**

```
#!/bin/bash
mail -s "Good News" bob@mycomputer -c $1 < memo1
```

3. **Save the program by using the Shift+ZZ key combination (and remember that the program is already executable from the last time you saved it).**

4. **Call the program and include the copy address on the command line as shown in the following example:**

```
mailprogram mary@mycomputer
```

The following steps describe what happens next:

1. Linux runs the bash shell because you enter #!/bin/bash on the first line of the program.

2. Next, Linux substitutes mary@mycomputer for the $1 (because you're sending Mary a copy of the e-mail).

   Remember that $1 represents the information that is passed to your program from the command line. You must place the $1 inside your program where the information passed from the command line is used if you typed it into the program. In this example, you place the $1 in the position where the copy address belongs in the instruction that calls the mail utility.

3. Finally, Linux calls the mail utility and sends the message that the memo1 file contains to bob@mycomputer and the mary@mycomputer copy address with the subject of Good News.

Passing the blind-copy address

The blind-copy address tells the mail utility to send a copy of the e-mail to this address without informing anyone else that the recipient at the blind-copy address is receiving a copy. (Flip through Chapter 20 to find out more about how the blind-copy address works.)

You can pass the blind-copy address to the program by making the blind-copy address a command-line value similar to the destination and copy address that I mention in the two preceding sections. Just follow these steps:

1. **Load the mail program into** vi **so that you can modify the program.**

2. **Change the mail program to look as follows:**

```
#!/bin/bash
mail -s "Good News" bob@mycomputer -b $1 < memo1
```

3. **Save the program.**

4. **Start the program by typing the program's name at the command prompt, making sure that you include the blind-copy address, as shown here:**

```
mailprogram boss@mycomputer
```

Note: If you're using the program from the section "Passing the copy address," earlier in this chapter, you can just save the program because it's already executable.

The following describes what's going on in these steps:

1. Linux follows your directions and runs the bash shell (#!/bin/bash).

2. Linux then substitutes boss@mycomputer for the $1. (The boss is receiving a blind copy of the e-mail.)

3. Finally, Linux calls the mail utility to send memo1 message to bob@mycomputer and to the boss@mycomputer blind-copy address with the subject of Good News.

Passing the subject

You want to give every e-mail a subject line that alerts the reader about the message that the e-mail contains. You can, of course, always exclude the subject and thus keep the reader in the dark about the e-mail message until he reads it.

Being the nice person that you are, however, you probably want to include a subject, and you can do so by passing the text of the subject to the program as a command-line value. Just follow these steps:

1. **Display the e-mail program in** vi.

2. **Modify the program from the section "Passing the blind-copy address," earlier in this chapter, as follows:**

   ```
   #!/bin/bash
   mail -s $1 bob@mycomputer < memo1
   ```

3. **Save the program by pressing Enter and then using the Shift+ZZ key combination, as I describe in the section "Passing the blind-copy address," earlier in this chapter.**

4. **Type the program's name at the command prompt and follow it by the subject, making sure that you include quotations around the subject, as shown here (remembering that the program is already executable because you use the same program in earlier sections):**

   ```
   mailprogram "Good News"
   ```

The following steps describe what's happening in the preceding steps:

1. Linux runs the bash shell first (`#!/bin/bash`).

2. Next, Linux substitutes Good News for the $1. (Good News is the subject.)

3. Finally, Linux calls the mail utility and then sends the memo1 message to bob@mycomputer with the subject of Good News.

Passing Multiple Arguments to an E-Mail Program

Writing your own e-mail program enables you to build in flexibility that you don't find by simply using the mail utility that Linux provides. Your own programs generally prove more flexible because you can probably think of different ways that you want an e-mail program to perform than are available in the Linux mail utility.

For one thing, you can pass multiple arguments to your e-mail program that you can substitute for features of the `mail` utility that you want to use. You can, therefore, write your program to meet your general needs, such as sending e-mails to all your friends, and then tailoring the program for each e-mail that you send.

Following are some of the common ways to add flexibility to your e-mail program:

- ✔ Change the subject and e-mail message from the command line.
- ✔ Change the subject, e-mail message, and destination address from the command line.
- ✔ Override default values of the e-mail.

The following sections describe these changes in more detail.

Changing the subject and e-mail message

I created an e-mail program that sends e-mails to all my friends. I purposely left out the subject and the e-mail message from the program, however, so that I can use the same program to send them any e-mail without needing to modify the program.

I can do so because I enter the subject and the file name that contains the e-mail message at the command prompt as I type the name of the program. I must, of course, first change the program to accept both arguments from the command line before I can run the program.

You use numbers to identify command-line arguments. The first argument is number 1, as you see in the section, "Passing an Argument to an E-mail Program," earlier in this chapter. The second argument is number 2 and so on. You refer to these arguments by placing a dollar sign ($) in front of the number that you want to use. The first argument is $1. The second argument is $2.

If I want to pass the subject and the name of the file that contains the e-mail message to the e-mail program, I use two arguments and refer to them as $1 and $2 in my program. The following example shows the modify program to accept two arguments from the command line:

```
#!/bin/bash
mail -s $1 bob@mycomputer < $2
```

I use the following command to call this program:

```
mailprogram "Good News" memo1
```

The following steps describe how the program works:

1. First, Linux runs the bash shell (#!/bin/bash).
2. Next, Linux substitutes Good News from the command line for $1.
3. Linux then substitutes the file name memo1 for $2 in the program.
4. Finally, the mail utility executes and sends the e-mail that memo1 contains to bob@mycomputer with the subject line as Good News.

Each time that I want to send Bob another e-mail, all I need to do is type the mailprogram name at the command prompt, following it with the subject and the name of the file that contains the e-mail message. I don't need to modify the program itself.

You can include additional destination addresses, copy addresses, and blind-copy addresses as part of your program by using the techniques that I describe in Chapter 20. I use only one address here to simplify the example.

Be careful and don't mix up the order of the arguments to your program. If you do, Linux may complain by displaying an error message or it may simply follow your directions, giving you unexpected results.

Imagine, for example, placing the filename as the first argument and the subject as the second. The mail utility then attempts to use the e-mail message as the subject line, which isn't your intent. In this case, the mail utility displays the filename that contains the message as the subject of the e-mail.

Changing the subject, e-mail message, and destination address

You can increase the flexibility of your e-mail program by passing the program the destination address along with the subject and e-mail message filename. After you modify your program, you can send an e-mail without directly using the mail utility.

You must change your program to accept three command-line arguments. The first argument is the subject; the second is the file name of the e-mail message; and the third argument is the destination address.

Within the program, you refer to each argument by number. $1 is the subject; $2 is the filename of the message; and $3 is the destination address. Here's how the program looks after you make these changes. You can save time and modify the program that you use in the section, "Passing the e-mail message," earlier in this chapter, rather than retyping instructions, as the following example shows:

```
#!/bin/bash
mail -s $1 $3 < $2
```

To call this program, use the following command:

```
mailprogram "Good News" memo1 bob@mycomputer
```

The following steps describe what's happening with this program:

1. After Linux runs the `bash` shell (`#!/bin/bash`), it substitutes `Good News` for $1 in the program.

2. Next, Linux substitutes the filename `memo1` for $2 in the program and substitutes the destination address `bob@mycomputer` for $3.

3. The program then calls the `mail` utility and sends `memo1` to `bob@mycomputer` with the subject line as `Good News`.

Each time that I want to send an e-mail, I type `mailprogram` at the command prompt along with the subject, e-mail message filename, and the destination address. The `mailprogram` then takes over and makes sure that the mail utility sends the e-mail.

Test your programming knowledge

1. What is the function of the $1 **variable?**

a. It tells you that the price is a buck.

b. It represents the second argument on the command line.

c. It represents the first arguments passed on the command line.

d. It stands for the amount of raise in pay that you get next year.

2. What does < $2 **mean in** `mail bob@mycomputer < $2`?

a. Use the file $2 as the e-mail message.

b. The $2 moves to the left one space.

c. Use the second word in the e-mail address.

d. $2 contains the second argument, which is the name of the file that contains the e-mail message.

Answers: 1) c. See "Passing an Argument to an E-Mail Program." 2) d. See "Passing Multiple Arguments to an E-Mail Program."

Overriding Default E-Mail Values

A common technique among programmers is to create a program with default values and then override those values by passing arguments to the program. You may, for example, want to always send e-mails to all of your friends, but sometimes you want only one of your friends to receive the e-mail.

You build the default destination addresses into your program and use them only if you *don't* include a destination address on the command line as you execute the program. A destination address that you enter on the command line automatically substitutes for the built-in destination addresses that your program contains.

Following are the modifications that you need to make in your program:

✔ Create default values in your program.

✔ Modify your program to accept command-line arguments.

✔ Insert logic into the program so that it knows when to use the command-line arguments.

Inserting default values

A *default value* is information that you always want the mail utility to use unless you give your program special instructions otherwise, such as placing a value on the command line to replace the default value.

Say, for example, that you always send e-mail to your best friends Bob and Mary, so you use their e-mail addresses as the default addresses for your e-mail program. To do so, you simply enter their e-mail addresses in the mail utility inside your program. The following example shows how this command looks:

```
#!/bin/bash
mail -s $1 bob@mycomputer mary@mycomputer < $2
```

Notice that you use the $1 and $2 variables as placeholders for the subject and filename of the file that contains the e-mail message. You can still pass the subject and filename to the mail program each time that you call the program. Because you probably want to send Bob and Mary various e-mails, you don't want to use a default value here.

The following example shows how you call this program:

```
mailprogram "Good News" memo1
```

The following steps describe what happens as the program runs:

1. Linux runs the `bash` shell (`#!/bin/bash`).

2. Linux substitutes `Good News` for $1 in the program and substitutes `memo1` for $2.

3. The `mail` utility uses the default destination address `bob@mycomputer` to send the e-mail.

Overriding default values

You can override default values by writing *logic* into your program to determine the number of arguments that are passing on the command line.

I decide, for example, that two arguments are to pass to the program whenever I want to use the default destination addresses, and three arguments are to pass if I want to override the default destination addresses. Suppose that your program contains a destination address that you use for every e-mail that you send by using your program. You can override the destination address by passing a new destination address from the command line whenever your call your program. Linux then uses the new destination address instead of the designation address written inside your program.

You must modify the e-mail program to determine whether two or three arguments are passing as you call the program. Basing its decision on the number of arguments, the program then executes one set of instructions or another set of instructions.

You must make the following three changes to the program:

✔ Determine the number of arguments on the command line.

✔ Determine which instructions to execute depending on the number of arguments.

✔ Insert two sets of instructions to handle two arguments and three arguments.

The $# variable contains the number of arguments that pass to the command line. You can use the $# as the number of argument itself.

You use the `if` *statement* to compare the value of $# with the number of arguments that's necessary to run each set of instructions. (See Chapter 7 for additional information about the if statement.) The following example shows how the program looks after the modifications:

```
#!/bin/bash
if [ "$#" -eq 2 ]
    then
        mail -s $1 bob@mycomputer mary@mycomputer < $2
    elif [ "$#" -eq 3 ]
    then
        mail -s $1 $3 < $2
    else
        echo "You did not enter the correct number of arguments."
fi
```

The following steps walk you through the program so that you can see how it works:

1. First, Linux starts the bash shell before it compares the number of command-line arguments.

2. Next, Linux determines whether the number of command-line arguments ($#) is equal to 2. If so, Linux uses the default destination address for the e-mail. Linux substitutes the subject passing as the first argument with $1. The filename of the e-mail message is the second argument and Linux substitutes it for $2. The first call to the mail utility in the program executes.

3. If the number of command-line arguments doesn't equal 2, Linux determines whether the number of arguments is 3. If so, it doesn't use the default destination address. Instead, it substitutes the third argument for the $3 and the second call to the mail utility in the program executes.

4. If the number of arguments is less than 2 or greater than 3, however, the e-mail doesn't go out and the program tells Linux to display an error message (because the e-mail program requires at least two and no more than three arguments).

Although the program reads the number of arguments passing on the command line, the program can't determine whether the argument contains the correct information. Nothing prevents someone from placing the arguments out of order, for example, as the program executes. In this case, you have no way of telling what can happen. The e-mail may not go out at all, for example, if the destination address is incorrect.

Using switches to identify arguments

You can identifying arguments passing to your e-mail program by using practically the same technique that the geeks who programmed the mail utility use. (Doing so doesn't really take much of an effort on your part.) The mail utility uses *switches* to identify the next value on the command line. (See the section "Passing an Argument to an E-mail Program," earlier in the chapter, for a quick reference or refer to Chapter 20 for more details.)

You, too, can use switches in your program to identify its parameters. Switches are a handy way to enable the person using your e-mail program to place arguments on the command line without regard to the order the arguments are to appear there.

You just make up the symbols that you use for switches. You simply use -s for subject, -f for the name of the file that contains the e-mail message, and -d for the destination address. Use the hyphen to differentiate the switch from other arguments on the command line. Linux doesn't care whether you decide to use the hyphen or leave it off.

You can use any characters for the switch symbol, although using characters that give a clue to the argument that the switch refers to makes sense. The s, for example, stands for *subject,* the f for *filename,* and the d for *destination address.*

Next, use the if statement to compare the number of ($#) arguments from the command line with a number that you expect. The number of arguments includes the switch symbol.

In the previous example, you reference two arguments if you want to use the default values. You use four arguments for the same amount of information if you're using switches. The first argument is the switch symbol; the second argument is the information that relates to the first argument; and the third argument is the switch symbol that relates to the fourth argument, which is the information.

After the if statement identifies the current number of arguments, you use a series of if statements to determine which switch symbol the program's using (see Chapter 7).

After the program identifies the switch symbol, you can tell the program to assign the value of the next argument to a variable by using the declare command (see Chapter 4). The name of the variable indicates the type of information that the variable contains.

I call one variable subject because I tell the program to assign the subject argument to the variable. The another variable I call file, and I have the program assign the file argument to it. And the third variable I call destination, which I assign the destination argument. The program then uses variables to provide the mail utility with the information it needs to send an e-mail.

The following example is an abbreviated version of my modified e-mail program. I limit this program to using the default values because I don't have sufficient room here to list the complete program. You can easily modify this program to include the destination argument by including if statements for all three arguments.

```
#!/bin/bash
if [ "$#" -eq 4 ]
    then
        if [ "$1" -eq "-s" ]
            then
               declare subject="$2"
        fi
        if [ "$3" -eq "-f" ]
            then
                declare file="$4"
        fi
        if [ "$1" -eq "-f" ]
            then
                declare file="$2"
        fi
        if [ "$3" -eq "-s" ]
            then
               declare subject="$4"
        fi
        mail -s $subject bob@mycomputer mary@mycomputer < $file
else
        echo "You did not enter the correct number of arguments."
fi
```

The following steps describe what's happening with this program.

1. The program tells Linux to run the bash shell (#!/bin/bash) before checking to see whether four arguments pass to the program from the command line.

2. If four arguments pass, the program uses an if statement to determine whether the first argument is -s. If so, the program creates the variable subject and assigns the second argument ($2) to the variable.

   Remember that the first argument is a switch symbol that identifies the type of information that the second argument contains.

3. The program uses an if statement to determine whether the third argument is -f. If so, it creates the file variable and assigns the fourth command-line argument ($4) to the variable. The third argument is also a switch symbol telling the program the type of information that the fourth argument contains.

4. The program determines whether the first argument is -f. If so, it declares the file variable and assigns the value of the second argument.

5. The program determines whether the third argument is -s. If so, the program declares the subject variable and assigns the value of third argument.

6. The program then calls the mail utility by using the variables $subject and $file. Linux substitutes the subject passing to the program for the $subject variable and the name of the file that contains the e-mail message for the $file variable before executing the mail utility.

You use the else statement in your program if four arguments don't pass to the program. Below the else statement is the error message that appears on-screen if the person fails to enter the minimum number of arguments necessary to run the program.

The program still isn't foolproof, because you assume that, if four arguments pass, they're the correct arguments. Nothing's stopping someone from using the -s switch, for example, and then entering the filename as the next argument. You must include many additional lines of instructions in your program to trap all the possible errors that can occur as the program runs.

Looping through addresses

A clever way to send the same e-mail to a list of friends is to call the mail utility for each name on your mailing list. The easiest way to do so is to use the for in loop in your program. See Chapter 11 for additional information. I also put it to work in this section to send e-mail to my friends.

You place e-mail addresses in the for in loop as a wordlist. Each time the for in loop executes, the for in loop takes the next e-mail address for the wordlist and assigns the e-mail address to the for in loop variable.

Linux uses the for in loop variable in place of the address in the mail utility. Each time the program calls the mail utility, the program replaces the for in loop variable with the contents of the variable, which is the e-mail address.

Here's how an e-mail program looks after inserting the for in loop into the program:

```
#!/bin/bash
for friends in  bob@mycomputer mary@mycomputer tom@mycomputer
   do
        mail -s $1 $friends < $2
done
```

The following steps describe what's happening in this program:

1. First the bash shell starts (#!/bin/bash).

2. Linux assigns the first e-mail address on the wordlist to the variable friend. The first e-mail address is bob@mycomputer.

3. Linux substitutes values for the three variables that the `mail` utility uses. The $1 variable is the first argument that passes from the command line as you call the program. This argument contains the subject line of the e-mail. `$friends` is the `for in` variable that contains `bob@mycomputer`. The $2 variable is the second argument that passes from the command line, which contains the name of the file that contains the e-mail message.

I removed the switches from this program to make it easier for you to read. Nothing's preventing you from leaving the switches in your program if you use the `for in` loop.

4. Linux then calls the `mail` utility, which sends the e-mail.

5. Linux reads the `done` command, which tells it to go to the top of the `for in` loop and read the next e-mail address on the wordlist. This address is `mary@mycomputer`. If it finds no more e-mail addresses, Linux executes the instructions following the `done` command. The program contains no more instructions, so Linux ends the program.

Test your programming knowledge

1. Why do you create your own switches for your program?

a. So that you can display arguments on-screen.

b. So that you can identify information passing as arguments to your program.

c. So that you can turn on and off switches by using your program.

d. Because you fancy becoming an electrician.

2. What's a wordlist?

a. The technical term that you use to describe switches.

b. The technical name for instructions written in your program.

c. A new type of word puzzle.

d. A list of values that you assign to the `for in` variable.

Answers: 1) b. See "Using switches to identify arguments." *2) d. See* "Looping through addresses."

Part IX

The Part of Tens

The 5th Wave   By Rich Tennant

After spending hours trying to get the system up and running, Carl discovers that everything had been plugged into a "Clapper" light socket when he tries to kill a mosquito.

In this part . . .

In this part, I get to tell you all sort of things that just don't come up in the regular chapters. Here you can find out about the most useful Linux utilities (and I know you're just waiting for the chance). You can also stumble across sources for more Linux programming information. And to top everything off, you even get a whole *potpourri* of topics that I can't fit elsewhere in the book.

Chapter 22

Ten of the Most Useful Linux Utilities

*O*ne of the biggest challenges that you face in building a Linux program is assembling a bunch of utility programs that you or someone else has written. The whole philosophy of Linux, in fact, revolves around creating small utility programs, each program performing one task very well.

Programmers distribute hundreds of utility programs for the Linux operating system, and even more are available on the Internet. This book isn't big enough to discuss all the utilities out there, but I want to show you my top-ten list of useful Linux utilities. (My list may, of course, vary from David Letterman's list.)

Accessing the Details

I present only the basic information for using each utility — just enough to whet your appetite. You can use the `man` pages in the online documentation (available on most Linux computers) to find out the details on how to use each of these utility programs.

To read everything that you can about the `troff` utility (which I discuss in the following section), for example, type the following command:

```
man troff
```

After you press Enter, Linux displays the manual pages that discuss the `troff` utility in detail.

You enter on the command line (at the Linux prompt) all the commands that I mention in this chapter. So if you're using the `bash` shell, your command looks as follows:

```
$ man troff
```

Printing Fancy Stuff: troff

Most of the printing that you do in Linux is of the plain-Jane type. Whichever fonts and type sizes are available on your printer are the ones that you use for your document. Linux can also do all that fancy stuff that you see in Windows and Mac programs, such as designing page layouts and using fancy type.

If you have a printer that offers these features, Linux can send instructions to your printer to make your documents look fancy. The trick is to use the `troff` utility. It interprets special codes into commands that tell the printer to use those fancy features.

If you want `Hello, world.` to appear in 12-point type in your document, for example, you type the following line in your document file. (A *document file* is a file on your computer's disk that contains the text that you want to print in your document. You can create this file by using a text editor such as `vi` or from one of your own programs.)

```
.ps 12
Hello, world.
```

The `.ps 12` special code tells the `troff` utility that, from this point on, you want to use 12-point size in your document. The `troff` utility then sends to the printer a printer code for 12-point size. If you want to change to another point size, you need to enter a different code into your document.

You use the troff utility to send a greeting to the printer, as follows:

```
troff greeting
```

And then you change the font to Roman, as in the following example:

```
.ps 12
.ft roman
Hello, world.
```

This example tells the troff utility that you want to use 12-point size (.ps 12) in the Roman font type (.ft roman). These settings remain in effect until you change the values by using the format commands .ps and .ft.

Keep in mind that using these codes in your documents involves one major drawback: Only the troff utility reads them. Don't forget that you use the lp utility, too, to print your document (refer to Chapter 17). The lp utility, however, prints all the characters that you enter into the document. The lp utility doesn't recognize, for example, that .ps12 is a special code that it's not to print because you're using the code to give the troff utility an instruction.

Checking Your Spelling: spell

Few people pose a threat to the national spelling-bee champion's crown, and the typical error-filled business document proves my point. A *misspelling* is where the writer doesn't know the correct spelling of the word. In comparison, a *typographical error* (typo) is where the writer knows the correct spelling of the word but inadvertently presses the wrong key on the keyboard while typing. Most people can come up with a host of excuses for such errors, as the following list attests:

- ✔ "My secretary is a poor proofreader." (Do you even have a secretary?)

- ✔ "I was in a rush and didn't catch that mistake." (You read the document ten times.)

- ✔ "He's never going to notice that it's misspelled." (Oh, how you wish that this one were true!)

- ✔ "She knows what I mean." (She also knows that you *don't* know — how to spell, that is.)

Now you have no excuse for misspellings or typos in the documents you create in Linux unless you're just too lazy to use spell. This simple spell-checker utility reads your documents and then displays the words that it can't find in its dictionary file.

Suppose that you type the following text in a document and then save the document in a file that you name `letter`:

```
Dear Mary,

We hab a goo time Saturday. Let's do it again soon.
```

Use the following command to have `spell` take a look at the file:

```
spell letter
```

The following lines then appear on-screen:

```
hab
goo
```

Using the `spell` utility has a few drawbacks, however, as I describe in the following list:

- The `spell` utility catches any word that it doesn't find in its dictionary file, but the word may not necessarily be a misspelling. The `spell` utility really compares the words in your document against those that the programmer entered into the `spell` utility's dictionary. In an address where the town is Ridgefield Park, for example, the `spell` utility reports that Ridgefield is an incorrect spelling. In fact, Ridgefield is correct but just doesn't appear in the `spell` utility's dictionary.

  The `spell` utility lists misspelled words — but because it doesn't show you where they appear in the document, you must find them yourself.

Sorting Stuff in Your Files: sort

Your programs can produce a list of names, but someone who uses your program may want you to sort the list. You can spend many evenings researching ways to write a program to sort the list, or you can simply use the `sort` utility.

Suppose that you place some names in a file that you call `names`. You can type the following line to sort the list:

```
sort names
```

The `sort` utility rearranges a list in ascending order (where the As come before the Bs and the 1s come before the 2s) and places a lowercase letter ahead of its equivalent uppercase letter. You also can change the utility to sort in descending order (where the Bs come before the As and the 2s come before the 1s) by using the -r option, as follows:

```
sort -r names
```

To set the sort utility to ignore the case distinction, use the -f option:

```
sort -f names
```

Another sort option (-n) tells the sort utility to order the file in numerical order. Still another sort option (-m) tells the sort utility to order by month. The -m sort option places January before February, February before March, and so on.

One drawback as you're using the sort utility is that the utility doesn't save the new, sorted list in the same file that contains the original, unsorted list. After you resort the names file, the results appear on-screen unless you use the redirection operator (>) to save the information to another file. (For a description of redirection operators, see Chapter 5.) If you want to save the results to a file, you must use the redirection operator.

What if you want to place the ordered information in the same file? The following example shows you how to do so:

```
sort -f names > newnames
mv newnames > names
```

The sort utility reorders the names file (ignoring the case distinction) and saves the sorted information in the newnames file. The last line renames the newnames file to the old file, names, by using the move (mv) command.

Checking Differences Between Files: diff

After you begin programming in Linux, you inevitably come across the problem of having two files with practically the same name that contain your program. You may have this problem if you save a backup copy of your work, modify one copy, and then forget which copy you modified. How do you find the differences between the files?

You can compare each file line by line yourself, or you can have the diff utility do it for you. If you type the following line on the command line, you tell the diff utility to read file1 and file2, compare the two files, and indicate the different lines in each file:

```
diff file1 file2
```

Say that you execute the diff utility from the command line. The following example shows what the diff utility may report back to you on-screen:

```
<programming is fun.
>I hate computers.
```

Lines that begin with the less-than sign (<) are lines that diff finds only in file1; lines that begin with the greater-than sign (>) are lines diff finds only in file2. Lines in either file that the diff utility doesn't display are lines that it finds in both files. (For more information about the < and > redirection operators, see Chapter 5.)

Comparing Files: cmp

At some point, you need to determine whether two files are the same. The best way to answer that question is by having the cmp utility compare the files. The cmp utility is similar to the diff utility except that the cmp utility displays which *character* on a line is different in the files. The diff utility simply shows you the actual *lines* that are different in each file.

The cmp utility matches both files line by line and issues a report that specifies where any differences occur. If you have two files that seem to refer to the same program, such as firstprogram and programone, you can type the following line to compare the files:

```
cmp firstprogram programone
```

The result may look something like the following example:

```
firstprogram programone differ: char 34, line 3
```

This line indicates that character 34 on line 3 of programone is different from character 34 on line 3 in firstprogram.

Changing Characters in a Large File: sed

If you try to modify an extremely large file, you may experience a serious problem — your computer runs out of memory in which to store the file (known as a *buffer*). Your computer has no memory (RAM) to store the text that the file contains.

Some text editors load a file into a buffer before you can begin editing the text in the file. If a file is too large for the buffer, you can't use the editor to change the text. This limitation isn't a problem for the sed utility. This text editor doesn't try to load the entire file into memory — it reads one line at a time from your file, makes changes to the line, and sends it back to the file on your hard disk.

Suppose that you want to remove all lines in the names file that don't contain the word *Bob*. (I wonder what Bob's friends did to deserve that treatment.) The sed utility normally displays the changed text on-screen. Because you want to store the changed information in the same file, however, sed by itself can't help you. So you must use the redirection operator (>) to redirect the output of sed to a file that you call names.tmp. After the changes are safely in this file, you can use the mv command to change the name of the names.tmp file to names. In doing so, you replace the old names file with the changed version of the file. The following example shows you how the code for this procedure looks:

```
sed '/Bob/d' names > names.tmp
mv names.tmp names
```

The target of your search is any character that you place between the slash marks (/). The d is the sed command for deleting a line.

Rather than delete lines that contains the word *Bob*, you can replace Bob with Mike by using the following code:

```
sed 's/Bob/Mike/' names > names.tmp
mv names.tmp names
```

The s is the sed command for substituting characters. This command replaces the characters that you type between the first two slash marks with the characters that you type between the second and third slash marks.

To remove just the word Mike, use the following code:

```
sed 's/Mike//' names > names.tmp
mv names.tmp names
```

This line is similar to the that of the preceding example, except that you don't type a value between the second and third slash marks. The reason is that you're telling the sed utility to substitute "nothing" for the name Mike.

Breaking a Large File: split

A large file can prove troublesome to work with in Linux because you sometimes can't load the complete file into memory. So why not break down the file into a bunch of other files that you can easily store into your computer's memory?

You can manually break down a file by copying and deleting the text in the file, but this process can become cumbersome. A better method is to make the split utility do the job for you. By default, split automatically divides your file into several 1,000-line files. It names the new files xaa, xab, and so on. `xaa` is the name the `split` utility gives to files it creates. Files begin with the letter x, which is followed by characters that represent the order of the files. For example, `xaa` is the first file and `xab` is the second.

Suppose that you have a file by the name of `phonebook` that contains 2,500 entries. (Boy, do *you* have a truckload of friends!) To break this file into several files, you type the following line:

```
split phonebook
```

The `split` utility then creates three files. The first two files contain 1,000 entries apiece. The third file holds only 500 entries (the entries that remain). The following list shows the filenames that the `split` utility creates from this file:

```
xaa
xab
xac
```

You can specify the maximum number of lines that each file contains by using the `-n` option, as follows:

```
split -n filename
```

Substitute the number of lines that you want for n. In the following example, I use the `split` utility to divide the `phonebook` file into smaller files. I want each of these smaller files to contain no more than 100 lines. (And if each line represents one entry in the telephone book, I'm telling the `split` utility to split the `phonebook` into files of 100 entries each.)

```
split -100 phonebook
```

Finding Information in a File: grep

What can you do if you want to know which file in the current directory contains the name *Bob*? You can use commands in a text editor to help find Bob — or you can use the `grep` utility. In the case of a text editor, you must first run the text editor and load the file before you can begin searching for Bob. If you use the `grep` utility, however, you specify the word that you want to search for as you execute this utility. The `grep` utility searches a file for a set of characters and displays on-screen all the lines that contain those characters.

If you want to find all the lines that contain `Bob` in the `namefile`, for example, you type the following line at the command prompt:

```
grep Bob namefile
```

Now suppose that you want to find in your files the name of a specific Bob — Bob Smith. If your search criterion contains a space, you must place quotation marks around the entire phrase, as in the following example:

```
grep "Bob Smith" namefile
```

Sometimes you don't know which file contains the name Bob. You know that it's one of the hundreds of files in the current directory, but you don't know which one. (That's what I call organization!) Type the following line:

```
grep Bob *
```

The asterisk (*) replaces the name of the file to search. The asterisk, which is a *wildcard,* tells the grep utility to search all the files in the current directory. (A wildcard is a symbol that tells Linux to search through any filename that it finds on the hard disk.)

Sending Files Electronically: ftp

You can ship your files electronically to any Internet location in the world by using the ftp utility. This utility enables you to link your computer to a remote computer and then send or receive one or more files. To begin, type the following line:

```
ftp othercomputer
```

In this example, the ftp utility tries to connect your computer to the computer by the name of othercomputer. If the ftp utility is successful, Linux prompts you to enter your login ID and password.

If the othercomputer accepts your login ID and password, you see the ftp command prompt, which looks as follows:

```
ftp>
```

You can then enter ftp commands that instruct the ftp utility to perform a task.

In this case, suppose that you want to transfer the datebook file from the othercomputer to your computer. Just type the following line:

```
ftp> get datebook
```

The ftp utility handles the file transfer for you. What happens, however, if you want to ship the same file to the other computer? The ftp utility is willing to help if you type the following line:

```
ftp> put datebook
```

As long as the datebook file resides in the current directory, the ftp utility does the rest of the work for you by copying the file to the other computer. The original copy remains on your computer.

After you finish transferring files, you give the ftp utility the following instruction to say good-bye to the other computer:

```
ftp> bye
```

The ftp utility then closes the transmission channel with the other computer and returns the Linux prompt to your screen.

Don't forget that you can find out more about the ftp utility (or any other utility, for that matter), by using the man utility that I explain at the beginning of the chapter.

Removing Fields from a Database: cut

A database file is similar to a regular file except that it organizes the information into columns and rows. (A column is also known as a *field*, and a row is known as a *record*.) You can remove fields from a database file by using the cut utility. (For more information about databases, refer to Chapter 16.)

Suppose that you have a database file by the name phonelist that contains the following information:

```
Bob Smith      555-1212
Mary Jones     555-5555
Tom Adams      555-7777
```

To remove the names to a file that you call names, you type the following line:

```
cut -f1,2 phonelist > names
```

The -f option tells the cut utility that you want to cut columns 1 and 2 from the phonelist file. The redirection operator (>) takes the columns that you cut from the phonelist file and places them in the names file. (To find out about the redirection operators, see Chapter 5.)

Chapter 23

Ten Sources of More Linux Programming Information

*B*ecause you're a beginner in the area of Linux programming, much more Linux is out there for you to discover than I can cover in this book. Even professional programmers must hit the books, take courses, and go to conferences to keep up with the latest changes in technology — and you can expect to do the same. In this chapter, I suggest a few ways that you can find out more about Linux programming.

Go Back to School at Your Local College

One of the better places to pick up some tricks and tips of the Linux trade is close to home, at your local college.

You don't need to go to MIT to find out about Linux programming, and you certainly don't need to become a computer nerd. As I mention frequently in this book, anyone with a little common sense and a great deal of patience can teach himself to program a computer.

Sometimes, however, you need more help in locating this type of information than a book can provide. You need someone to look over your shoulder until you get on the right track — and that person (the instructor) is usually at your local college.

Many four-year universities and community colleges offer courses in Linux programming. Give your local college a call to find out when the next course is starting. Then make sure that you find out how to register for the course.

You don't need to go for the whole college degree. These institutions love to have students who just want to brush up on their skills by taking a course or two. (They hope that you get hooked and come back for more.)

Attend a Conference

A good source for the latest information about Linux and Linux programming is a computer conference. Computer professionals, vendors, and nerd wannabes gather at these meetings to exchange ideas. Linux is such a hot topic these days that Linux and Linux programming are usually discussion topics at conferences that don't even have Linux in their names.

Trade publications such as *PC Week* and *InfoWorld* widely advertise popular conferences, such as the Linux World Expo hosted by IDG. Keep your eyes open for these ads, which usually list scheduled speakers and topics. Some presentations cover topics that may prove of interest to you (and others that you can live without!).

Plan to pay for this experience. Conferences usually take place in major cities (and in Hawaii). You must pay for airfare, accommodations, and a fee to get into the conference. You may also need to pay for each presentation that you attend.

Visit Yahoo!

Yahoo! (at www.yahoo.com) covers various aspects of Linux and Linux programming so make sure that you stop by the site whenever you can to read the latest about Linux. Yahoo! also offers links to many sites that provide assistance to Linux programmers such as yourself.

You can find the Linux section of Yahoo! by typing www.yahoo.com in your browser and then, at Yahoo!'s site, entering the search word **linux**. You can also type http://fullcoverage.yahoo.com/Full_Coverage/Tech/Linux/ into your Web browser's Address text box if you want to go directly to the Linux Web pages.

Find a Newsgroup on the Internet

Usenet news is the part of the Internet that you can tap for sources of information from around the world. Each of the newsgroups that comprise this service focuses on a particular topic. (If you're still unsure of this Internet stuff, consider a book such as *The Internet For Dummies*, by John Levine and Carol Baroudi, available from IDG Books Worldwide, Inc.)

Thousands of newsgroups are available. You can use your Internet browser to skim through the available newsgroups and then choose the ones to which you want to subscribe (for free!).

Every time that you visit Usenet news, your browser displays your list of newsgroups. After you choose one in which you want to participate, your browser shows you all the postings for that group.

To find newsgroups, you use keywords with your browser's built-in search feature to quickly skim the list for newsgroups in which you may have an interest. If you enter the keyword **Linux**, for example, a large list of newsgroups that contain information about Linux appears on-screen.

After you enter a newsgroup, a list of subjects appears that briefly describes the related messages people have posted. (The messages can contain anything from meaningful information to just plain garbage.) Skim the subject list to see whether any of them seem interesting. If you find one, open the message and see what that person had to say.

You can post (send) your own message to a newsgroup by using your Internet browser. You can comment on other messages, post questions, or answer questions that other people post.

You may need to wait a while for the newsgroup to post your messages. Be patient. After they appear, keep watching the subject listings for the newsgroup to see whether anyone responds to your posting.

A word of caution: Just because someone posts something doesn't necessarily mean that it's true. Even someone with good intentions can post incorrect information.

Review Online Documentation

If you have questions about Linux programming or any of the Linux utilities, you want answers to your questions quickly and accurately. Where can you find a response, however, especially if you're sitting in front of your computer at 2 a.m.?

Ask your computer! One of the best features of Linux is its `man` utility, which displays the *man*ual pages for the operating system. If you're unsure about how to use the `sort` utility, for example, just type the following at the Linux command prompt:

```
man sort
```

Your computer then displays the manual for the `sort` utility. Although the manual isn't as well written as this book (ahem), it does provide a complete discussion of topics, including how to implement all the options. What more can you ask for (except for someone else to do the programming!)?

Read Other Books about Linux

You want to expand your knowledge of Linux in two directions: programming and the operating system. This book covers the programming aspect of your Linux education. But Linux also runs many computers, the same way that Windows does. To find out more about the Linux operating system, pick up a copy of *Linux For Dummies*, by John R. Levine and Margy Levine Young (published by IDG Books Worldwide, Inc.).

Subscribe to Computing Magazines

Hit the newsstands and search the racks for computer magazines. A vast array of magazines is available for just about every imaginable aspect of computing.

Don't limit yourself to newsstands — bookstores and major computer stores also offer a wide selection of computer magazines. Keep your eyes open for articles and columns about Linux and Linux programming. Those magazines are the ones that you want to subscribe to.

Also check out trade magazines, such as *Linux World*, *PC Week*, and *InfoWorld*. They talk about the latest developments in the computer industry and the world of technology and are must-reads for serious programmers.

Join or Create a Linux Programming Club

You're probably not the only person in your town or city with an interest in computer programming. Computer clubs are a common gathering place for like-minded folks.

Computer clubs are great places to exchange ideas about all sorts of aspects of computers, including Linux programming.

Ask around to find your local computer club. Start with the computer teachers in your local school district and the manager of your local computer store. They usually know whether a club exists. If you can't find a local club, ask the teacher or manager to help you organize one.

Ask for Technical Help at Your Local College Computer Lab

If you end up in a bind, stop by the computer lab at your local college or university. All sorts of nerds hang out there who're usually more than happy to give you an opinion about how to solve your problem.

Try to build a friendship with a few of these folks. Before long, you become part of the family.

Computer labs are usually open to members of the general student body. Teaching assistants or advanced computer science majors looking to make a few extra dollars oversee the labs. Taking a course or two to become an official student also helps gain access to these labs.

Send E-Mail to Authors of Articles about Linux Programming

One way to quiz the experts is to send an e-mail message to them. Most authors of computer articles and books now include their e-mail address as part of their bylines. If you have a question about an article or book topic, ask your question in an e-mail message.

Authors are usually happy to hear from their readers and do their best to answer questions. Keep in mind, however, that they don't want to become your tutor or your pen pal. Because authors may also be busy with other projects, your request can have a low priority with them.

Chapter 24

Ten Linux Programming Topics That Didn't Fit Anywhere Else

*N*ow that you're at the end of this book (even if you haven't read it yet and just skipped back here to see the possibilities), you're probably wondering whether the information in this book includes everything that you need to know about Linux and Linux programming.

No, this book is just the beginning. This chapter contains some tidbits that you may find useful and interesting as you continue your quest to build that killer Linux program (the one that makes you more money than Bill Gates has).

Creating Programs That Run in the Background

You can make your Linux program one of those sneaky, stealth applications that quietly goes about doing its thing inside the computer while other programs are running. This type of program, known as a *daemon (de-mon)*, lives inside your computer somewhere and can do mischievous things. (Not really — you wouldn't think of writing a program that may destroy your own computer.)

You frequently use a daemon program to process information that doesn't require the use of the keyboard or the screen. An example is a payroll program that crunches numbers in a database and then prints checks. No one must do anything other than start the program as a daemon by using the following command:

```
payroll &
```

You insert an ampersand (&) after the name of the program to tell your computer to run the program in the background. In other words, you run it as a daemon (you little devil).

One problem with a daemon is that it stops running if you log off the computer. You can keep it running after you're long gone by using the nohup command, following it with the name of the program, as in the following example:

```
nohup payroll
```

Stopping Your Program in an Emergency

You must keep ready to jump into action if your program goes wild. Every programmer experiences this situation while building a new program. During a test, the program keeps running and running (and sort of resembles the Energizer bunny).

A number of problems can cause this situation — an endless loop, for example, waits for a response that never comes (see Chapter 12). Before you can find out what went wrong, however, you must stop the program.

Don't turn off a computer that's running Linux to stop a program. Other things may be happening in the background that you must not interrupt that way. (If you do, your system file can get out of sync and someone — usually a system administrator — must reset it before you can use your computer again.) Instead, you tell the computer to stop your program by using the kill command.

If you use the kill command, you must also identify the program that you want to stop. *You* know what name you gave the program, but you must also find out how your computer identifies it.

You do so by running the jobs command, as follows:

```
jobs
```

Running this command displays a list of all your active programs, as shown in the following example:

```
[1] + Running payroll
[2] + Running vi
```

The jobs command shows you the status of your programs. In this example, two of your programs are running: payroll and vi. You use the numbers at the beginning of each line to identify each program. To stop a program from running, you use the appropriate number with the kill command, as follows:

```
kill %1
```

This example tells the computer to kill program 1. (Notice the percent sign before the job number. This tells the kill utility that the value to the right of the percent sign is the job number.) After Linux carries out your order, the kill command reports back to you that it stopped the program so that you can begin to investigate the cause of the problem, as shown in the following example:

```
[1] + Terminated payroll
```

Sharing Shell Variables

Whenever you call a subprogram from your program, a common problem that you may experience is that a variable you create in your program isn't available to the subprogram. Suppose, for example, that your program creates the following string variable:

```
declare name="Bob Smith"
```

You can call the subprogram that you name payroll from your program, as follows:

```
declare name="Bob Smith"
payroll
```

The payroll program doesn't know that the variable name exists. The reason is that your computer starts another shell known as a *subshell*.

Here's how this shell works. (And, no, it's not under the middle one.) As you log on to your computer, your computer starts a shell. A *shell* is the program that translates your commands to your computer. For more information about shells, refer to Chapter 3.

Your computer creates another copy of the shell for each program that you run. Guess what happens as your program runs a subprogram: Another shell starts. After your program or subprogram finishes running, its shell closes.

Variables that you create in each shell are *local,* which means that only that shell can use the variables. (For more information about local variables, refer to Chapter 4). You can make shell variables available to other shells, however, by changing the variable to an environment variable, as in the following example:

```
export name="Bob Smith"
payroll
```

In this example, the payroll program can access the name variable. Either the program or the subprogram can change the value of name. The change, however, affects the other copy of the name variable. Both the program and the payroll program, for example, can access the name variable with the value Bob Smith because the program makes the name variable an environment variable (see Chapter 4).

The payroll program can assign Joan Jones to the name variable that affects the name variable in the program — that is, the value of the name variable in the program changes to Joan Jones.

The next time that your subprogram isn't working correctly, double-check to see whether it's using a variable that it can't access.

Keeping Other People's Hands off Your Code

A major weakness in a Linux shell program is that your code is available to prying eyes and that some folks just like to change other people's code. Anyone who has a copy of your Linux shell program can look at your code by using vi or any other text editor, because your Linux shell program is text — instructions that you write in English. Linux translates it into machine language as your program reads each instruction in itself.

This problem doesn't exist in most programs that you write in other programming languages. The program starts out as text, just as your Linux shell program does, but then a program known as a *compiler* translates the program into machine language. You store this compiler in a file that you give to anyone who wants to run the program. You don't, therefore, give out a copy of the code that anyone other than real nerds can see.

Although you can't convert your shell program into machine language, you can make Linux prevent unauthorized persons from seeing the code of your program by using the chmod command. You use the chmod command to give everyone else permission only to execute your program. They can't read nor write to your program file. The following example shows how you use this command:

```
chmod o+x payroll
```

This line tells Linux that anyone can execute your payroll program, but they can't look at your program file and they can't write to your program file. (Refer to Chapter 1 for a few more details — along with alternative commands — for the chmod utility.)

If you really want to lay down the law, you can also limit access to just the owner of the program by using the following commands, which remove read and write privileges to everyone except the program's owner. (The g stands for group rights and x makes the program executable):

```
chmod g+x payroll
chmod o-rw payroll
chmod g-rw payroll
```

Only a member of your group can now execute your program. (The person in charge of your computer, known as the *system administrator*, determines who's in your group.)

Copying Files between Windows and Linux

Your Linux program may need to use a bunch of information that's on your personal computer running Windows. Say, for example, that you have a list of your friends that you save in a text-file format on your Windows PC. (A *text file* is a file that you create by using an editor, such as WordPad, or a word processor that doesn't use any special formatting characters in the file. The file consists of just text. And that's where the name comes from.)

Now the problem is that you want to save the file to a floppy disk and then copy the file onto your computer that's running Linux. This process sounds simple, and you've probably done it thousands of times from one Windows PC to another. But if you try simply copying the file to Linux, it doesn't work! I don't go into the details here, but trust me: It just doesn't work because the formats aren't compatible.

You can easily overcome this problem: Just use the mcopy command to handle all the necessary translations (and indicate a source drive, as I do here with drive A), as follows:

```
mcopy a:windata unixdata
```

This line tells your computer to copy to Linux the `windata` file that's in Windows format on your floppy disk. During the copying process, your computer performs the translation and renames the file in Windows to `unixdata`.

The following line shows you how to copy a file from Linux to your Windows floppy disk (again indicating a drive, and in this case, I'm indicating the A drive):

```
mcopy unixdata a:windata
```

Your computer copies the `unixdata` file to the Windows floppy disk and, in the process, translates and renames the file.

Finding Lost Files

After you reach your stride in creating Linux programs, you eventually end up knee-deep in files. They're everywhere on your hard disk: Some you can find immediately, but others lie buried in subdirectories.

Finding the file that you want can prove a huge chore, but you can simplify this task by using the `find` command to do all the work for you. Suppose that you want to find the `payroll` program (the one you haven't touched in more than a year). As long as you can remember the name of the program, you can use the `find` command to search your hard disk, as follows:

```
find ~ -name "payroll" -print
```

The tilde (~) tells the computer to begin the search in your home directory. The `find` command begins looking in that directory and continues through all the subdirectories in your home directory. The `-name` option tells the computer that the next word is the name of the program, which is `payroll`. Finally, the `-print` option tells the computer to display the location on-screen.

Creating Your Own Place on the Disk

After you find out how to create programs in Linux, you start with just one program file. Programs, however, seem to grow on their own. First, you add a subprogram and then another. Because a program requires information, you may create a database file. You also eventually create different versions of your program as you make changes to it.

Keeping track of all the files necessary to run your programs is vitally important. How do programmers keep things organized? They create subdirectories in their home directory. Give each of the programs that you create its own subdirectory on your hard disk to isolate it from other programs you're building.

To create a subdirectory, use the `mkdir` command, as follows:

```
mkdir payroll_proj
```

This line tells your computer to set aside a section of your disk and call it `payroll_proj`. In this area, you put all the files that relate to your payroll project.

You can access this new area of your hard disk by using the `cd` command. This command tells your computer to change to that directory, as in the following example:

```
cd payroll_proj
```

After the new directory appears on-screen, you can create other subdirectories. Each subdirectory houses a different type of file. The following example shows how a programmer typically organizes files for a program:

```
mkdir payroll_proj
mkdir payroll_proj/release_version
mkdir payroll_proj/version1
mkdir payroll_proj/data
mkdir payroll_proj/documents
```

As you start a new programming project, use the `mkdir` command to create a project directory as a branch of your home directory (what's happening in the first line of this example). The new programming project is `payroll`, so I call the project directory `payroll_proj` to clearly identify the contents of the directory.

Beneath the `payroll_proj` directory lie additional subdirectories that contain specific information about the project. I create four such subdirectories as branches of the `payroll_proj` directory. One of these subdirectories is to contain the release version of the program. I call this subdirectory `release_version`. After I finish writing and testing my payroll program, I place the program in this directory so that I always have a copy of the program ready for anyone who asks for it.

The *release version* of the program is also known as the *current version* of the program. Every time that you change the instructions in the program, you create a new version of the program. Windows, for example, comes in versions 3.1, NT 4.0, and so on. These are version numbers, and each one signifies that changes were made to the previous version of the program. To help me keep track of versions of my own program, I create a subdirectory for each version and then place the appropriate version of the program in that subdirectory. In this example, I have only one version of my program, so I need to create only one subdirectory, which I name `version1`.

Two other subdirectories that programmers commonly create for new programming projects are those for data and documentation. *Data* is the information that the program needs to complete the task. Frequently, you keep this information in a file on your hard disk — and store it in the data directory. Similarly, you use the documentation subdirectory to store files that contain instructions for using the program and notes about the design of the program, such as flow charts.

This setup is just the typical subdirectory layout that I use as I begin a new programming project. You need to keep your program files organized, and this example gives you a head start in creating your own subdirectory layout for your programming projects.

Changing the Characters in a File

This section presents a trick that can save you a great deal of programming time. If you ever need to perform a global search and replace for information in a file, you can do so by using the `tr` command. This command changes the information efficiently.

If you want to change all the lowercase letters in a data file to uppercase, for example, type the following command:

```
tr "[a-z]" "[A-Z]" < dataInput > dataOutput
```

The first argument, `"[a-z]"`, is the information that your computer searches for.

The information that you want to replace the first argument in the file is shown in the second argument, `"[A-Z]"`.

The third argument, `dataInput`, is the file that you want to search.

The computer places the modified information in the `dataOutput` file, which is the last argument.

Check out the `man` pages (manual pages) about the `tr` command to discover more neat tricks, by using the following command:

```
man tr
```

Maintaining Your Code

To store your programs and their related files safely and professionally, save them in an *archive file*. You manage an archive file by using the `ar` command, which enables you to place several files under one name. It's like having a file drawer that contains all your programs and files. You can refer to the label on the file drawer if you need to look at any of the files that you store in the drawer. In this case, the file drawer is really an archive file with its own name. Inside the archive file are all your other files that relate to your program.

Suppose that you're building the payroll program that I mention in the section, "Stopping Your Program in an Emergency," earlier in this chapter. The program consists of a program file and subprograms, data files, and documentation files.

You can organize these files by creating subdirectories, or you can save them in an archive file by typing the following command:

```
ar q payroll_lib payroll
```

The q command tells the computer to append the file *q*uickly to the library file, while payroll_lib is the name of the library file, and payroll is the file that the command places in the library file.

Whenever you want to use the payroll file, you ask your computer to retrieve it from the library file, as follows:

```
ar x payroll_lib payroll
```

The x command tells the computer to extract the file from the library. After you finish with the file, you return it to the library by using the r command, as follows:

```
ar r payroll_lib payroll
```

Pausing Your Program

You can make your program pause at any time by using the sleep command. This command temporarily stops the execution of your code until a specified number of seconds passes, as in the following example:

```
echo "How do you get 4 elephants into a compact car?"
sleep 10
echo "Two in the front and two in the back."
```

In this example, your computer first asks a question, and then the program tells it to pause for ten seconds. Then the punch line appears on-screen. (That's a sick one.)

Part X
Appendixes

The 5th Wave

By Rich Tennant

Re·al Pro·gram·mers

Real Programmers love to talk "computer-eze" while ordinary citizens are listening.

In this part . . .

Here's some very useful information at your fingertips. This part contains a glossary that helps you
understand terms that Linux and Linux programming use,
info to help you sharpen your skills as a master of the vi
text editor (good luck!), a handy cross-reference that you
can use to convert your bash shell programs to the C
shell, and lots of exercises (with the answers) to challenge
your newly developed bash programming skills.

Appendix A

Glossary

anonymous FTP

Many computer systems enable anyone to log in as anonymous and then transfer files without a formal user name on the computer. After connecting with the remote computer, type **anonymous** in response to the user ID prompt; you then type your e-mail address as your password. The transfer of files is made possible through the use of the file transfer protocol (FTP).

application

A program that does real-world work, such as a payroll program or a word-processing program.

argument

Information that you enter on the command prompt along the name of the program. In the command `rm myfile`, for example, `myfile` is an argument to the program `rm`, which removes the file from your disk. An argument is information that Linux sends to your program after your program begins.

background

Describes a program that runs behind the scenes while other programs are running on your computer. Many programs can run at the same time in Linux.

backslash (\)

What you use in Linux to identify the character to the right of the backslash as a special character. If you see \n, for example, it indicates a new line on-screen. Technically, the backslash tells Linux to ignore the way that you normally handle the next character and to treat it in a special way. (The normal way that Linux handles the n is to display the letter n on-screen.)

backup

An extra electronic copy of your program or data that you keep in a safe place; you can use a backup to restore the program or data in case a problem of some kind erases the information.

bash (which stands for Bourne Again shell)

An enhanced version of the Bourne shell. You can start the bash shell by typing **bash** at a command prompt and pressing Enter. bash is the default shell for many Linux distributions, including Red Hat Linux.

bit

The smallest piece of information that your computer understands — you represent it as a 1 or a 0. You normally throw a bit together with seven other bits to form a byte.

Bourne shell

A shell that enables you to enter commands into Linux. It's the forerunner of the bash shell, and uses the $ symbol as its prompt. You can begin the Bourne shell by typing **sh** at a command prompt and pressing Enter:

Bourne Again shell

See bash.

BSD Unix

The version of Unix that the University of California at Berkeley developed. *BSD* stands for *B*erkeley *S*oftware *D*istribution.

buffer

A place in memory where the computer temporarily stores information until a program needs it. Text editors use buffers to store a copy of your file while you edit it; printers use buffers to store the file that it's printing.

byte

A collection of eight bits that you use to represent information. Eight bits enable 256 different combinations of eight 1s and 0s (256 is 2^8). Many computers use the ASCII code to translate characters on the keyboard to a unique pattern of 1s and 0s.

C shell

A program that enables users to enter commands into Linux. The C shell uses the % as its prompt. You can begin the C shell by typing **csh** at the prompt and pressing Enter.

central processing unit (CPU)

The brains of the computer that performs all the "thinking" for the computer. Some command central processing units are the Pentium, SPARC, and 80486.

command

A word that you type at a shell prompt to direct Linux to do something productive. Commands are names of things that the shell knows how to do. They're also names of programs that you or someone else writes by using a shell script language.

command mode

A mode in a text editor where you enter commands. Pressing Esc while using vi, for example, places the text editor into the command mode.

CPU

See central processing unit.

current directory

See working directory.

current job

The job Linux marks with a plus sign after you enter the job command at the shell prompt. A job is a program or command that's running.

cursor

A character on-screen that indicates the current position on-screen. The actual character that appears on-screen varies with the program that you're using. Typically, a flashing underscore character or box serves as the cursor.

daemon

(Pronounce it "demon.") The daemon is a program that runs in the background without requiring any input from you. Daemons perform housekeeping functions, such as printing files that are waiting in the queue.

data

Information that Linux or your program uses to complete a task. Your password is data to the program that verifies that you have access to the computer.

directory

A collection of files that you identify by a single name on your hard drive.

disk

A round, flat platter where you can electronically store information in much the same way that you can record your voice on an audio tape. A single flat platter resides inside a floppy disk and multiple flat platters reside inside hard disks.

editor

See text editor.

Escape key

The key on your keyboard that reads *Esc* or *Escape*. The function of the Esc depends on the program that's running. In the vi editor, for example, Esc places vi in the command mode.

executable file

A file that Linux can run. Executable files include programs and shell scripts.

external command

A program with the same name as a shell command.

file

A hunk of information that you store under the same name in memory or on your drive.

file system

The organization of files on your hard drive. A file system begins with the root directory and branches to many other directories known as subdirectories. You store files in either the root directory or a subdirectory.

filter

A Linux program that changes the way information in a file appears. The sort program, for example, changes the order in which the information appears. The sort program is a filter.

foreground

A program that's running — you can communicate with the program and the program can communicate with you. Another way to run a program is in the *background* (where you can't communicate with the program).

FTP (file transfer protocol)

A program that enables you to log into a remote computer and transfer files to or from the remote computer. *See* anonymous FTP.

gateway

A connection between two different kinds of computer networks.

home directory

The directory that you're in after you log in to your computer. Your home directory is usually a subdirectory of /home.

input mode

A setting in a text editor that enables you to enter text. In the vi text editor, for example, pressing **i** while in the command mode places you in the insert mode.

I/O (input/output)

Information going into your computer or program or leaving your computer or program.

job

A program that's running in a shell.

keyboard

The device you use to type characters into your computer.

kill

A Linux command that enables you to stop a program that's running. The kill %payroll command, for example, stops the payroll program (and nobody gets paid!).

Korn shell

An improved version of the Bourne shell that uses the $ as the prompt. Type **ksh** the command prompt and press Enter to start the Korn shell:

line editor

A text editor that enables you to edit text one line at a time. The ed program is a line editor.

Linux

A free version of the Unix operating system that a Finnish student named Linus Torvalds developed while he was studying at the University of Helsinki, on the premise that Unix shouldn't be so darned expensive.

log in

The process of identifying yourself to the computer. This process requires you to enter a user ID and a password that Linux validates before you can use the computer.

memory

A short-term storage area inside your computer that holds information temporarily (just while you're working on it). You lose the contents of this storage memory after you turn off your computer. You use your disks (including your hard drive) and CDs for long-term storage.

menu

A list of tasks from which you can choose one for Linux or your program to perform.

Motif

A development library that you use with the C programming language for building graphical user interfaces for applications. Motif pretty much just gives Linux the look of Microsoft's Windows operating system. The Open Software Foundation distributes Motif and bases it on the X Window System.

nerd

You, if you spend too much time working on your computer.

Open Look

A development library that gives Linux the look of Microsoft Windows. It's similar to Motif.

operating system

A program or group of programs that take over your computer's hardware and enable you to give your computer instructions to follow.

option

A symbol that tells a program or command to do something different from what it normally does. An option is sometimes known as a *flag* or *switch*. The command ls, for example, lists files in a directory. You can, however, use an option — in this case -l — to make ls display an expanded list of information. You type **ls -l** at the command prompt and press Enter.

parent directory

A directory that contains subdirectories, or the name for the directory directly above the one you're in. (That is, if you're in folder a/b, a is the parent directory of b).

password

A secret word that only you and your computer knows about (you hope). A combination of your user name and your secret password can gain you access to the computer.

pathname

A list of directories and subdirectories in which Linux should look for programs that you tell Linux to run. Linux starts with the first directory on the pathname and, if the program isn't found, continues to look into all the directories/subdirectories on the pathname until the program is found. If the program still isn't found after looking into all the specified directories/subdirectories, Linux displays a message on the screen telling you that the program can't be located.

permissions

A list of symbols associated with a file or directory that specifies who can access the file or directory. The three kinds of permissions are *read*, *write*, and *execute*. The read and write permissions enable someone to read a file and write to a file. The execute permission enables someone to run a file (for example, a program that you create).

pipe

Redirects the output of a command from the screen to input into another command. The | character symbolizes a pipe. The `cat myfile | sort` command, for example, redirects the display of the contents of `myfile` from the screen as input to the `sort` program.

process

A program that's running in Linux.

prompt

An on-screen character that tells you that Linux is waiting for you to do something. In the `bash` shell, for example, you see the $ prompt.

read-only

A file that a user can read and copy but not write to or change. Read (which means the same thing) is one of the permissions that Linux enables you to specify for a file or directory.

redirection

A way to change the normal flow of information into and out of a program. *See* pipe.

root directory

The top-level directory on your hard drive. All other directories branch out from the root directory.

screen editor

A text editor that fills your entire screen with text of your file. The vi text editor is a screen editor.

shell

A program that enables you to talk to Linux, which in turn talks to your computer hardware.

shell script

A file containing a list of shell commands that you can run like a program.

slash (/)

The character that you use to separate directories and subdirectories in the pathname, such as /payroll/year1996/myvacation.

software

Programs that contain instructions that tell your computer to perform a task.

Solaris

A version of Unix for use on a Sun workstation.

subdirectory

A directory within another directory.

superuser

A user with the power to really mess up the computer — and do a lot of good things, too. A superuser is also known as the *root*.

system administrator

The person responsible for keeping your computer and Linux running.

System V

The version of Unix that AT&T developed and that UNIX System Labs, which is part of Novell, later distributed.

text editor

A program that enables you to create and edit files. One popular Linux text editors is vi (although many programmers hate to use it).

text file

A file that contains ASCII characters and no control characters. (Control characters are symbols that word processors use to make your text fancy, such as font and type size.)

UNIX

A multiuser processing system developed in 1972 at Bell Laboratories.

Unix

An accepted term for generic Unix-compatible operating systems, such as Sun's Solaris and Linux.

UNIX International (UI)

A group of vendors who support System V.

username

The name that you enter as you log into Linux. Linux then compares your username and password with its list of known users to determine whether you can access the computer.

utility

A program that comes with Linux and performs one task very well. The cmp utility, for example, compares two files and tells you where these files differ. Find out about any utility by using the manual pages. If, for example, you want to know more about cmp, type **man cmp** at the command prompt and press Enter:

wildcard

A symbol that takes the place of any character if you use it in a filename or pathname. The two symbols that you use as wildcards in Linux are * and ?.

working directory

The current directory that you're working in. You can use the pwd command to ask Linux to tell you the name of the working directory.

X Window System (or just X)

A program that enables you to break Linux into several windows on-screen. Each window is running a shell and permits you to run different programs in each window.

Appendix B

When the Moon Hits Your Eye Like a Big Piece of vi

. . . .

*T*o create a Linux program, you must type all the instructions necessary for the program to carry out the task that you want into your program file.

You enter those instructions in your program file by using a text editor. The text editor in Linux that people probably use most widely (and sometimes hate the most because of the awkwardness of entering text-editor commands) is known as vi. (I even give you a brief introduction to vi in Chapter 3.)

Although vi isn't normally a discussion topic in a Linux programming book (because it's usually a topic in a more comprehensive book about Linux), I think that you can benefit from a quick overview of how to use vi to write your programs. This appendix serves as your basic introduction to vi (and as a good review if you're already familiar with vi.

Become comfortable using vi because you may find that it's the only text editor available on your copy of Linux.

Launching vi

You can start up the vi editor in either of two ways. The first way is to simply type vi at the command line and press the Enter key. Here's how you do it using the bash shell — which the $ prompt indicates — as an example:

```
$ vi
```

This keyboard gymnastics causes vi to open an empty document on-screen. Give the document a name before you save the document to a file.

The other way to begin vi is to specify the name of the file as you start up vi. Say, for example, that you want to create a file that you call myfirstprogram. Type the following on the command line:

```
$ vi myfirstprogram
```

The vi text editor first tries to find the myfirstprogram file in your current directory. If it finds the file, Linux displays the first page of the file on-screen within the vi text editor. If it doesn't find the file, however, Linux displays an empty page.

If you later want to save myfirstprogram to a file, you don't need to specify the name of the file, because the vi text editor automatically saves your work with the name that you specify as you start vi.

No Mouse!?

All of us face life's disappointments.

The vi text editor is primitive if you compare it to today's standards for text-editing programs. You don't find any conveniences that you expect to see with a word processor. For one thing, you can move your mouse all you want, but the vi text editor ignores it (how dare it!) unless you're running vi in an X Windows environment. (X Windows is software that enables you to open multiple windows on-screen at the same time.)

So you must settle for either using the arrow keys or issuing one of the vi text editor commands to move the cursor around the page.

You can avoid frustration in trying to move the cursor in the vi text editor by forgetting the way you move the cursor in other programs. The sooner that you become comfortable using the arrow keys or issuing the necessary vi text editor commands, the sooner you can start writing your Linux program.

The Mode-us Operandi of vi

The vi text editor interprets what you type in three different ways. At first contact, you may think that you and the vi text editor are experiencing difficulties in communicating with each other. That's true as you first begin using vi. After you practice awhile, however, you get on the right wavelength to communicate with vi.

The three modes of vi are as follows:

- **Command mode:** In this mode, vi interprets everything that you type on your keyboard as a command telling it to do something. Pressing the letter **j** in the command mode, for example, tells the vi text editor to move the cursor down one line on-screen.

  Note: The vi text editor starts in the command mode. You can also enter the command mode from any other mode at any time by pressing Esc.

- **Input mode:** Everything that you type on your keyboard goes on-screen and in the file as you save the pages (just as with a regular word processor). Pressing the letter **j** while the vi text editor is in the input mode, for example, displays the letter j at the cursor.

  You can enter the input mode from the command mode by pressing **i** or **a**. Pressing the letter *i* inserts characters on the page at the cursor, and pressing the letter *a* appends characters to the page directly after the cursor.

- **Last line mode:** In this mode, vi interprets everything that you type on your keyboard as a last-line command. In other words, the characters appear on the last line of the vi text editor at the bottom of your screen.

  You can enter the last line mode from the command mode by entering a colon (:).You can press the letter **q** in the last line mode, for example, which tells the vi text edtior to exit (quit).

Waiting for your command, sir

If you start the vi text editor without opening a previously saved file, you see a nearly empty page on-screen; the tilde (~) character repeats down the left margin (see Figure B-1).

This look gives you the incorrect impression that the tilde is the vi text editor's way of telling you where a line on the page begins. The tilde actually signifies that these line are *empty* lines. But don't think that an empty line is a blank line: It isn't. An empty line means that the line doesn't really exist — whereas a blank line means that the line exists but doesn't have any characters on the line.

Remember that the vi text editor starts up in the command mode: It interprets anything that you type as a command. This feature is quite different than that of other text editors such as Windows Notepad, which starts up in the insert mode. (Notepad doesn't even have a separate command mode!)

Figure B-1:
The vi text
editor
welcomes
you.

Not remembering this command mode versus input mode stuff is a common mistake many Linux programmers make as they first start using the vi text editor. The programmer often begins typing away without looking at the screen. If he does glance at the screen, only part of the text appears. Why? Because as the programmer is typing, the vi text editor is in the command mode. The vi text editor interprets each letter as a command and not as text. So vi ignores most of the letters because the letters aren't commands. As soon as the programmer enters an **i**, however, vi enters the insert mode and enters all the subsequent letters directly on the page.

Get me out of here!

You can exit the vi text editor by using one of several commands. The fastest way is to press the Esc key to enter the command mode and then type **ZZ** (make sure that you press and hold the Shift key to make the Zs capitals!) This action saves any changes to the file that you make and exits the vi text editor. If you don't make any changes, you don't save the file, but you still exit vi.

Moving Around Inside Your File

Here's a good way for you to pick up the various vi commands that you use to get you around your files. Find a large text file on your hard disk. A text file is almost like a word-processing file, except those special symbols that control things such as the font and size of the letters are missing from the file. Try to find a readme or readme.txt file on your hard disk. These files sometimes come with other software to keep you up-to-date on the latest changes occurring with the program.

If you can't find any text files, however, you can use vi to create one. Just begin vi; press **i** to enter the input mode, and then type a whole bunch of lines on the page. Hey, why not just type some of the Linux code that you see in this book? You may go on to the next page if you go overboard with your typing — but that's just fine.

Just line up

The vi text editor displays your text on lines shown on-screen. It automatically places the cursor on the first character of the first line of the text. Each line of text (including those lines that can't fit on-screen but exist in the file) has a number. The first line is number 1; the second line is number 2; and so on.

You can display the number of the line that the cursor is on by pressing Ctrl+G. I do that in Figure B-2, where I have myfirstprogram open. Notice that the line number appears at the bottom of the screen. (The cursor is on line 3 of a 14-line file.)

```
set flag = "go"
while ($flag == "go")
   echo "Enter your name or type stop to end: "
   set friend = $<
   if ($friend == "stop") then
      set flag = "stop"
      break
   endif
   if ($friend == "Tom") then
      continue
   endif
   echo "Hello, $friend ."
end
echo "Good-bye!"
~
~
~
~
~
~
~
~
~
"myfirstprogram" [Modified] line 3 of 14 --21%--
```

Figure B-2: The bottom of vi's screen reveals the line number for the cursor's position.

To see the line numbers beside each line on-screen, as shown in Figure B-3, type **:set number** and press Enter while you're in the command mode. (This text is really a command in last-line mode, but you must start in command mode.) Now you see the number for each line, which is an important navigational aid if you want to move around quickly in vi.

```
 1   set flag = "go"
 2   while ($flag == "go")
 3      echo "Enter your name or type stop to end: "
 4      set friend = $<
 5      if ($friend == "stop") then
 6         set flag = "stop"
 7         break
 8      endif
 9      if ($friend == "Tom") then
10         continue
11      endif
12      echo "Hello, $friend ."
13   end
14   echo "Good-bye!"
~
~
~
~
~
~
~
:set number
```

Figure B-3:
Line numbers at a glance make for easy navigation.

You can move the cursor to any line in your text by using one of the commands shown in Table B-1. Before you type any of these commands, make sure that vi is in the command mode by pressing the Esc key. Notice that some of the commands in Table B-1 contain the letter *n*. Say, for example, that you want to move the cursor to line 12 in your text. Use the command *n*G to tell the vi text editor to move the cursor to a particular line number. You must, however, replace the letter *n* with the number of the line where you want the cursor to move. In this case, type **12g** and press Enter. The cursor moves to the beginning of line 12 in your text. (In Figure B-4, I did these very steps, and my cursor rests at the beginning of line 12.)

```
 1   set flag = "go"
 2   while ($flag == "go")
 3      echo "Enter your name or type stop to end: "
 4      set friend = $<
 5      if ($friend == "stop") then
 6         set flag = "stop"
 7         break
 8      endif
 9      if ($friend == "Tom") then
10         continue
11      endif
12      echo "Hello, $friend ."
13   end
14   echo "Good-bye!"
~
~
~
~
~
~
~
~
~
:set number
```

Figure B-4:
The cursor's
now jumped
from line 3
to line 12.

Keep in mind that the vi text editor commands are *case sensitive,* so you must use the commands in either upper- or lowercase as they appear in the table.

Table B-1	Commands for Moving through Text Line by Line
Command	**What It Does**
*n*G	Moves to the line that you specify as *n*. If you specify no line, the cursor moves to the last line in the text.
n (# of lines to move)	Moves up the number of lines that you specify as *n* while remaining in the same column of the line.
n (# of lines to move)	Moves down the number of lines that you specify as *n* while remaining in the same column of the line.
H	Moves to the first line of the page shown on-screen.
M	Moves to the middle line of the page shown on-screen.
L	Moves to the last line of the page shown on-screen.
+ or Enter	Moves to the first nonwhite space on the next line. A *nonwhite space* is a character that you can see in your text. A white-space character is a character that you can't see, such as a tab character.
−	Moves to the first nonwhite space on the previous line.

Picking up speed

Faster ways of moving around text exist than moving line by line. The vi text editor has another set of commands that you can use to move a screen full of text at a time. These commands are known as screen-control commands and are shown in Table B-2.

A screen full of text, which you sometimes refer to as a *page,* is all the text that can appear on-screen at the same time. In Windows, for example, you can fill your screen with a different part of your text by using the Page Up and Page Down keys or by using the vertical scroll bar.

These Windows, however, methods don't work if you use the vi text editor. Instead, you must use the screen-control commands such as Ctrl+F to move to the next screen and Ctrl+B to move to the previous screen.

If you're using the vi text editor on a workstation (a computer that's between a mainframe computer and PC in terms of power), exactly what constitutes a screen may confuse you. Some workstations have many windows (with X Windows) on-screen at the same time. Each window runs a different application, and vi may be only one of these applications. In this case, the screen-control commands affect only the window showing the vi text editor. These screen-control commands don't affect the other windows.

Table B-2	Screen-Control Commands
Command	*What It Does*
Ctrl+B	Moves to the previous screen.
Ctrl+D	Moves down half the current screen. You can enter the number of lines that you want to move down before pressing Ctrl+D to instruct the vi text editor to move down a specific number of line.
Ctrl+E	Moves the screen down one line.
Ctrl+F	Moves to the next screen.
Ctrl+L	Clears the screen.
Ctrl+U	Moves up half the current screen — and as with Ctrl+D, you can specify the number of lines that you want to move down.
Ctrl+Y	Moves the screen up one line.
Z	Repaints the screen, placing the current line at the middle of the screen.
Z (press Enter)	Repaints the screen, placing the current line at the top of the screen.

The word, sentence, and paragraph jump

You can fine-tune your movements around your text by using the *word, sentence*, and *paragraph* commands. You need to be in the command mode for these to work. (As if I need to tell you that again after you read this appendix.) Table B-3 contains a list of these additional commands.

Table B-3	Word, Sentence, and Paragraph Commands
Command	*What It Does*
W	Moves forward one word.
Shift+W	Moves forward one word that ends with a blank space.
B	Moves back one word.
Shift+B	Moves back one word that begins with a blank space.
E	Moves to the end of the current word.
Shift+E	Moves to the end of the current word that ends with a blank space.
)	Moves to the beginning of the next sentence.
(	Moves to the beginning of the previous sentence.
}	Moves to the beginning of the next paragraph.
}	Moves to the beginning of the previous paragraph.
%	Finds the matching parenthesis (the cursor must be on a parenthesis for this command to work).

Just a character at a time

You can move the cursor throughout your text a character at a time by using the character commands of the vi text editor. Table B-4 shows you these commands.

Table B-4	Character-Control Commands
Command	**What It Does**
^ (caret)	Places the cursor on the first nonwhite character on the current line.
0 (zero)	Places the cursor at the beginning of the current line.
$ (dollar sign)	Places the cursor at the end of the current line.
l (or spacebar)	Moves the cursor right one character.
h (or Ctrl+H)	Moves the cursor left one character.

I don't mean that

You're sure to make a mistake or two as you use the vi text editor. Even professional Linux programmers find themselves needing to undo something they enter into the text. You can undo a mistake in either of the following two ways:

- ✔ Press **u** to undelete anything that you delete by using the dd or x command.
- ✔ Press **U** to undelete the current line.

Around the text I search for you

Locating the character or word that you need in pages of text is often difficult, especially if you're trying to find a specific line in your Linux program — the code is a jumble of Linux-ese and English.

The vi text editor can come to your rescue if you find yourself in such a jam. You can command vi to locate the information that you need in your text. Say, for example, that you want to find the word *bye* in your program (don't ask me why). You are, of course, in the command mode and ready to give some orders. You can then type **/bye** if you know that this word must fall somewhere after your current cursor position. This command appears at the bottom of your screen, ready for you to press Enter (see Figure B-5).

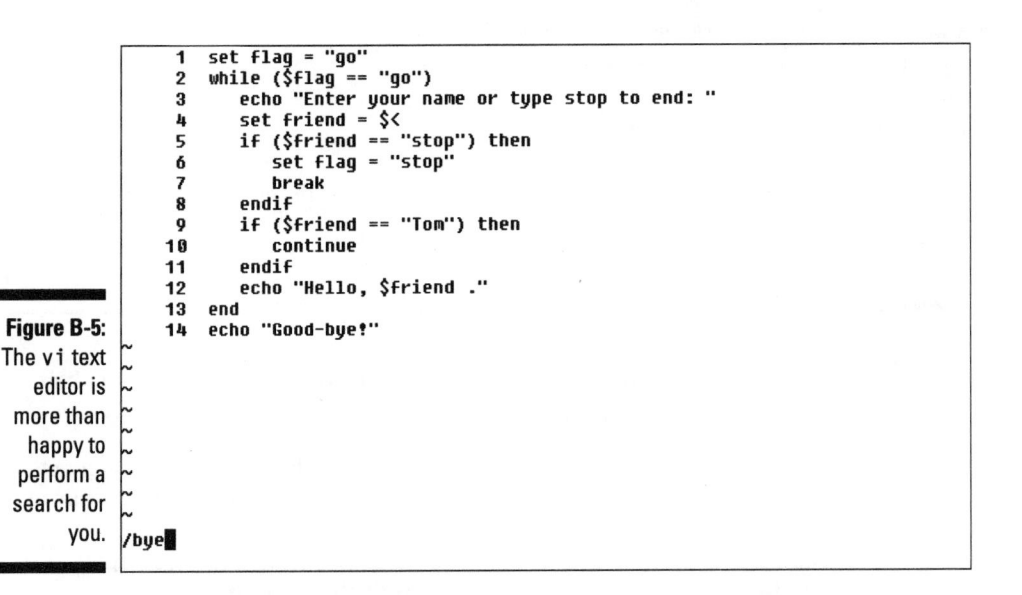

```
 1  set flag = "go"
 2  while ($flag == "go")
 3     echo "Enter your name or type stop to end: "
 4     set friend = $<
 5     if ($friend == "stop") then
 6        set flag = "stop"
 7        break
 8     endif
 9     if ($friend == "Tom") then
10        continue
11     endif
12     echo "Hello, $friend ."
13  end
14  echo "Good-bye!"
~
~
~
~
~
~
~
/bye█
```

Figure B-5:
The vi text
editor is
more than
happy to
perform a
search for
you.

After you press Enter, notice that the cursor jumps to the beginning of the search item — in this case the word bye, as shown in Figure B-6. (Of course, this demonstration is more impressive if you have really big and complex text, but you get the idea.)

```
 1   set flag = "go"
 2   while ($flag == "go")
 3      echo "Enter your name or type stop to end: "
 4      set friend = $<
 5      if ($friend == "stop") then
 6         set flag = "stop"
 7         break
 8      endif
 9      if ($friend == "Tom") then
10         continue
11      endif
12      echo "Hello, $friend ."
13   end
14   echo "Good-Bye!"
~
~
~
~
~
~
~
~
~
/bye
```

Figure B-6:
vi proudly
places the
cursor at
the
beginning of
the search
item.

Table B-5 contains the commands that you need to instruct vi to conduct a search of your text or program.

Note: Words that appear in *italics* in the commands in this table you must replace with the characters or words that you're trying to locate in your text.

Table B-5	Search Commands
Command	*What It Does*
/pattern	Begins the search from the cursor position for the characters that compose the pattern you're searching for.
/pattern/+n	Places the cursor on the *n*th line after the line that contains the characters or words that you're searching for. (Replace *n* with the number of the line.) Typing /Bob/+3,for example, places the cursor on the third line below the line where vi finds the word *Bob*.
?pattern	Begins the search at the cursor and continues to search backward through the text.
?pattern?-n	Places the cursor on the *n*th line before the line that contains the characters or words that you're searching for. Typing ?Bob?-3, for example, places the cursor on the third line above the line where vi finds the word *Bob*.
N	Repeats the last / or ? command.
Shift+N	Repeats the last / or ? command but reverses the direction of the search.

Using the Input Mode

By now, you probably know all you ever want to know about vi commands. Your sleeves are up and you're ready to plow into inserting text into your page. Before you can tackle this chore, however, you need to know — what else? — a few more vi commands.

I begin by showing you the various ways for you to enter the input mode from the command mode. Table B-6 contains the commands that you need to know before you begin typing away.

Table B-6	Entering the Input Mode
Command	**What It Does**
A	Places new text after the cursor position.
Shift+A	Places new text after the end of the current line.
I	Places new text in front of the cursor position.
Shift+I	Places new text in front of the current line.
O	Places new text below the current line at the beginning of the next line.
Shift+O	Places new text on the line above the current line at the beginning of the line.
R	Replaces the character at the cursor with the next character that you enter at the keyboard. Typing rb, for example, replaces the character at the cursor with the letter b.
Shift+R	Overwrites the text beginning with the character over the cursor. You can stop overwriting the text by returning to the command mode (by pressing Esc).
cw*word*+Esc	Replaces the word at the cursor with another word. If the cursor is on the word Bob, for example, and you enter **cwMary** and press Esc, vi replaces the word Bob with the word Mary.

Copy-editing the vi way

The vi text editor has a wealth of editing commands that make changing whatever you type into your text a breeze. All these commands require that you place vi in the command mode by pressing Esc; otherwise, you insert all the commands that you type into your text. Table B-7 contains text-editing commands. (Make sure that you replace *n* with an actual number.)

Table B-7	Text-Editing Commands
Command	*What It Does*
*n*X	Deletes *n* (meaning a number that you specify) characters beginning with the character at the cursor.
*n*Shift+X	Deletes *n* characters backward from the character at the cursor.
Shift+D	Deletes the line from the cursor to the end of the line.
DW	Deletes the word at the cursor position.
DD	Deletes the line on which the cursor sits.
Shift+J	Combines the line on which the cursor sits with the next line. The next line goes at the end of the current line.
. (period)	Repeats the previous editing command.

Cut and paste text without scissors and glue

You're probably familiar with the cut-and-paste features of Macs and PCs running Windows. You highlight the text that you want to cut, select Cut from the Edit menu, and the text disappears from the screen. Then you move the cursor to the spot in your text where you want to insert the text and select Paste from the Edit menu. Right before your eyes, the text that disappeared appears again.

The vi text editor has similar features known as *yank* and *put*. Yank is the same as Cut and put is the same as Paste in Windows. Table B-8 contains the yank and put commands. (Remember to replace *n* with a number.)

Table B-8	Yank and Put Commands
Command	*What It Does*
*n*YY	Removes *n* (a number that you specify) lines from the text and places those lines into your computer's memory.
*n*YyL	Removes *n* characters, beginning with the character at the cursor, and places those characters into your computer's memory.
P	Places the text that you yank after the cursor.
Shift+P	Places the text that you yank before the cursor.

Using the Last-Line Mode

The *last-line mode* enables you to read files into the vi text editor so that you can edit them. This mode also enables you to write files to a disk (the same as saving a file) after you finish editing the file. You use the last-line mode to exit vi.

You can enter the last-line mode by first placing vi in the command mode (by pressing Esc). After you're in the command mode, press the colon (:). This command places vi in the last-line mode.

All the commands that you enter in the last-line mode appear at the bottom of the screen (and *that's* where the name comes from). After you enter the command, you must press Enter for the command to execute. Table B-9 contains last-line mode commands.

Table B-9	Last-Line Mode Commands
Command	*What It Does*
R *filename*	Reads the file that you name in the command into the vi text editor and places the first character of the file at the current cursor position.
E *filename*	Edits the file that you name in the command and stops editing the file currently in the vi text editor.
E!	Discards changes made to the file since you last saved the file and begins to edit the file again.
E#	Changes between the two files most recently edited. You must save the file that you're editing before you can switch to the other file.

Practicing safe file editing

You can prevent yourself from catching the fatal disease that strikes many new Linux programmers. It's known as "I lost my files!" The disease hits you as you least expect it. You spend hours typing away, entering code into your vi text editor. Then, suddenly, without warning, your computer goes blank. It's as if someone turns off the power switch, and you lose all your hard work forever.

The best defense against this disease is protection. Always save your files regularly while working in vi. Table B-10 shows you the save-file commands.

Note: You must be in the last-line mode for these commands to work. First, make sure that you're in the command mode by pressing Esc and then type a colon (:), following it with the command.

Table B-10	Save-File Commands
Command	*What It Does*
W	Writes the current file to disk and overwrites the contents of the copy of the file that's on the disk.
W *filename*	Writes the current file to disk using the filename that you specify in the command. Make sure that you replace *filename* with the name of the file that you want to use for the current file.
W! *filename*	Writes the current file to disk using the filename that you specify in the command and overwrites the contents of the copy of the file that's on disk.

Bailing out of vi

Stop, already. Here are some ways to exit the vi text editor. All these commands require vi to be in the last-line mode, and you must press Enter to execute the command. Table B-11 contains exit commands for the vi text editor.

Note: You can simply press **ZZ** in the command mode (without pressing Enter) to exit vi and save changes to your file.

Table B-11	Exit Commands
Command	*What It Does*
:Q	Exits v i only if you save changes that you make to the file you're editing to the disk.
:Q!	Exits v i regardless of whether you save changes to the file to the disk.
:X	Has the same effect as the ZZ command.

Appendix C

Shell Conversion

● ●

*T*hroughout this book, I show you how to write a program by using the bash shell. You may, however, want to try your programming skills with the C shell, another very popular Linux shell. (You find both bash and the C shell in most versions of Linux.)

How to Use This List

The tables in this appendix can help you convert popular bash commands and statements to their C shell equivalents. After you write your program by using the techniques that you pick up in this book, you can match the bash shell keywords with their C shell equivalents. Notice that the bash shell and the C shell commands are usually similar — indeed, both shells sometimes have the same commands.

Note: This list is by no means exhaustive; in fact, it just scratches the surface. Some commands in the C shell have no equivalents in the bash shell. I'm not even going to get into that now!

Table C-1	Command Conversions	
Command Function	*bash Shell Command*	*C Shell Command*
Starting the shell from a program	`/bin/sh`	`#!/bin/csh`
Setting a variable	`variable=variable name`, `declare variable = variable name`, or `let variable = variable name`	`set variable variable name`, `let var[1]=100`, or `echo $var[1]`
Resetting a variable	`unset variable`	`unset variable`

(continued)

Table C-1 *(continued)*

Command Function	bash Shell Command	C Shell Command
Referring to a string variable	$*variable*	$*variable*
Picking out data from a string array	declare -a var= (1 2 3 4), echo $ {var[1]}	set var =(1 2 3 4), echo $var[1]
Making Linux wait (suspends script for *n* seconds)	sleep *n*	sleep *n*
Appending standard output to a file	>> *filename*	>> *filename*
Taking standard input from a file	< *filename*	< *filename*
Sending standard output to a file	> *filename*	> *filename*

Table C-2   **Operator Conversions**

Operator	bash Shell Operator	C Shell Operator
Equal to	-eq	==
Not equal to	-ne	!=
Less than	-lt	<
Less than or equal to	-le	<=
Greater than	-gt	>
Greater than or equal to	-ge	>=

Table C-3	Statement Conversions	
Statement	*bash Shell Form*	*C Shell Form*

if	if[*condition*]
	then
	command(s)
	fi
		if (*condition*) then
		command(s)
		endif

if else	if [*condition*]
	then
	command
	else
	command(s)
	fi
		if (*condition*) then
		command(s)
		else
		command(s)
		endif

if else if	if [*condition*]
	then
	elif [*condition*]
	command
	else
	command(s)
	fi
		if (*condition*) then
		command
		elseif (*condition*)
		command(s)
		else
		command(s)
		endif

switch case	case variable in case value: *command(s)* ;; *) esac	switch(*value*) *command(s)* breaksw default: *command(s)* endsw

Table C-4	Loop Command Conversions	
Loop or Loop Command Function	*bash Shell Form*	*C Shell Form*
while	while [*condition*] do *command(s)* done	while (*condition*) *command(s)* end
foreach	for *variable* in list do *command(s)* done	foreach *variable* (list) *item(s)* *command(s)* end
Breaking out of a loop	break	break
Resuming a loop	continue	continue

Appendix D
Linux Programming Exercises

● ●

*N*ow you actually must put your knowledge to use to solve the exercises in this appendix. But don't fear! This task is an open-book activity — and I provide the answers right after the question. You can peek if you want.

Note: I group the exercises by chapter, but not all the chapters have corresponding exercises.

Chapter 3: Writing Your First Linux Program

1. **How do you start the** vi **text editor?**

   Type **vi**, following it by the name of the file that you want to create or modify, as follows:

   ```
   vi myfile
   ```

2. **What is the first line in a** bash **shell program?**

   ```
   #!/bin/bash
   ```

3. **What is the second instruction you want to give the computer in most programs that you write?**

   ```
   clear
   ```

   This command clears the screen of characters that are left from the preceding program.

4. **Write a program that displays the name *Bob Smith* on-screen.**

   ```
   #!/bin/bash
   echo "Bob Smith"
   ```

5. **Make a program that you name** myprogram **into an executable program.**

   ```
   chmod 777 myprogram
   ```

Chapter 4: Getting Indecisive with Variables

1. **Say that you want to write a Linux program to keep track of your personal telephone list. Before you can solve this problem, you need to list all the pieces of information that you need to create the telephone list. What information do you include?**

   Answer: First name, last name, street, city, state, Zip code, home phone.

2. **Each piece of information on your list in the preceding exercise you must identifiy in your program as a variable. Write down possible names of the variables that you can use for each piece of information on your list. (Remember the guidelines for naming Linux files.)**

   Answer: FName, LName, Street, City, State, Zip, Hphone.

   Of course, your names may vary somewhat.

3. **Which of these piece(s) of information can you use to look up a telephone number?**

   Answer: LName, FName.

4. **Write the instruction that tells the computer to assign the name *Bob* to the FName variable.**

   ```
   declare FName="Bob"
   ```

5. **Write the instruction that tells the computer to declare the FName and LName variables without assigning a value to these variables.**

   ```
   declare FName, Lname
   ```

Chapter 5: Interfacing with the User

1. **Write a program that prompts someone to enter his name by using the keyboard and then have the program read the keyboard.**

   ```
   #!/bin/bash
   clear
   echo "Enter your name"
   read response
   ```

2. **Modify the program in the preceding exercise so that a personal greeting appears on-screen. Change the program to display** Hello **and then name the person entering at the keyboard.**

```
#!/bin/bash
clear
echo "Enter your name"
read response
echo "Hello $response"
```

3. **Write a program that asks a person how much money he wants to make this year.**

```
#!/bin/bash
clear
echo "How much money do you want to make this year?"
read salary
```

4. **Modify the program in the preceding exercise. Add 100 to whatever amount the person enters into the keyboard.**

```
#!/bin/bash
clear
echo "How much money do you want to make this year?"
read salary
let salary="$salary + 100"
```

5. **Modify the preceding program. Display a message on-screen reading, "I think you can earn ___," and then display the amount they enter plus 100.**

```
#!/bin/bash
clear
echo "How much money do you want to make this year?"
read salary
let salary=$salary + 100
echo "I think you can earn $salary"
```

Chapter 6: Who Were Those Masked Operators?

1. **Write an expression that asks the computer whether the values of two variables are the same.**

```
$Var1 -eq $Var2
```

2. **Write an expression that asks the computer whether the values of two variables are different.**

```
$Var1 -ne $Var2
```

3. **Write an expression that asks the computer to add the values of two variables and assign the sum to another variable.**

```
let Var3="$Var1 + $Var2"
```

4. **Write an expression that asks the computer to divide the values of two variables and assign the results to another variable.**

```
let Var3="$Var1 \$Var2"
```

5. **Write an expression that asks the computer to determine whether the value of the variable SALARY is greater than $30,000.**

```
$SALARY -gt 30000
```

Chapter 7: The if, if else, and if elif Statements

1. **Write an if statement that displays the message** Higher **if the value of** SALARY **is lower than 30,000.**

```
if [ "$SALARY" -lt 30000 ]
   then
     echo "Higher"
fi
```

2. **Write an if statement that displays the personal greeting** Hello, Bob **if the** FName **variable contains the value** Bob. **Otherwise, display the message** You're not Bob.

```
if [ "$Fname" -eq "Bob" ]
   then
     echo "Hello, Bob"
else
     echo "You're not Bob"
fi
```

3. **Modify the following program from the first exercise. Write an instruction that tells the computer to display** Higher **if** $SALARY **is less than 30,000 and display** Lower **if the** $SALARY **is greater than 30,000.**

```
if [ "$SALARY" -lt 30000 ]
   then
     echo "Higher"
fi
```

Answer:

```
if [ "$SALARY" -lt 30000 ]
   then
     echo "Higher"
elif [ "$SALARY" -gt 30000 ]
   then
     echo "Lower"
fi
```

4. **Modify the preceding program so that the message** Right On **appears if** $SALARY **is equal to 30,000.**

```
if [ "$SALARY" -lt 30000 ]
  then
    echo "Higher"
elif [ "$SALARY" -gt 30000 ]
  then
    echo "Lower"
else
    echo "Right On"
fi
```

5. **Write an** if **statement that displays the message** Right On **if** $SALARY **is 30,000. You can't, however, use the -eq operator (**$SALARY -eq 30000**). You must use the less than operator (**-lt**) and the greater than operator (**-gt**) in a single expression.**

```
if [ "$SALARY" -gt 29999 ] && [ "$SALARY" -lt 30001 ]
    then
    echo "Right On"
fi
```

Chapter 8: The case Statement

1. **Write a** case **statement that displays** New York, Chicago, Boston **if the value of the variable** $city **contains the corresponding value.**

```
case $city in
  "New York")
        echo "New York"
        ;;
  "Chicago")
        echo "Chicago"
        ;;
  "Boston")
        echo "Boston"
        ;;
esac
```

2. **Modify the** case **statement from the preceding exercise to display** Incorrect city entered **if none of the cities reflect the selection.**

```
case $city in
  "New York")
        echo "New York"
        ;;
  "Chicago")
        echo "Chicago"
        ;;
  "Boston")
        echo "Boston"
        ;;
    *)
        echo "Incorrect city entered."
esac
```

3. **Write instructions for the to computer display the following menu items. (Make sure that you include a menu item to quit running the program.)**

   a) Search by name

   b) Search by telephone number

   c) Search by employee number

   Answer:

   ```
   echo "a) Search by name"
   echo "b) Search by telephone number"
   echo "c) Search by employee number"
   echo "q) Quit"
   ```

4. **Modify the program in the preceding exercise and include instructions that tell the user to make a selection from the menu; include instructions for the program to read the user's selection from the keyboard.**

   ```
   echo "a) Search by name"
   echo "b) Search by telephone number"
   echo "c) Search by employee number"
   echo "q) Quit"
   echo " "
   echo "Enter your selection: "
   read selection
   ```

5. **Modify the program in the preceding exercise to include instructions that determine which selection the user makes and display the name of the selection on-screen.**

   ```
   echo "a) Search by name"
   echo "b) Search by telephone number"
   echo "c) Search by employee number"
   echo "q) Quit"
   echo " "
   echo "Enter your selection: "
   read selection
   case $selection in
    "a")
           echo "Search by name"
           ;;
    "b")
           echo "Search by telephone number"
           ;;
    "c")
           echo "Search by employee number"
           ;;
    "q")
           echo "Quit"
           ;;
        *)
           echo "Incorrect menu selection."
   esac
   ```

Chapter 10: The while Loop

1. Write a program using a `while` loop that continues to add 1 to the `$sum` variable until the `$sum` variable equals 10.

```
let sum=0
while [ "$sum" -lt 10 ]
  do
    let sum="$sum + 1"
done
```

2. Modify the program in the preceding exercise so that the computer displays the current value of the `$sum` variable each time the value increments.

```
let sum=0
while [ "$sum" -lt 11 ]
  do
    let sum="$sum + 1"
    echo "$sum"
done
```

3. Modify the program in the first exercise so that the computer displays the message `sum is equal to 10` only if this statement is true.

```
let sum=0
while [ "$sum" -lt 11 ]
  do
    let sum="$sum + 1"
    if [ "$sum" -eq 10 ]
       then
       echo "sum is equal to 10"
    fi
done
```

4. In Exercise 5 for Chapter 8, you build a program that displays a menu, prompts the user to enter a selection, reads the selection the user enters from the keyboard, and then displays the selection on-screen. Modify the following program with a `while` loop so that the program continues until the user selects q to quit the program.

Here's the original program:

```
echo "a) Search by name"
echo "b) Search by telephone number"
echo "c) Search by employee number"
echo "q) Quit"
echo " "
echo "Enter your selection: "
read selection
case $selection in
 "a")
        echo "Search by name"
        ;;
 "b")
        echo "Search by telephone number"
        ;;
 "c")
        echo "Search by employee number"
        ;;
 "q")
        echo "Quit"
        ;;
     *)
        echo "Incorrect menu selection."
esac
```

Answer:

```
declare flag="1"
while [ "$flag" -eq "1" ]
  do
  clear
  echo "a) Search by name"
  echo "b) Search by telephone number"
  echo "c) Search by employee number"
  echo "q) Quit"
  echo " "
  echo "Enter your selection: "
  read selection
  case $selection in
 "a")
        echo "Search by name"
        ;;
 "b")
        echo "Search by telephone number"
        ;;
 "c")
        echo "Search by employee number"
        ;;
 "q")
        set flag = "0"
        ;;
     *)
        echo "Incorrect menu selection."
  esac
done
```

5. **Create an endless** while **loop that alternates displaying the messages** Green **and** Red **on-screen.**

```
let flag="1"
let color=0
while [ "$flag" -eq "1" ]
    do
        if [ "$color" -eq 0 ]
            then
                clear
                let color=1
                echo "Green"
        fi
        if [ "$color" -eq 1 ]
            then
                clear
                let color=0
                echo "Red"
    fi
done
```

Chapter 11: The for in Loop

1. **Write a program that uses the** for in **loop to display the cities you travel to during your vacation: Paris, Rome, and London. (Bon voyage!)**

```
for city in Paris Rome London
    do
        echo "$city"
done
```

2. **Use a** for in **loop to display a personal greeting to your friends Bob, Mary, and Joan.**

```
for friend in Bob Mary Joan
    do
        echo "Hi, $friend"
done
```

3. **Modify the preceding program to include each person's first and last name: Bob Smith, Mary Jones, Joan Adams.**

```
for friend in "Bob Smith" "Mary Jones" "Joan Adams"
    do
        echo "Hi, $friend"
done
```

4. **Write a** for in **loop that displays the message** Here is my friend **on one line. On the second line, identify your friends by name, using the names Bob Smith, Mary Jones, and Joan Adams.**

```
for friend in "Bob Smith" "Mary Jones" "Joan Adams"
    do
        echo "Here is my friend"
        echo "Hi, $friend"
done
```

5. **Modify the** `for in` **loop of the preceding program so that you display the message** `She's great!` **only if you assign Mary Jones to** `$friend`.

```
for friend in "Bob Smith" "Mary Jones" "Joan Adams"
   do
      echo "Here is my friend"
      echo "Hi, $friend"
      if [ "$friend" -eq "Mary Jones" ]
         then
            echo "She's great!"
      fi
done
```

Chapter 12: Nested Loops and Quick Exits

1. **Write a program that asks someone to enter his name and then end the program only if the person enters the word** `stop`.

Hint: Use the `break` keyword to end the loop in the program.

```
#!/bin/bash
declare flag="go"
while [ "$flag" -eq "go" ]
   do
      clear
      echo "Enter your name or type stop to end: "
      read friend
      if [ "$friend" -eq "stop" ]
         then
            break
      fi
done
```

2. **Modify the preceding program to make the computer return to the top of the loop if the person enters the name** `Tom`.

Hint: Use the `continue` keyword.

```
#!/bin/bash
declare flag="go"
while [ "$flag" -eq "go" ]
   do
      clear
      echo "Enter your name or type stop to end: "
      read friend
      if [ "$friend" -eq "stop" ]
        then
            break
      fi
   if [ "$friend" -eq "Tom" ]
     then
        continue
   fi
done
```

3. **Modify the preceding program so that a personal greeting appears only if the user doesn't enter the name Tom and doesn't enter the word stop.**

```
#!/bin/bash
declare flag="go"
while [ "$flag" -eq "go" ]
  do
    clear
    echo "Enter your name or type stop to end: "
    read friend
     if [ "$friend" -eq "stop" ]
     then
       break
    fi
    if [ "$friend" -eq "Tom" ]
    then
       continue
    fi
    echo "Hello, $friend ."
done
```

4. **Write a program using the if statement to determine whether a last name is Smith and then determine whether the first name is Bob. If they match, say Hello to Bob Smith on-screen.**

   Hint: Use nested if statements.

```
#!/bin/bash
declare fname="Bob"
declare lname="Smith"
if [ "$lname" -eq "Smith" ]
  then
     if [ "$fname" -eq "Bob" ]
     then
       echo "Hello Bob Smith"
    fi
fi
```

5. **Write a program that displays** *name* has these *degree* degrees **but substituting Bob, Mary, and Joan for** name **and BS, MS, and Ph. D. for** *degree.*

   Hint: Use a nested for in loop.

```
#!/bin/bash
for name in Bob Mary Joan
  do
          for degree in BS MS Ph.D.
            do
             echo "$name has these $degree degrees"
          done
done
```

Chapter 14: Getting Down with Subprograms

1. **Create a subprogram with the name** `greeting` **that displays** `Hello` **and then create a program to call the** `greeting` **subprogram.**

   Program:

   ```
   #!/bin/bash
   greeting
   ```

   Subprogram: `greeting`

   ```
   echo "Hello"
   ```

2. **Write a subprogram with the name** `addition` **that adds 5 and 6 and then displays the results on-screen. Create a program to call the subprogram.**

   Program:

   ```
   #!/bin/bash
   addition
   ```

   Subprogram: `addition`

   ```
   let sum="5 + 6"
   echo "$sum"
   ```

3. **Write a subprogram with the name** `name` **that displays** `Bobby`. **Write a program that displays** `Hello` **and then calls the subprogram.**

   Program:

   ```
   #!/bin/bash
   echo "Hello"
   name
   ```

   Subprogram: `name`

   ```
   echo "Bobby"
   ```

4. **Modify the programming in the preceding exercise to display** `He's my friend.` **after the name** `Bobby`.

   Hint: The subprogram must display only the name `Bobby`.

   Program:

   ```
   #!/bin/bash
   echo "Hello"
   name
   echo "He's my friend."
   ```

Subprogram: name
```
echo "Bobby"
```

5. **Modify the preceding exercise so that a second subprogram (with the name** name2) **displays the words** He's my friend.

Program:
```
#!/bin/bash
echo "Hello"
name
name2
```

Subprogram: name
```
echo "Bobby"
```

Subprogram: name2
```
echo "He's my friend."
```

Chapter 15: Understanding Arguments . . . Not the Ones with Your Mother-in-Law

1. **Write a program that accepts a person's name as an argument and then displays the name on-screen.**

Call the program:
```
name Bob
```

Program: name
```
#!/bin/bash
echo "$1"
```

2. **Modify the program in the preceding exercise to accept and display the person's first and last name.**

Call the program:
```
name Bob Smith
```

Program: name
```
#!/bin/bash
echo "$1 $2"
```

3. **Modify the preceding exercise to accept the first and last name as one argument.**

Call the program:
```
name "Bob Smith"
```

Program: name

```
#!/bin/bash
echo "$1"
```

4. **Modify the following program and subprogram so that the subprogram receives the name that the subprogram displays as an argument.**

Program:

```
#!/bin/bash
echo "Hello"
name
```

Subprogram: name

```
echo "Bobby"
```

Answers:

Program:

```
#!/bin/bash
echo "Hello"
name Bobby
```

Subprogram: name

```
echo "$1"
```

5. **Modify the following program and subprogram so that the information that both subprograms display pass as arguments to the subprograms.**

Program:

```
#!/bin/bash
echo "Hello"
name
name2
```

Subprogram: name

```
echo "Bobby"
```

Subprogram: name2

```
echo "He's my friend."
```

Answers:

Program:

```
#!/bin/bash
echo "Hello"
name Bobby
name2 "He's my friend."
```

Subprogram: `name`

```
echo "$1"
```

Subprogram: `name2`

```
echo "$1"
```

Chapter 16: Working with Database Files

1. **Write a program that saves the string** `Hello World` **to the file** `myfile`.

```
#!/bin/bash
echo "Hello World" > myfile
```

2. **Write a program that saves the name** `John Smith` **to the file** `myfile` **and then appends the name** `Mary Jones` **to the same file.**

```
#!/bin/bash
echo "John Smith" > myfile
echo "Mary Jones" >> myfile
```

3. **How do you run the program** `greeting` **so that the output of the program prints to the file** `myfile`?

```
greeting > myfile
```

4. **Repeat the preceding exercise and append the output of the program** `greeting` **to the file** `myfile`.

```
greeting >> myfile
```

5. **Write a program that saves the following information to the file** `mydata`. **Then use the** `gawk` **utility to find and display the information for** `Mary Jones`.

Bob Smith 555-1212

Mary Jones 555-5555

Tom Adams 555-7777

John Smith 555-4444

```
#!/bin/bash
echo "Bob Smith 555-1212" >> mydata
echo "Mary Jones 555-5555" >> mydata
echo "Tom Adams 555-7777" >> mydata
echo "John Smith 555-4444" >> mydata
gawk '$2 ~ /^Jones/ {print $1, $2, $3}' mydata
```

Chapter 17: Making Your Program Print Stuff Out

1. Send the words Hello world **to the printer.**

```
echo "Hello world" | lp
```

2. Print the following data to the printer:

Bob Smith 555-1212

Mary Jones 555-5555

Tom Adams 555-7777

John Smith 555-4444

```
echo "Bob Smith 555-1212" | lp
echo "Mary Jones 555-5555" | lp
echo "Tom Adams 555-7777" | lp
echo "John Smith 555-4444" | lp
```

3. Write the data in the preceding exercise to a file with the name mydata **and then print the contents of the file.**

```
echo "Bob Smith 555-1212" >> mydata
echo "Mary Jones 555-5555" >> mydata
echo "Tom Adams 555-7777" >> mydata
echo "John Smith 555-4444" >> mydata
cat mydata | lp
```

4. How can you print a formatted file (that's to say, change its fonts)?

Use a Linux utility such as troff, which enables you to specify margins, fonts, and other formats for text that you're printing.

5. Modify the following program so that the data the gawk **utility selects prints rather than appears on-screen.**

```
#!/bin/bash
echo "Bob Smith 555-1212" >> mydata
echo "Mary Jones 555-5555" >> mydata
echo "Tom Adams 555-7777" >> mydata
echo "John Smith 555-4444" >> mydata
gawk '$2 ~ /^Jones/ {print $1, $2, $3}' mydata
```

Answer:

```
#!/bin/bash
echo "Bob Smith 555-1212" >> mydata
echo "Mary Jones 555-5555" >> mydata
echo "Tom Adams 555-7777" >> mydata
echo "John Smith 555-4444" >> mydata
gawk '$2 ~ /^Jones/ {print $1, $2, $3}' mydata | lp
```

Chapter 18: Getting Chatty with Comments

1. **Modify the following program by explaining (in the program) what the** echo **command does.**

```
#!/bin/bash
echo "Bob Smith"
```

Answer:

```
#!/bin/bash
#The echo command displays the name on-screen.
echo "Bob Smith"
```

2. **Modify the following program to include comments for each action the program must take.**

```
#!/bin/bash
clear
echo "How much money do you want to make this year?"
read salary
let salary="$salary + 100"
echo "I think you can earn $salary"
```

Answer:

```
#!/bin/bash
#clear the screen
clear
# prompt the user to enter a salary
echo "How much money do you want to make this year?"
#read characters from the keyboard
read salary
# add 100 to the value of the salary variable and assign the new value to
          the salary variable.
let salary="$salary + 100"
#display the message and salary on the screen
echo "I think you can earn $salary"
```

3. **List two ways that you can add a comment about this instruction:** read salary.

   Answer 1: By placing the comment on the line above the instruction:

```
#read characters from the keyboard
read salary
```

   Answer 2: By placing the comment on the same line but to the right of the instruction:

```
read salary #read characters from the keyboard
```

4. How you use can *pseudo*-code as comments for your program? (Yes, this one *is* an essay question!)

Answer: You can list instructions that are necessary to complete a task as pseudo-code (that is, the instructions that you write in real English) in your program file. Linux, of course, doesn/t understand English. You can, however, place a number sign (#) as the first character of the pseudo-code, which converts the pseudo-code into a comment.

Chapter 19: Stamping Out Bugs in Your Program

1. What's the problem with the following code?

```
#!/bin/bash
clear
declare name="Bob"
if [ "$name" -eq "Tom ]
    echo "Hello Tom"
fi
```

Answer: The if statement is missing the then keyword.

2. What's the problem with the following code?

```
#!/bin/bash
clear
declare name="Bob"
while "$name == "Tom"
  do
    echo "Hello Tom"
done
```

Answer: You must enclose the expression $name == "Tom" within brackets:

```
while [ "$name" -eq "Tom" ]
```

3. What's the problem with the following code?

```
#!/bin/bash
clear
declare name="Bob"
if [ "$name" eq "Tom" ]
  then
    echo "Hello Tom"
    if [ "$name" -ne "Tom" ]
    then
        echo "You're not Tom."
fi
```

Answer: This code actually contains two problems. The second if statement never runs because the condition requires that the $name not be Tom — the if statement, however, nests inside another if statement that executes only if the $name *is* Tom. The second if statement is missing the fi keyword.

4. **What's the problem with the following code? (Are you noticing a pattern with the questions for this set of exercises?)**

```
#!/bin/bash
clear
case $city in
 "a")
        echo "Search by name"
        ;;
 "b")
        echo "Search by telephone number"
        ;;
 "c")
        echo "Search by employee number"
        ;;
 "q")
        declare flag="0"
        ;;
     *)
        echo "Incorrect menu selection."
```

Answer: You're assigning no value to $city. And the case statement requires the esac keyword, which is missing from the last line of this program.

5. **What's the problem with the following code?**

```
#!/bin/bash
clear
for friend in Bob Smith Mary Jones Joan Adams
    do
      echo "Hi, $friend"
done
```

Answer: You need to enclose the names Bob Smith, Mary Jones, and Joan Adams within quotation marks:

```
for friend in "Bob Smith" "Mary Jones" "Joan Adams"
```

Appendix E

Surfing for Sample Code

• •

*I*f you detest typing as much as I do, you're going to be happy to know that I took the larger bits of code from this book and slapped it up on the Web for you to download and save yourself from typing your fingers blue.

The code is available on the Web at the following URL:

```
www.idgbooks.com/extras/dummies/linuxprog.html
```

You can download it just by clicking the handy little `Click here to download sample code` button on the page. The file that you download is a zip file containing text files with the name of each chapter. If you see some code in the book that you don't want to type, follow these steps:

1. **Navigate to the directory on your computer (or wherever) you extract the zipped text files.**

2. **Find and open the text file corresponding to the chapter number where you find the code that you want in the book.**

3. **Find the code that you want and then copy and paste the code from the text file into whatever compiler (or other program) you want to use the code in.**

I don't included every little snippet of code from the book in these text files — just the bigger chunks. So if the code you're looking for isn't in the corresponding text file (if one's there — a few chapters didn't have any code to put up), it's probably just a line or two that I thought you can type out faster yourself.

If you have trouble with the sample code and need assistance, please call the IDG Books Worldwide Customer Service phone number: 800-762-2974 (or outside the U.S.: 317-572-3342).

Index

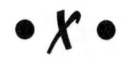

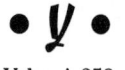

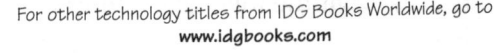

IDG BOOKS WORLDWIDE
BOOK REGISTRATION

Register This Book and Win!

We want to hear from you!

Visit **http://my2cents.dummies.com** to register this book and tell us how you liked it!

🖊 Get entered in our monthly prize giveaway.

🖊 Give us _____ est, what y_____ or and u_____

🖊 Let us _____ n.

Your feed_____ s what coverage_____ er we're me_____ host valu- able res_____

Not on t_____ *The Internet* _____ tailers everywh_____

Or let us_____ a letter _____

*For Dum*_____
Dummie_____
10475 C_____
Indianap_____